Gold
of the
Pharaohs

BARNES
&NOBLE
BOOKS
NEW YORK

Gold
of the
Pharaohs

Hans Wolfgang Müller
Eberhard Thiem

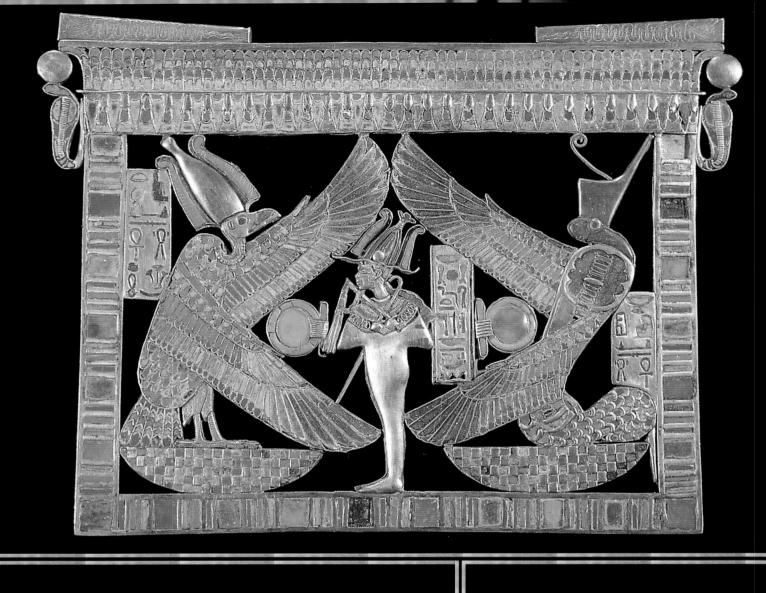

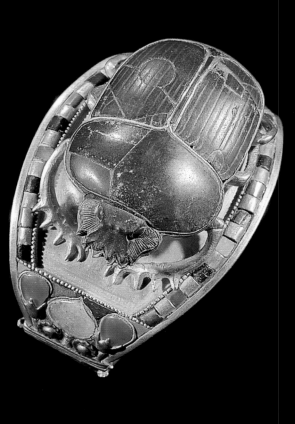

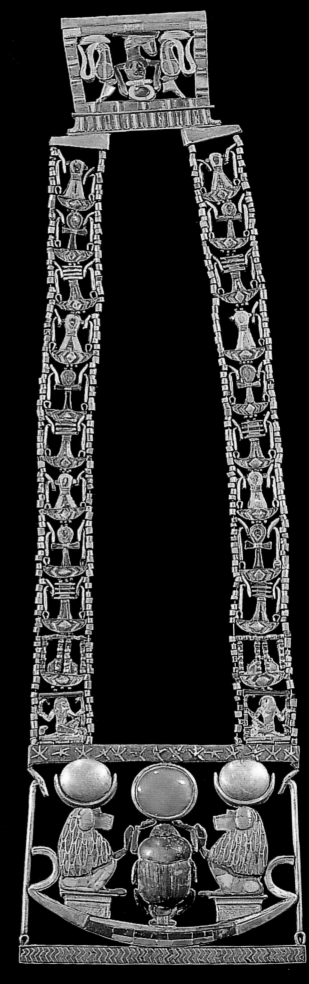

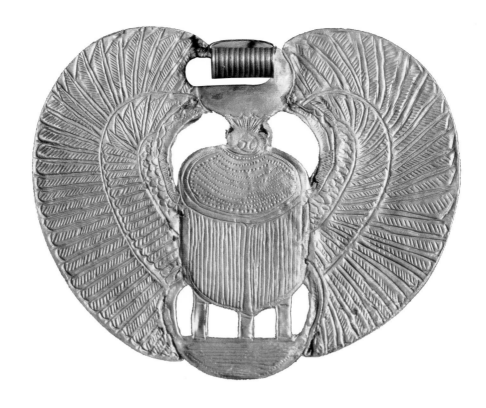

Acknowledgements

Illness and an untimely death prevented Hans Wolfgang Müller from finishing this manuscript. I thank wholeheartedly his pupils and colleagues who, in honour of their former teacher and mentor, generously contributed their time and expertise in order to complete the book: Dr Birgit Schlick-Nolte, who agreed to Hans Wolfgang Müller's request to act as consultant for the entire project as well as working on the Third Intermediate Period and the Late Dynastic Period; Professor Dr Abdel Ghaffar Shedid, who acted as consultant for the illustrations; Petra Illenseer, who drew the line drawings; Dr Alfred Grimm, for helpful advice in a range of different areas of the project; Rosemarie Klemm MA and Professor Dr Dietrich Klemm, for their invaluable advice on ancient gold mining and for acting as consultants on the subjects of coloured stones and their origins. Special thanks are also due to Karin Gruhl for her support throughout the project, and of course to Eberhard Thiem, whose idea the entire project was and who worked unstintingly to assemble the photographs.

Maleen Müller von Saalfeld

llustrations on pages 1–18:

Endpapers: 1 Tutankhamun and Ankhes-en-pa-Amun, from a statue-shrine; Page 1: 2 Golden head of Hathor from the tomb of Prince Sheshonq; Page 2: 3 Tutankhamun wearing the crown of Lower Egypt; Pages 4–5: 4 Vulture pectoral of Tutankhamun; Page 6: 5 Seated king figurine from the tomb of Tutankhamun; Page 7: 6 Diadem of Tutankhamun; Page 8: 7 Osiris-pectoral, 8 Counterweight with figure of eternity, 9 Scarab bracelet; Page 9: 10–11 Double receptacle in the form of a cartouche from the tomb of Tutankhamun, 12 Scarab bracelet, 13 Clasp or counterweight with the throne-name of Tutankhamun, 14 Scarab pectoral; Pages 10–11: 15 Metamorphosis pectoral of Tutankhamun; Page 12: 16 Bracelet of Psusennes I, 17 Bracelet of Sheshonq I; Page 13: 18 Bracelet of Queen Ahhotep, 19 Bead bracelet of a wife of Thutmosis III; Page 14: 20 Emblem of the falcon Gemhesu and statuette of the god Amun; Page 15: 21 Female head from the throne of Princess Sit-Amun; Pages 16–17: 22 Backrest of the throne of Princess Sit-Amun; Pages 18–19: 23–24 Reverse and obverse of a scarab pendant of Tutankhamun

Foreword

Hans Wolfgang Müller was passionately involved in the study of Egyptian Art History for more than half a century. His depth of understanding and knowledge of Egyptian art was unrivalled. As Professor Emeritus of Egyptology in Munich he founded a world-renowned school of Egyptian Art History, and as director of the Egyptian Collection he then oversaw the expansion of the school into a museum. His meticulous observation and analysis of objects of art, and his feeling for the subject as a whole, gave him such judgement in both value and dating of objects that his initials, HWM, have become a kind of seal of authority in the world of art history. His many published works convey his enormous knowledge and sophisticated methodology to pupils and colleagues alike. His books about Egyptian art and painting have a concise style and comprehensive coverage that set a high standard for other historians of art.

In recent years HWM concentrated increasingly on the study of artwork in metal. He was as interested in the techniques used for making weapons and figurines in copper and bronze as he was in the age-old Egyptian tradition of work in gold. The land of the pyramids, a 'state fashioned in stone' and the cradle of artforms such as monumental sculptures and stone reliefs, was also the golden land of Antiquity. It was the land of Pharaoh the 'Horus of gold', the 'god of gold', the king who held the monopoly over the sacred metal. Gold-mining techniques and the technical skills needed to create the jewellery that celebrated the images of the gods and helped to preserve the mummified bodies of dead pharaohs, were developed early in Egyptian history, and were improved steadily.

HWM's last work was devoted to this subject, first in research and then in publishing his findings. As 'sacred gold' was an Egyptian symbol for eternity, so may this last work make Hans Wolfgang Müller and his achievements timeless and unforgettable.

Rainer Stadelmann
First Director of the German Archaeology Institute, Cairo

Preface

Praise to you, oh Re,
in your beauty and perfection,
wherever you are,
in your shimmering gold

Divine Gold

Divine Gold: what is meant is not some blasphemous adoration, or even the Biblical worship of a golden calf. Instead, the term is an attempt to convey to modern readers the fundamental belief of the ancient Egyptians in the sacredness and magic power of gold, the substance of gods and kings. The symbolic power that was associated by the Egyptians with gold – because of its shine and its enduring qualities – was similar to the power invested in alchemy, which was transmitted by Arab alchemists to Europe during the Middle Ages.

The ancient Egyptians are the only people in the world whose belief in the magic of gold was given expression in the material world. Only when we understand this can we fully understand the form and meaning of the pieces of jewellery that were worn by Egyptian kings and their wives, princes and princesses, officials and servants, both in life and in their graves. Gold was a divine metal that not only decorated but also imparted magic power.

These ideas could be supported only by gold in abundance. Only in a land with rich supplies of gold could its divine power have been a credible belief.

Precious stones and their artfully fashioned substitutes in coloured glass or faience were also closely linked to the idea of gold as magical. Each colour had a beneficial and protective function.

Images and texts from surviving murals in tombs and temples provide rich insights: reports of

expeditions in search of gold; biographies and titles of the officials dealing with gold and its processing; goldsmiths at work in their workshops; the uses and ways of wearing jewellery; royal decrees awarding gold... all these scenes and inscriptions show us the social and religious importance of gold jewellery in ancient Egypt.

The shining golden sarcophagi and jewels in the tombs all guaranteed immortality to the deceased, because gold was of the same material as the eternal sun. It is now hard to imagine the value of the treasures that once lay buried in the the great pyramids and in the tombs of the Valley of the Kings, when even the tomb of such a relatively insignificant pharaoh as Tutankhamun revealed such overwhelming wealth. It is amazing that after thousands of years of tomb-robbery there are still treasures to be found.

Of the immense treasures produced under the pharaohs only fragments now survive. These pieces – lost for ages – give us an insight into the highly developed skills of the ancient Egyptian goldsmiths. The pieces found bear witness to political, religious and historical changes, each detail holding a special meaning. Each piece of jewellery also reflects the extraordinary organizational abilities of the Egyptian state in mobilizing the enormous workforce that were needed to mine and transport the gold. This book is intended to give the reader an insight into the true scale of this achievement.

Contents

The Magic of Gold

The most ancient cultures of the Near East go back as far as the 7th and 6th millennia BC, but the earliest archaeological traces of settlement on the edges of the Nile Valley date only to the end of the 5th millennium BC. Up to then, the sparse rainfall had allowed development, in what is now the Western Desert, of a savanna-like vegetation in which the trees and grasses supported a wide variety of wildlife, and its human population had been able to win a fairly comfortable living by hunting game and raising scanty crops of cereals. Humans had lived on the elevated rim of the Nile Valley since the Stone Age, but as rain grew more scarce and finally stopped altogether, the savanna gradually turned to desert, and these populations now descended towards the river itself. The valley did not present a very inviting prospect then for, although the river had already sunk to its present level and produced the narrow flood-plain alongside, it overflowed its banks every summer. It was only toward the end of the 5th millennium BC, that the inhabitants of the valley had begun to understand the annual timetable of the floods and had started to settle on the higher reaches of ground within the valley, out of reach of the high summer water.

25 'Horus-falcon over the palace façade' (the serekh)

26 Sunrise on the Nile

The Magic of Gold

The imagination of these now sedentary people remained marked for a long time by the memory of their earlier lives as hunters.

Jewellery of the Prehistoric Period

In prehistoric times, jewellery was made of crystals, shells, stones and coloured pebbles from the desert; gold, silver and copper were also sometimes used. Nomads from the Eastern Desert bartered such materials for the produce of the sedentary farmers of the Nile Valley, who also traded with the Semitic nomads who inhabited the Sinai Peninsula, where malachite and turquoise were to be found. Semi-precious blue lapis lazuli had been made into jewellery in Egypt since the very earliest times, but has never been found in the Egyptian mountains; it probably reached Egypt from Afghanistan, along the extensive trading routes that ran through Mesopotamia. There was a considerable demand for such semi-precious stones, for much jewellery was usually interred with its owner as a burial offering.

Indeed, jewellery from the late 5th and the 4th millennium BC is known only from such burials, which have yielded necklaces (often featuring a pendant), armlets, bracelets, anklets and girdles. A clay figurine intended as a 'companion for the dead' in the hereafter shows how women of the period adorned themselves (27): the bead anklets can be clearly distinguished, and the marks on the right upper thigh, the shoulders and the breasts represent tattoos.

From the beginning, jewellery was worn not simply for ornament but as an amulet, a life-giving charm that provided protection from danger. As these amulets were worn at work, they had to be made of durable materials.

Coloured Stone and other Natural Materials

There is hardly a natural stone in Egypt that was not turned into beads or amulets in prehistoric times. Beads were strung on thin leather thongs or on cords of linen or animal hair. Necklaces and belts consisting of several rows of beads were held together by narrow bars of bone or other material drilled with tiny holes through which cords were threaded.

27 Predynastic female figure with painted anklets

Amulets were thought to exercise their protective and life-giving powers in different ways, depending on their characteristics. Semi-precious stones were credited with particular magical qualities associated with their colours. Red was the colour of pulsing blood and of vigilant defence, and carnelian was very often used as an amulet, as were the deep-red garnet and red jasper. Green was the colour of plants – the papyrus in particular – which sprang up from the earth, died off, and grew up again. It was a symbol of flourishing health, of freshness, rebirth, and unending life and joy. Among the green stones were turquoise, from the Sinai Peninsula, and malachite, which although rarely made into beads has been found in great quantity ground up on palettes for use in eye make-up. Feldspar came from the Eastern Desert, and a green variant of jasper was used. Blue was a divine colour; of the semi-precious stones used in Egypt only lapis lazuli is deep blue, and according to later accounts the hair of the gods was made of this stone. The golden-yellow calcite, or Egyptian alabaster, was closely related to gold, and in later texts the name 'House of Gold' was given to the most important calcite quarry, in central Egypt. As well as beads, natural objects, such as curiously shaped snail shells from the Nile Valley and sea shells from the shores of the Red Sea and the Mediterranean, were strung together as amulets.

Sometimes tiny stones would be placed in sea shells, which would then quietly tinkle with each movement of the body. Cowry shells have most often been found in women's graves on the girdles worn on the hips and the lower abdomen. Fabricated cowry shells, made of thinly beaten sheet gold, reappear during the Middle Kingdom, at the beginning of the 2nd millennium BC, on the precious belts worn by princesses; these shells protected the lower abdomen from disease and miscarriage. A similar significance was attributed to acacia seeds, both natural and made up in other materials; they are often found as ornamental links in bead girdles. The shells of ostrich eggs, which were trimmed, perforated and then shaped into small discs, were also very popular for stringing into girdles and necklaces.

28 Predynastic- and Early Dynastic-period necklaces and armlets

Magical protective powers were also ascribed to animal teeth – for instance, the canine teeth of the hippopotamus – and to the horns of smaller animals. The claws of birds of prey were worn over the ankle bone. As time went on, representations of animals were increasingly incorporated as amulets in necklaces and bracelets: figurines of hippopotami and frogs were thought to bring fertility, while the porcupine, the enemy of snakes and scorpions, would protect the wearer from danger. In the late Prehistoric Period, amulets in the form of falcons, symbol of the god of the heavens, begin to appear.

The Making of Beads
Tens of thousands of prehistoric beads made of various stones have been preserved; their manufacture presupposes the existence of specialized workshops in the settlements of the Nile Valley. The primitive tools and methods of bead-making remained unchanged until about 1500 BC, and the excavated remains of a bead factory from the beginning of the 2nd millennium BC – with broken stones, unfinished beads at every stage of production, and drilling tools of flint and copper – show the painstaking processes involved.

29 Drilling and polishing carnelian beads on a tomb relief

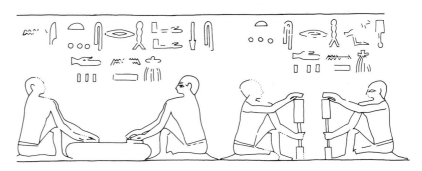

The Magic of Gold

Coloured pebbles from the desert and semi-precious stones from Egypt or elsewhere were skilfully broken into fragments of the required size, and these rough pieces ground into beads of various shapes on sandstone or quartz slabs with smooth, ribbed or grooved surfaces. They would then be cemented into small depressions and pierced with a drilling tool, which would usually be worked from both ends towards the centre. A relief from the Old Kingdom (29) shows drills consisting of a thin wooden rod with a flint tip, which the operator forced through the

30 Umm el-Qa'ab, the tomb of Dewen

stone by rotating it while holding the handle at the top. Drilling like this ground up the hard stone to a fine powder. The beads were then burnished to a high sheen with abrasives. In this relief, the tools and beads have been magnified for clarity. The inscription above the left-hand group reads, 'Polishing carnelian beads'.

Glazes and Faience
In the early 4th millennium BC, the Egyptians had already succeeded in producing imitations of

31 Umm el-Qa'ab, the tomb of Khasekhemwy

blue-green stones. Beads and pendants of steatite and quartz were glazed green and blue. Glazing was probably discovered by chance, the result perhaps of an accidental encounter on an open fire between pulverized malachite (used as eye make-up) containing copper oxide and desert sand containing sodium carbonate – the copper oxide, sodium carbonate and quartz sand combining and fusing to form a glaze. Steatite beads were particularly suited to glazing, because steatite does not explode on heating.

Another discovery made not much later was 'Egyptian faience'. It was made of calcareous desert sand, with copper compounds to provide the colour, and with sodium carbonate, binder and water. The paste was kneaded, shaped into beads, dried and presumably in early days baked in an oven under a layer of calcite powder, alkaline vegetable ash and copper compounds. Beads would be shaped around a straw to avoid the difficult process of drilling.

Gold, Silver and other Metals
The metals used to make beads were gold, silver and copper, and also small quantities of meteoric iron.

32 Umm el Qa'ab, the tomb of Qa'a

Pure silver was probably imported to the Nile Valley from the Near East – although much of it has now disintegrated through oxidation. Gold beads, which were produced by hammering nuggets of gold into foil and winding the foil into small straw-like tubes, are rarities. Egyptian gold, which contains appreciable amounts of silver, melts at approximately 1768°F (1000°C); as this temperature was achieved only towards the end of the 4th millennium BC, the earliest metal beads cannot have been cast, but must have been worked cold.

The Early Dynastic Period

Towards the end of the 4th millennium BC the last hunters abandoned their hunting grounds. The rock drawings that they left behind in shady resting places along their routes show the game that they hunted: elephant, rhinoceros, giraffe and other animals. With the weapons of the time, large game could be hunted only through tightly organized co-operation and expert leadership: the experience and social organization of the hunters who now moved into the Nile Valley equipped them for imposing a hierarchy on the population and commanding collective action. With these advantages and with a sense of belonging to a superior caste, they stamped their rule on the sedentary population of the Nile Valley, establishing a social order and living as an upper class benefiting from the labour of their inferiors.

33 Stone ointment jar with gold lid

From the first, the upper Nile Valley was too narrow for these hunter tribes. They were used to wide open spaces and they now looked towards the richer north, to which the focus of cultural development had shifted since the later Prehistoric Period. They advanced as conquerors as far as the wide landscape of the Nile Delta. Their leaders appear on palettes of the period, depicted as having the powers of wild animals: lions tearing the Lower Egyptians limb from limb, or wild bulls trampling them under their hooves.

In the Nile Delta the new masters came into contact with the objects and motifs of Near Eastern art. At first they maintained the centre of their realm in Upper Egypt, where their more demanding commissions spurred artisans on to new levels of achievement. Images of African big game created with unprecedented artistic ability suddenly appear among the archaeological finds in Upper Egypt, on knife-handles artfully carved from ivory or hammered out of gold foil. This cultural advance is also noticeable in the quantity and fine finish of new forms of bead.

The triumphal image on the Narmer Palette (37, 38), which may be a votive offering to Horus, god of the heavens, illustrates a decisive advance in figurative art: the invention of hieroglyphic writing. This made it possible to show in stylized images not only earthly and heavenly powers, but also all the phenomena of everyday life.

On the obverse of the palette (37), Narmer, wearing the tall crown of Upper Egypt, is represented symbolically smiting a defeated chieftain from Lower Egypt with his mace. At the centre of the upper margin of the palette the name *Nar-mer* is engraved, and flanking it on either side is the goddess of the heavens, who has a woman's face and a cow's ears and horns. Behind the king stands his sandal-bearer, his rosette and the accompanying hieroglyphics designating him as a 'servant of the King'. The pectoral that he wears – a pendant consisting of a short crossbar with two short verticals suspended from a necklace – was to undergo continuous artistic development throughout the entire pharaonic period. The motif of the king smiting the defeated enemy recurs in relief sculptures and in jewellery as a symbol of the order guaranteed by the king and of victory over chaos.

34 Carnelian ointment jar with gold lid

35 Breccia ointment jar with gold lid

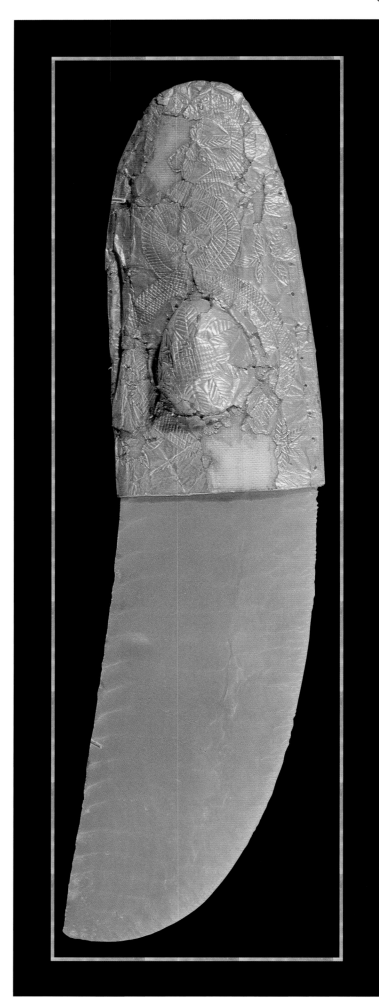

36 Flint knife with gold foil handle

On the reverse of the palette (38), the principal motif is formed by the intertwined necks of two fabulous panthers. In the upper register Narmer is shown wearing the low crown of Lower Egypt, going in procession to visit the place of execution of decapitated rebels. The ceremonial beard, an artificial beard that formed part of the king's regalia, was now also an attribute of the Egyptian gods. In his right hand the king holds a flail, a symbol of kingship like the sceptre that developed from the shepherd's crook. From his belt hang rows of beads and a protective pendant terminating in a tiny bird.

Every sign and every pictorial motif of the new figurative art is stamped by the divinely ordained order (*ma'at* in Egyptian) that now rules and that also governs the actions of the king. The fine arts – and also the art of the jeweller – become a propaganda instrument for the kings of Egypt, whose role is to make visible the divine order on earth.

Royal Tombs of the Early Dynastic Period

Royal tombs dating from the period of the unification of the two kingdoms (the so-called '0' Dynasty) and of the first two dynasties have been uncovered in the vicinity of Abydos, in Upper Egypt, and near the city known at the time as 'White Walls' (later Memphis), in Lower Egypt. As a few kings' names from the graves at Abydos reappear on the tombs at Memphis, it is possible that these kings, the 'lords of the two lands', built themselves tombs in both Upper and Lower Egypt. The true tombs were probably at Abydos (30–32), in accordance with tradition, and a cenotaph, an empty tomb, in Lower Egypt, where the princes who acted as governors of Lower Egypt, and queens, were in fact buried.

The cemetery of Umm el-Qa'ab, near Abydos, is the oldest known royal burial site in dynastic Egypt. It is here that the tombs of Narmer and the other rulers of the '0' Dynasty, as well as the tombs of almost all the kings of the first two dynasties, were discovered. These royal tombs, dug into the desert surface and walled with clay bricks, with a roof supported on wooden beams surmounted by a flattened mound, had already been plundered and destroyed in pharaonic times.

The earliest excavation of these tombs, carried out by Émile Amélineau in the late 19th century, was more of a treasure hunt than a scientific investigation. At the turn of the century the British archaeologist William Matthew Flinders Petrie dedicated himself to the excavation of these tomb structures, which were very important for the investigation of the earliest history of Egypt. Flinders Petrie discovered tombs that his predecessors had overlooked, and made highly significant new finds in those that had already, albeit inexpertly, been excavated.

Among these finds were important items of jewellery. When the excavators uncovered the burial

The most important of the four bracelets was made of alternating links of gold and green turquoise (25, 44). The front and back of each element represent the king's title: 'Horus-falcon over the palace façade (the *serekh*)'. On the gold links the falcon appears in the later, upright form, which remained the classic shape until the end of the pharaonic period. The turquoise king-falcons are artfully cut and polished. The gold links are cast in two parts and the architecture of the palace is engraved with a sharp tool. The regular shape of each

37 Narmer Palette, obverse, showing triumphant king

38 Narmer Palette, reverse, with round depression for grinding

chambers of Djer, they found hidden away a woman's severed arm, bound in linen bandages. Concealed beneath the bandages, truly royal jewels encircled the wrist: there were four different bracelets, of gold, lapis lazuli, amethyst, and turquoise (43). This was a unique find of women's jewellery, which had been provided for a royal wife or a female member of the royal family to use in the afterlife.

gold falcon indicates that they are casts. The links of this bracelet were perforated twice diagonally, and they were strung on two threads, which also passed through small holes drilled in the two end pieces, made of hollow beaten gold; the threads emerged at each end of the bracelet and were knotted together.

The bracelet worn above that with the king-falcons (41) is made up of two unequal parts linked at the

39 Tomb relief of a princess of the 2nd Dynasty

The third bracelet (40) is made up of a single row of beads with an unusual shape. Two large, flat links of green turquoise, like the smaller ones with the same shape and in the same material, may have been modelled on acacia seeds, which in the prehistoric

41 Bracelet with gold rosette

side of the wrist with cords of gilded animal hair. The part worn on the outer side of the wrist has a symmetrical design, with a gold rosette in the centre. Three short rows of beads on both sides show a regular alternation of tiny gold beads and larger ones made of turquoise, ending in a large, spherical bead of lapis lazuli. The gold beads are made of hemispheres beaten from gold foil, soldered together lengthwise in groups of three and strung on the three cords. The fastening would have been completed with a loop that was pulled over the individual gold beads.

The gold rosette in the centre of the bracelet (41), in the shape of the pistil of a lotus flower (42), is a masterpiece of early goldsmiths' work. The outer corona surrounds a plate lower down with a tiny round bulge in the middle, from which engraved lines radiate to the edge. In order to create precise forms, this part of the rosette would have been made by pressing the gold into a die.

The underside of the rosette consists of a box constructed of gold foil and filled with stucco. The lotus flower was closely linked to the sun-god. It is not known, however, whether this golden flower was seen as the symbol of the sun in the Early Dynastic Period. It was worn above the king-falcon bracelet and had the function of an amulet.

period were thought to protect a woman's health. Golden links with two wider, funnel-shaped ends join the beads together. The links, in the form of double cudgels that are set in four groups of three, are unique. The two outer links in each group are cast in solid gold, while those in the centre are made of translucent amethyst. These double-cudgel links are not drilled through but are caught in a double string of gold wire twisted round an annular notch with raised edges. Although the double cudgels bear some resemblance to the emblem of the goddess Neith, their significance remains uncertain.

42 Pistil of the lotus flower

The fourth bracelet (45), worn nearest the wrist, below the three others, also consists of three strands

43 Forearm of the body of woman, with four bracelets, from the burial chambers of Djer

40 Single-strand bracelet with double-cudgel links

44 Bracelet links with Horus-falcon over the palace façade (serekh)

divided into three groups. The central section is emphasized by the use of larger beads. Here, too, three large, spherical beads of beaten gold have been soldered into single elements. Totally new forms of beads can be seen, displaying the inventiveness of the early jewellers: from sections of gold wire that taper from a thick centre to progressively thinner ends, small, spirally wound drum-like beads were formed. The grooving on the three large beads of lapis lazuli in the centre imitates this goldsmith's work. Spirally wound beads of gold wire of exactly the same type were also found among the gold jewellery of a queen of Ur, in Mesopotamia, although she lived 500 years later. The correspondence between the two is remarkable, not least because this bracelet is the only known object in Egypt in which spirally wound gold beads are found.

These four bracelets from the royal burial ground at Abydos show a multitude of ideas in the design of their elements, in their structure, and in the perfection of their execution. They were much admired by Flinders Petrie when this unique assemblage of early Egyptian jewellery was discovered by chance.

The queen or princess upon whose wrist these treasures were discovered would also have worn a necklace and anklets of beads, and probably also a golden diadem on her head. Although all the jewellery had been plundered from the tomb of Queen Neithhotep (probably the wife of Aha, an early ruler of the 1st Dynasty), who was buried at Naqada, nine small ivory tablets were found there; on them were listed the necklaces and other jewellery originally buried with her, a record of stolen property that was to have been hers for eternity.

At Saqqara, the necropolis of Memphis, a 2nd Dynasty stela decorated in relief with a representation of a king's daughter (39) was found; it provides an idea of the jewellery that a lady of the royal house would have worn in life. The original paint on the relief, which might have indicated the nature of the materials used for these pieces, has unfortunately not survived. Around the abundant mass of her hair the princess wears a diadem in the form of a zigzag. From her neck hang three simple bead necklaces, the lower one with a pendant recognizable as an animal claw and worn as an amulet. Her right hand is outstretched to receive the offerings for the dead, and this wrist is adorned by a bracelet. On each ankle is a bead anklet. The large bow that hangs at the left shoulder holds her robe together.

Also from the 2nd Dynasty are finds from the tomb of Khasekhemwy, the last ruler to be buried at Abydos (31). Under the collapsed brickwork of this royal tomb several small ointment jars were found; they were made of various grained stones, fitted with gold lids (33–35). The lids are of thin, gold foil cut in circles, stretched like parchment over the lipped tops of the jars, and tied with twisted gold wire. The jars were sealed with a lump of clay applied to the ends of the wire.

Also among the finds in the tomb of Khasekhemwy was a plain bracelet of gold foil, an example in precious metal of a type of jewellery found in prehistoric graves, carved in ivory and later made in copper. There was also a royal ceremonial staff, perhaps a sceptre. Rods of black carnelian are fastened to a copper stick with golden clamps. The one surviving end has a gold cap. The sceptres from Tutankhamun's tomb, which were similar in construction, are significantly shorter.

Like those at Abydos, most of the royal tombs at Saqqara, near Memphis, have been plundered. Excavations carried out in the 1930s by Walter Bryan Emery yielded no jewellery. But in one burial chamber, dating from the time of Djet, the successor to Djer, precious metal was used in a new way, for the pillars of the burial chamber were covered with thin strips of

45 Triple-stranded bracelet with spiral beads of gold wire

The Magic of Gold

gold leaf; the metal of the sun would have lit up the darkness of the tomb for the deceased. About one thousand years later an inscription relating to Amenemhet I records that he had built his tomb as a 'golden house'. Yellow paint on the walls and ceiling of the tomb was used to imitate the magical effect of the precious metal.

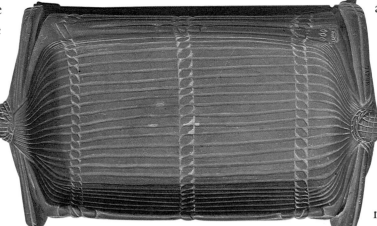

46 Small stone 'basket' with engraved hieroglyph for 'gold'

a tomb whose ceiling had fallen in and which had therefore escaped the attentions of grave robbers. The skeleton lying on the floor of the underground chamber had been crushed by the masonry, and the skull was surrounded by numerous pieces of jewellery made of gold with beads of coloured stone, and among them was a gold circlet.

Gold from Non-Royal Tombs

Ownership of jewellery made of gold and coloured stones was not restricted to members of the royal house. This is suggested by inscriptions on the Palermo Stone, a basalt stele dating from the 5th Dynasty, which mention, among other events, the twice-yearly collection of taxes and the counting of the gold in the kingdom. So gold was also the property of private individuals, perhaps because it was given as a reward for particular services or as a gift to loyal followers from the king's 'treasure house'. This is confirmed by a significant find in Upper Egypt.

During the excavation of a severely damaged burial site of the Early Dynastic Period at Nag ed-Deir, on the eastern bank of the Nile opposite Abydos, the American archaeologist George A. Reisner came upon

The necklaces found included a chain of twenty-four links made of shells of thick gold foil (47) – a successor to the real shells worn as ornament in prehistoric times. The gold shells are highly realistic, and may have been produced by taking a plaster impression from a real shell and pressing the gold foil into the hollow forma. The spiral on the outside of the shells was reworked with a gouge. The inside was filled with plaster and the opening covered with soldered gold foil. Reisner places great emphasis on the exceptionally careful way in which loops have been soldered on to the narrow sides of the shell.

Two pectorals (50–51), one in the form of a male oryx, the other in the form of a bull, which were discovered in the tomb, are unique in Egyptian art. They are beaten out of thin gold foil in high relief, the backs are filled with pink stucco and sealed with

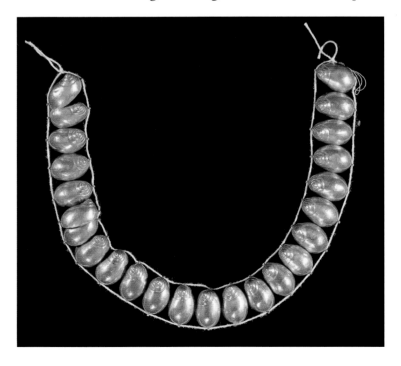

47 Gold necklace
48 Stone relief with the emblem of the goddess Neith
49 Amulet in the form of a beetle with the emblem of the goddess Neith

gold foil, which is held in place by the inward-turned edges of the front portion of foil. Two loops are soldered on the reverse of each pectoral, so that they can be worn on a ribbon or string of beads. A bow hangs down from the wide neckband of the oryx: this is the hieroglyph *tjet* ('life'). The bull, whose horns have been broken off, carries on a wide belt around his neck the emblem of Bat, goddess of the heavens: a woman's face with a cow's ears and inward-curving horns, and under this a wide bead frontlet. In Early

contrasts with the gold background is that of the material used to fill the inside of the beetle.

The beetle has been classified as a species of click beetle (*Elaterida*). Its association with the goddess Neith of Sais is shown on an early stone tablet (46), where it appears twice alongside Neith's emblem. During the Old Kingdom both these motifs often appear in jewellery and in decorative patterns (170, 171). The click beetle may be a precursor of the scarab, or dung beetle (*Ateuchus sacer*), which appears

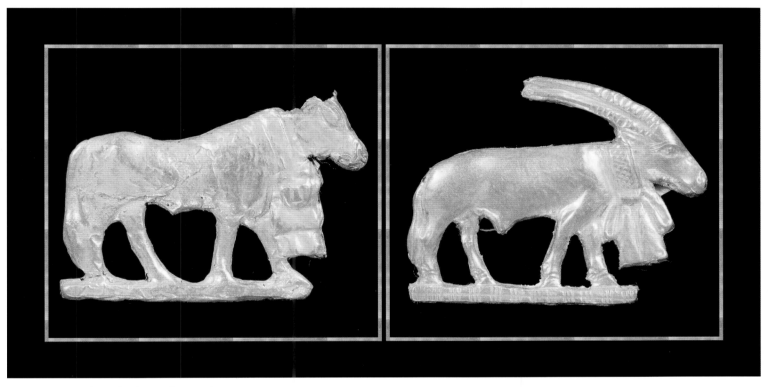

50–51 Pectorals in the form of animals

Dynastic times the goddess of the heavens had appeared as a magical protectress on the girdle of Narmer (38), and she reappears in the same role on a fragment of a statue of Djoser (119). The emblem of Bat was also the sign of the seventh province of Upper Egypt. Later, Bat entered into a close identification with the cow-goddess Hathor, of the neighbouring sixth province.

A particularly interesting piece from this tomb is the amulet in the form of a beetle (49). This amulet has been beaten out of gold foil into a two-part relief, an upper and a lower. The two parts are soldered together at their edges. The head was broken off – presumably when the ceiling of the tomb collapsed. On the underside, stylized beetle legs are clearly visible. The emblem of the Lower Egyptian goddess Neith is cut into the wing-covers; the blue that

from the end of the 3rd millennium BC, and the amulet would have signified life and rebirth.

The size of the tomb of Nag ed-Deir suggests that its occupant was close to the king. The jewellery that it contained, preserved in its entirety, shows how richly the tomb was furnished, and, compared to the sparse remains of royal burials, it demonstrates how much has been lost through grave-robbing.

The Hieroglyph for 'Gold'

From around 3000 BC, near the beginning of the Early Dynastic period, the hieroglyph for 'gold' takes the form of a beaded necklace, the item of jewellery most often worn by the pharaohs and their contemporaries, both men and women.

In its earliest form this necklace consists of semicircular rows of beads that hang down over the

The Magic of Gold

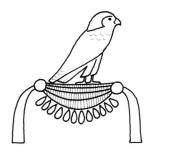

52 The Horus-falcon on the hieroglyph for 'gold'

53 Seth, squatting over the hieroglyph for 'gold'

breast, continue over the shoulders and are tied by two ribbons at the back of the neck. The lower edge of the necklace has a row of droplet-shaped pendants.

No such necklace dating from the Early Dynastic Period has yet been found; neither is it seen in pictorial representations of that period. Only in the 3rd Dynasty, during the reign of Djoser, does it appear – as an item of jewellery in an image of a deity (55) in a chapel at Heliopolis – but even then not in reliefs or statues of Djoser. From the beginning of the 4th Dynasty, the beaded necklace was part of the king's costume, as shown in pictorial representations, and it was also worn by members of the royal family.

The oldest coloured representation of this type of bead necklace is preserved on the seated statue of the princess Nofret (132). The rows of beads are painted in alternating blue, green and red, which may depict beads of lapis lazuli, turquoise and carnelian. The blue and green may, however, represent faience beads (red-glazed faience would have appeared only later).

54 Isis kneeling on the hieroglyph for 'gold', on the lower end of the sarcophagus of Queen Hatshepsut

During the Old Kingdom, the strands of beads in the necklace hieroglyph for 'gold' end in circular end-pieces. In all real necklaces, however, these terminals are almost oval, and the necklaces represented on statues also have oval end-pieces. From the later part of the Old Kingdom onwards, the end-pieces sometimes take the form of falcons' heads.

How was it, then, that a necklace, which was strung with beads of faience and coloured stones and made only partly of gold (as shown in surviving examples and in pictorial representations), could have come to signify gold? Several attempts have been made to answer this question.

The bead necklace was perhaps originally an ancient emblem for the 'gold town' of Nubt (now Naqada) on the west bank of the Nile, at the end of the roads leading to the gold mines in the region of Koptos. In inscriptions the bead necklace designated the god Seth as 'the one from Nubt', and he was also represented as squatting above it, as was his counterpart, the king-god Horus (52–53).

Another explanation of the original meaning of this hieroglyph is that it could be derived from the early Egyptian language. The root of the word for 'gold' (*nb*) and that for 'glowing embers' are the same. Gold is the metal of the blazing sun and gold is melted in 'glowing embers'.

These attempts at interpretation do not take into account the circular gold end-

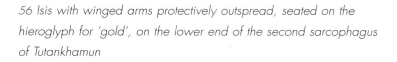

55 Deity with necklace and solar disc

pieces of the necklace, which in the hieroglyph are sometimes shown with a dot within the circle and may be symbols of the sun. If the two circles are taken in this sense, they can be seen as the rising and setting sun, and the strings of beads as the sun's rays. Blue and green are the colours of the rising and setting sun and of its nocturnal journey through the underworld. Red is the colour of the blazing daytime sun, the same colour as that of the inlay of solar discs on pectorals of the 12th Dynasty (219, 220, 233, 234). The blue and

56 Isis with winged arms protectively outspread, seated on the hieroglyph for 'gold', on the lower end of the second sarcophagus of Tutankhamun

green cylindrical beads of the necklaces found on the chest of the dead in tombs suggest the nocturnal underworld and the daily rising and setting of the sun. Necklaces worn by the living also have red carnelian beads, uniting the two phases of the sun's journey, through day and night.

The Gold Mines

Of all the great civilizations of antiquity, that of the Egyptians was the richest in gold. The ancient civilizations of the Near East, which flourished in the Fertile Crescent in the basins of the Tigris and Euphrates rivers, had to obtain all the precious metals and the stones that they needed for their jewellery from the Caucasus Mountains, Iran and the mountainous regions of Asia Minor, regions that all lay beyond the limits of their power.

Egypt, however, was blessed with numerous deposits of gold within its own boundaries – in the Eastern Desert of Upper Egypt and in the ancient rock formations along the shores of the Red Sea. Gold is found in veins of white quartz wherever slate and granite meet, and the deposits extend much further than Egypt's southern borders at the First Cataract, through Ta-Nub, the Land of Gold (Nubia) and deep into the Sudan. Nubian gold was already brought as tribute to the kings of the Old Kingdom.

The mountains of the Eastern Desert, whose sometimes rounded and sometimes much more precipitous summits rise to more than 6,500ft (2,000m), are cut through with dry valleys, or wadis,

in which only sparse vegetation – a few tamarisks, acacias and low bushes – can survive. Moisture that rises as clouds from the Red Sea and gathers around the highest mountaintops brings local rain from time to time, and the occasional heavy rainstorm. The wadis are then transformed into raging torrents, which may be dammed up in small lakes whose water gathers in crevices in the rock. Here it remains fresh for a long time. The damp ground supports sparse green grasses and becomes colourful with flowers, which wither quickly in the scorching sun. In the 3rd millennium BC, rainfall was significantly more frequent in the Eastern Desert than it is today.

The climate change that in prehistoric times caused drought in most of North Africa, resulting in the gradual formation of the sterile Sahara, did not have such a drastic effect on the mountains along the shores of the Red Sea. In the Old and Middle Kingdoms the climate was more favourable than it is today. In areas that later turned to desert there was a greater number of water sources along the trails and at the mines in the mountains, far from the Nile Valley, and as a result more vegetation and game. Hundreds, even thousands, of workers could remain in these areas for several weeks if mining expeditions and the necessary supplies were carefully planned and organized by the state administration, and particularly if the workforce was recruited from among the undemanding nomads who were used to the harsh life of these arid mountains. Over-exploitation of the vegetation and the felling of trees – both for firewood

57–59 Tribute: Nubians bring gold nuggets and rings, and Asiatics bring magnificent gold vessels

and to shore up the tunnels of the underground mines – gradually turned the wadis of the eastern mountains into barren wastes.

Gold Deposits – Exploration and Approaches

From prehistoric times, the nomads who lived in the mountains had brought precious stones and lumps of gold to barter in the Nile Valley. In the earliest hieroglyphic inscriptions they are depicted as men, called *Sementiu*, sitting on the ground, holding leather purses in outstretched hands. In the 1st Dynasty they seem to have been taken into the service of the Egyptian state to explore mineral resources and trade routes in faraway regions that were difficult to reach.

Alongside these explorers prospecting for gold and precious stones, there was also a desert guard, whom the royal administrators of Central and Upper Egypt had probably set up in early times.

The most northerly group of gold deposits in the mountains along the Red Sea coast lies approximately parallel with the southern tip of the Sinai Peninsula and the city of Minya, in the Nile Valley. These deposits can be reached from the city of Qena, which lies at the apex of the Nile loop, northwards through the Wadi Qena or ten days' march eastwards from

Pages 38–39: 60 The huts of pharaonic miners near the Fawachir gold mine

The Magic of Gold

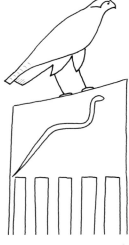

61 Horus-name of Djet and royal snake

Minya. The mine at Fawachir (60) yielded significant deposits of gold. The oldest routes to the mine probably started in the city of Koptos (modern Qift) and passed through the Wadi Hammamat. The god Min, who was worshipped at Koptos and was already represented in statues of the Late Prehistoric period, was lord of this city and also protector of the desert routes that led east through the Wadi Hammamat and to a port on the Red Sea, modern Quseir.

Koptos, on the east bank of the Nile, was vulnerable to attacks from nomadic tribes of the Eastern Desert and was therefore unsafe for storing gold. On the edge of the desert, facing Koptos and protected by the Nile, lay the metropolis of Nubt, the main area of settlement in prehistoric Upper Egypt. It was here, it appears, that the gold obtained from the Eastern Desert was stored and processed. The god Seth, who took the form of a strange desert animal (53), was the Lord of Nubt, an earlier king-god and the opponent of the falcon king-god Horus of Nekhen (Hierakonpolis).

There are also several routes providing access to gold deposits from the city of Nekheb (El Kab), south of Koptos. Since earliest times the city had been surrounded by walls, which still encircle the ancient ruins of houses and temples today. Nekhbet, the main goddess of the city, who took the form of a white vulture, was worshipped as the protector of the White Crown of Upper Egypt. A relief from the mortuary temple of the pharaoh Sahure at Abusir shows the goddess granting the king the right to 'wash silver and gold in the eastern mountains'.

In a niche in the rock of Wadi Barramiyeh, on the route to the gold deposits accessible from Nekheb, the name of one of the earliest Egyptian pharaohs, Djet, is carved (61). This suggests that gold was already being mined there on the king's orders in the Early Dynastic period. On the west bank of the Nile, not far from Nekheb, is Nekhen (Hierakonpolis), the royal capital of the earliest Egyptian kings. From here, on the opposite bank of the Nile, there was also a route to the gold mines lying to the east of Nekheb. The elevation of the Upper Egyptian chieftains to the rank of kings was perhaps in part based on the ownership and exploitation of these gold deposits.

There was another way in to the southerly deposits at present-day Kom Ombo. The three mining districts

62 Mortar for grinding in the Wadi Margh
63 Nugget from a find of the 4th Dynasty
64 Gold mine in Wadi Barramiyeh
65 Gold-bearing quartz at Um Ud
66 Gold-washing installation at Faras, Nubia

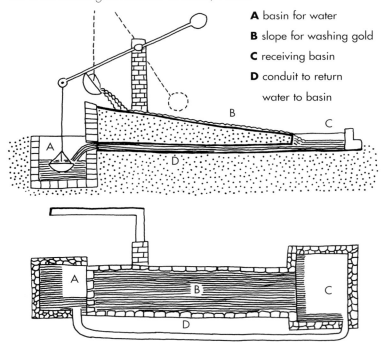

A basin for water
B slope for washing gold
C receiving basin
D conduit to return water to basin

The Gold Mines

67 Beam balance in a goldsmith's workshop, surmounted by an image of the goddess Ma'at

accessible from Qena, Quft, Nekheb and Kom Ombo, delivered the 'gold of Koptos'. About seventy mining sites in use from pharaonic times to the Roman period (and occasionally as late as the Islamic Middle Ages) have been discovered. Exploration of individual mines has only just begun. As well as determining mining techniques and methods used for breaking up the gold ore and washing and melting the gold, the aim of these investigations is to determine the periods in which the mines were being exploited.

In inscriptions, Nubian gold and precious stones are designated 'royal jewellery'. From the foundation of Egypt, Nubia – the land to the south, between the First and the Second Cataracts of the Nile – had regularly to be prevented from encroaching on the southern borders of Egypt and forced to pay tribute in gold. The royal governors on the southern borders of Egypt near Elephantine explored this far country with their troops and brought back 'royal jewellery'.

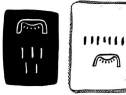

68 Stone weights for weighing gold, 12th Dynasty

Gold-mining Expeditions and Techniques

In principle, all mining operations were carried out for the sole benefit of the pharaoh. He equipped the expeditions at royal expense and all gold obtained as a result would be deposited in the royal treasury. The nature of the preparation and organization of such an expedition in the 3rd millennium BC can be deduced only roughly from present-day knowledge of the administrative structure of ancient Egypt, for few written records of such enterprises have as yet been found by archaeologists.

Newly discovered gold deposits were reported by the explorers, the *Sementiu*, to the administrative centre of the nearest province. The provincial administrator would investigate the approaches, the likely yield, and the water supply en route and at the location of the mine. He would then report this to the administration of the treasure house at the royal capital, which during the Old and Middle Kingdoms was at Memphis, in

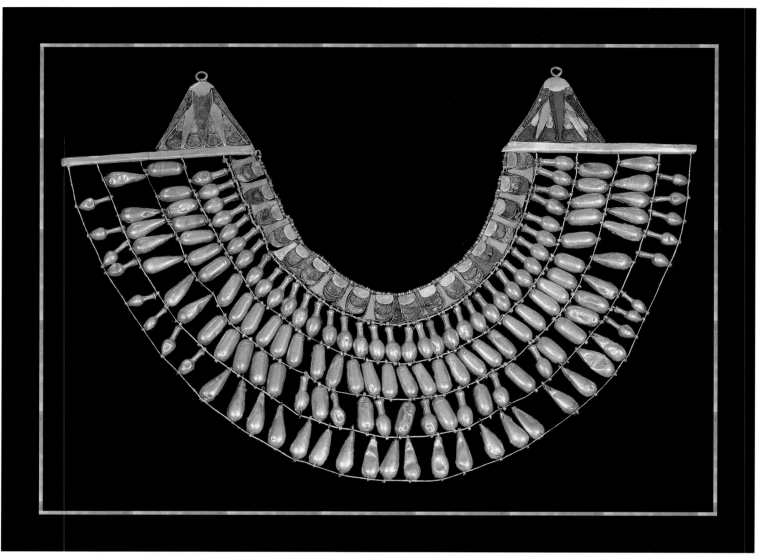

69 Bead collar of King Smenkhare, 18th Dynasty

Lower Egypt. Here, at the king's command, the men and resources needed would be assembled: the officials who would lead the expedition, the scribes to keep records of the provisions consumed and gold obtained, and the skilled workers with their tools; enough provisions carried from the granaries of the royal capital for the thousands of workers; and the ships and crews to transport all these to Upper Egypt, to the starting-point of the overland march.

At the same time, the provincial administrator had to find labourers from his own province – generally nomads from the adjacent Eastern Desert – and provide donkeys for the land transport of provisions and equipment. Supplied with daily rations of water and bread, the labourers made the long journey on foot. Each expedition would usually spend only a few days at the mines.

Along the route of the march, and at the gold mines in particular, sufficient water had to be

available for people and animals, and also for washing the gold. It was necessary to dig wells quickly in order to access ground water, and when the rare storm rains occurred water would be collected in cisterns or in dammed valleys.

The labourers were divided into gangs and housed in small huts of rough stone, whose low walls were presumably roofed with vegetation or tenting (60). They were protected against attacks from nomadic tribes by the desert guard, who acted as overseers and were also responsible for transporting the gold from the mining site to the Nile, loading it on to ships and for its transportation by river to the royal capital.

For those involved in these expeditions, working conditions in the hot mountainous regions were extremely harsh. Despite all the planning and provisioning by the state, the labourers had to be driven relentlessly. The majority of them were probably of nomadic origin.

The Gold Mines

The ancient gold mines have been prospected in modern times by European and Egyptian mining companies, whose engineers have reported that hardly any gold deposits were overlooked by the explorers of antiquity. The mines themselves are astonishing, with shafts up to 330ft (100m) deep and hundreds of feet of corridors and pillared galleries.

Here and there in a few of the gold mines in the Eastern Desert of Upper Egypt and Nubia, evidence of ancient mining techniques has been found. Traces of workings were left behind, and there are surviving items of equipment, such as stone mortars (62), mills and washing installations (66). In the course of the millennia these mines were exploited over and over again, most recently in the Islamic Middle Ages. Mining techniques, however, remained the same – except for the introduction of iron tools, which

70 Ring with cloisonné-work, 18th Dynasty
71 Girdle from the tomb of Queen Mereret, 12th Dynasty
72 Scarab bracelet, 18th Dynasty
73 String of golden shells and ducks, 18th Dynasty

appeared in Egypt in about 200 BC – and it is only possible to identify the periods when the mines were operated from the rare surviving inscriptions and from the form of mortars and grindstones.

The miners of ancient Egypt worked the exposed veins of auriferous quartz in open trenches (64–65). This 'open-cast' mining must have been the earliest technique in use, and was employed in the Old and Middle Kingdoms. Once such deposits had been exhausted, around the middle of the 2nd millennium BC, the miners had to work underground, driving shafts and tunnels into the depths of the earth to follow the veins of gold (99). The gold-bearing quartz was probably first fractured by heating with fires, and the loosened rock prized out with dolerite hammers and copper chisels, and hardened through constant annealing. In the diorite quarries of the Nubian Western Desert (north-west of Abu Simbel) copper chisels have been found dating from as early as the time of Cheops and Chephren (4th Dynasty).

The gold-bearing rock obtained from the quartz veins was broken down into pea-sized lumps by pounding in stone mortars, then reduced to dust by grinding with a stone against flat stone slabs. To separate the gold from the quartz the mixture was tipped on to a slightly inclined stone table, with a shallow lengthways trough in the middle, and washed down several times with water. During this process, the heavy gold sank to the bottom and was caught on the rough stone surface, while the lighter quartz dust was washed away. The gold would be swept together, packed into leather pouches and weighed, the weight being recorded by scribes.

Gold could also be obtained from the auriferous sands of mountain slopes and wadis, which would be dug to a depth of approximately 6½ft (2m) and the tiny gold particles washed out using the method described above. This 'alluvial gold' was therefore much easier to obtain than the mined gold extracted from veins of quartz.

As water was scarce in the mountains along the Red Sea coast, it might be supposed that the gold dust would be washed again when it reached the banks of the Nile, at the site of the start of the land-journey, and such a washing installation has been found in Nubia on the banks of the Nile, but the equipment probably dates from the Byzantine period (66).

Gold was weighed with special weights made of stone. Surviving examples of these weights (68) are inscribed with the sign for 'gold' and a number and sometimes also with the name of the king. The number indicates the weight in *deben*, the unit used to weigh gold since the time of the early kings (1 *deben* = ½oz = 13–14gm).

As a rule it was only in the Nile Valley, where fuel was more abundant than at the mines in the mountains, that gold dust was melted into rings and bars of officially prescribed weights.

The Quality of the Gold

The gold obtained from Egyptian and Nubian mines is of varying quality. It is rarely pure '24 carat' gold, and usually contains a significant proportion (20–40 per cent) of silver and a small amount of copper. As well as 'good gold' – that is, pure gold – the ancient Egyptians distinguished two further qualities, named for their colour: 'light gold' and 'white gold'. What the Egyptians called 'white gold' we call by the Latin name *electrum*, itself derived from *elektron*, the Greek word for amber. The Egyptian 'white gold', with its very high silver content and an appearance that is hardly distinguishable from silver, should not be confused with our own 'white gold', which is an alloy of platinum and nickel. As early as the Old Kingdom, the quality of gold might also be specified as a fraction representing the ratio of gold to silver: 'one-third' (8 carats) and 'two-thirds' (16 carats).

Pure 24 carat gold is extremely soft and scratches easily. Gold that contains silver is harder and is ideal for making jewellery. Pure gold melts at a temperature of 1920°F (1065°C), silver at 1740°F (965°C) and, with a high silver-content, Egyptian gold could be melted at a temperature of around 1768°F (1000°C).

Only later on did the Egyptians learn how to 'refine' gold – that is, to separate gold from silver by cupellation. Deposits of pure silver (90 per cent or higher) are not found in the Eastern Desert of Egypt or Nubia, and from prehistoric times silver was imported from the Near East. After the Egyptian conquest of territories in that region, great quantities came to Egypt as booty or tribute. During the Old and Middle Kingdoms the scarcer silver was more highly prized than gold.

Gold in Private Hands

As mentioned above, the exploitation of mineral resources in general – and of gold and coloured stones in particular – was a royal monopoly. The existence of jewellery made of beads and gold and used for the adornment of the dead shows that small quantities of gold had already made their way into private hands as early as the 3rd millennium BC, and records of the

74–75 String of carnelian beads with gold pendants, 18th Dynasty

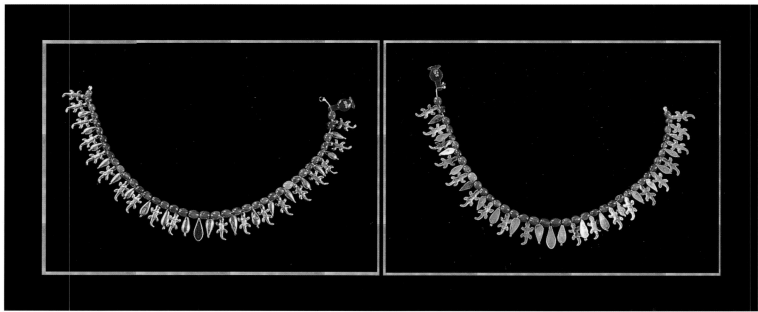

76 Necklaces of the late Ptolemaic period

2nd Dynasty show that the king regularly conducted a 'census of all the fields and all the gold in the land'.

Throughout their history, the ancient Egyptians of the Nile Valley were supplied with gold and precious stones, either by the nomads of the Eastern Desert or from their own explorations. Large-scale expeditions could be equipped and sent out only by the king.

A royal instruction issued to the vizier, the highest official of the kingdom, presumed to date from after 1800 BC, permits the mining of gold against a request made in writing in advance. There is no evidence to indicate to what extent the provincial administrators who commanded access to the gold deposits may have sent out smaller expeditions on their own account.

Bead-makers' workshops, where gold was also worked into jewellery for the living and the dead, existed in all the larger towns, but all the more sophisticated gold jewellery found in the private tombs of the Old and Middle Kingdoms must, however, have been 'gold of favour', a gift from the king.

Historical Evidence
Sesostris I, the second ruler of the 12th Dynasty, elevated a loyal follower named Sirenpowet to princely rank as governor of Elephantine, an island below the First Cataract on the southern frontier of Upper Egypt. An inscription in Sirenpowet's rock tomb on the steeply sloping western bank of the Nile,

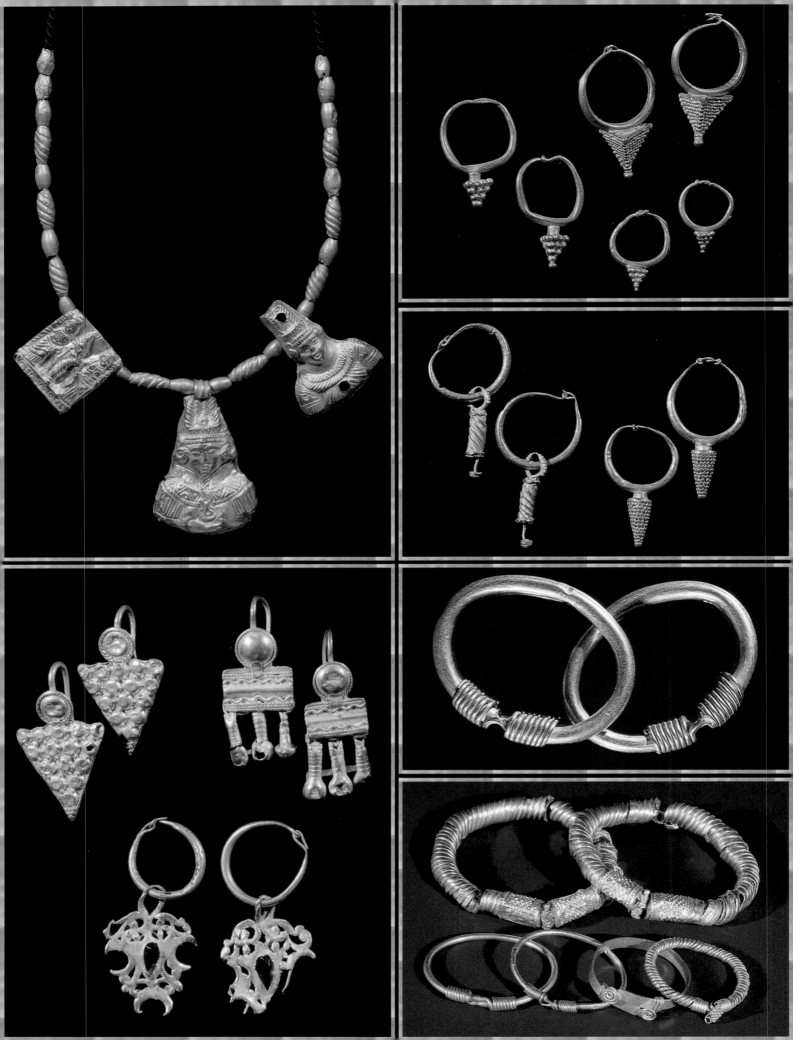

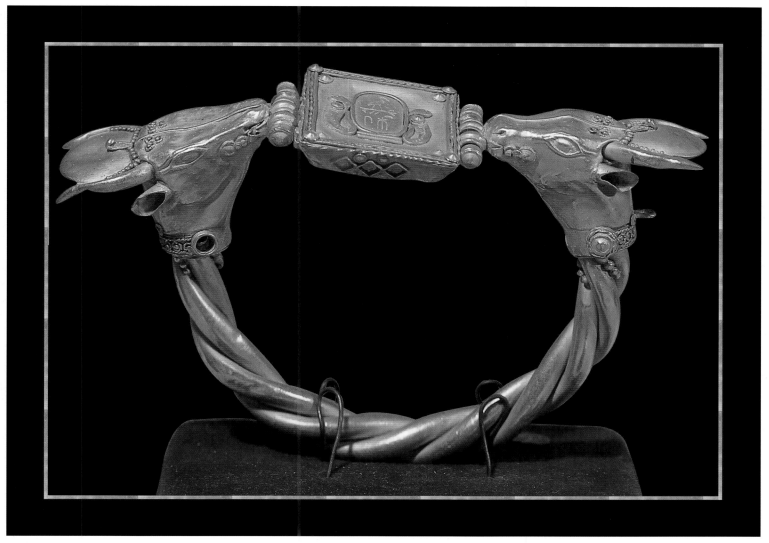

83 Ptolemaic bracelet with cow's heads of Hathor and a decorative plate with a royal cartouche

just north of Elephantine, details his responsibilities in connection with gold-deliveries from Nubia: 'amid the jubilation of the Egyptians and their prince and governor, the wondrous things from the land of the Medes [Wadi Allaqi]' came by ship through the rapids and whirlpools of the First Cataract to arrive at the 'Foreigners' Gate' above Elephantine Island. Embarked with his entourage on the ship of the gods, the cultic barge of the god Khnum, Sirenpowet sails 'on the turbulent waters' to meet the arriving tribute of 'royal jewellery'. The gold delivery is handed over at the temple of Khnum, in a strictly ritualized ceremony, before the eyes of the god himself.

As the god of creation, Khnum of Elephantine was also responsible for gold and everything made of it. The ancient Egyptians believed that he formed gods

77–82 Gold jewellery of the Ptolemaic period: chain with pendants, earrings and bracelets

and people on the potter's wheel in the 'house of gold', and brought them to life by magical rites. At Elephantine, a 'priest of Khnum of the royal jewellery' was entrusted with the ritual for the melting of the gold and the production of golden or gilded statues. The god would be 'born anew' in this golden form. Vessels destined for cultic use were made in accordance with the same ritual. The 'priest of Khnum of the royal jewellery' was then responsible for the onward transportation of the gold, which he accompanied to the treasury in the royal capital.

If we understand Sirenpowet's inscription correctly, on the day of the great feast he would spend the night in the temple and receive gifts of precious objects, like the ones given by the king at his palace. He, like the temple of Khnum, must surely have received his part of the gold delivery. This inscription in Sirenpowet's tomb is the only one that tells of the rituals associated with gold; and it was only these that imbued such costly materials – gold and precious stones – with their life-preserving, protective powers.

In an inscription of about the same date, found in a tomb at Beni Hasan in Middle Egypt, a provincial governor boasts: 'I sailed southwards by ship to obtain gold for His Majesty King Sesostris I, together with the prince and heir to the throne, Ameni, the eldest son of the King [later King Amenemhet II].'

> I sailed southward with 400 chosen men from my army. I returned home in peace, without any losses among them. I brought the gold as I had been instructed, and for this I was praised in the King's house and the King's son thanked me.

84–85 Foundation plaque from the Serapeum in Alexandria, from the time of Ptolemy III and IV, 3rd century BC

With a military escort, Ameni, had brought gold from Nubia to store in such strongholds as Buhen and Semna. Barely a century later, on a memorial stela from Abydos, an official under Amenemhet III confirms that gold mining was imposed on the subjugated indigenous chiefs of Nubia: 'I forced the chiefs of Nubia to wash gold'.

Around 1285 BC King Sethos I had a watering station and a small temple with a colonnaded façade constructed by a shady rock face (100) at Kanais in the Wadi Mia, en route to the Barramiyeh mines. The inscription testifies to the king's interest in gold mining and his concern for the mining expeditions:

His Majesty inspected the desert as far as the mountains. His heart wished to see the mines which furnished the gold. After His Majesty had gone many miles, he rested along the way in order to take counsel with his heart. He said: 'How arduous is a path on which there is no water … who quenches the thirst of those who march? The valley of the Nile is far away and the desert is endless. How can I care for them and do something that will revive them, so that for years to come they may praise God and my own name … because of my prudence and my care for the travellers?'

> After His Majesty had spoken these words in his heart, he travelled about the desert and searched for a location for a reliable watering place. God however directed him and brought him success. Masons were commanded to dig a well in the mountains whose water would cool and encourage the exhausted, and the heart of him who is burnt by the heat. This watering station was thus erected in the great name of Men-Ma'at-R[e] [the regnal name of Sethos I]. It gave abundant water, like the cave of springs in Elephantine [whence sprang the Nile, according to ancient Egyptian belief].

The following words in the inscription are clearly a warning against any attempt at misappropriation:

> Gold is the flesh of the gods. It is not your business. Beware of saying what Re said when he began to speak: 'My skin is pure gold.'

A temple was built in the vicinity of the well. In its inscriptions all rights to the exploitation of the gold deposits and all revenue from this mining area are granted exclusively to the great temple of Sethos I in Abydos, which at that time was still in the process of being built. The gold-washers, described as 'belonging to my temple' (of Abydos), had the responsibility of producing the gold required for the gilding of the statues. The inscription ends with a warning to future kings who might claim the rights to the gold from the mines at Barramiyeh, or wish to use the gold-washers on other tasks. For these gold-washers were to be 'exempted and protected', and were not to be disturbed 'by any person in the whole land, by no Commander of the Gold, by no Inspector of the Desert. The head of the gold-washers … shall be independent and shall send his deliveries of gold directly to the temple in Abydos.' Similar royal ordinances assigning gold mines to temples – the temple of Amun in Karnak, and many others – were also set down in tomb inscriptions.

The Gold Mines

An official report from the days of Sethos'
successor, Ramesses II, survives. It deals with the
difficulties involved in exploiting rich deposits of gold
in the Nubian Eastern Desert. It is inscribed on a
memorial the king had erected at Quban in Nubia.
Here, on the western shores of the Nile, Sesostris I
had already built a stronghold to protect the gold
mines of the Wadi Allaqi, at which fortress the gold
obtained was also securely stored until its
transportation to the Egyptian frontier station on the
island of Elephantine. Within the walls were gold-
washing facilities and weights for weighing the gold.
This stronghold was rebuilt several times and
continued to fulfil its function until the end of the
Ramesside period.

The memorial was erected by the Viceroy of Kush,
the Egyptian official responsible for the mining of
gold in Nubia. The text, which is given here almost
word for word, clearly describes the situation on the
roads to the gold mines and the difficulty in
obtaining water:

> In the year 3, in the first month of the sprouting of the
> seed [December], on the fourth day, in the reign of the
> Horus … Ramesses II, in Memphis, on a feast day
> celebrated there. His Majesty thought of the lands from
> which gold is brought, and he decided to have wells dug
> along the road which is without water, for he heard it said
> that there might be much gold in the land of Akita [the
> area of the Wadi Allaqi] but that the way there was
> without water. When expeditions of gold-washers went
> there only half arrived. They would die of thirst on their
> way, together with the donkeys they took with them for
> transport. On the march there and back to the Nile Valley
> sufficient supplies of drinking-water could not be found
> for their skins. Therefore no more gold could be brought
> from this region without water.

*86–87 Gold stater of Nectanebos II: galloping horse, and the
hieroglyphs nefer nub, 'pure gold'*

*88–89 Five-drachm coin: portrait of Ptolemy I Soter. Eagle on
thunderbolt*

*90–91 Eight-drachm coin with portraits of royal couples. Obverse:
Ptolemy I Philadelphos and Arsinoe II. Reverse: Ptolemy I Soter and
Berenice*

*92–93 Eight-drachm coin: portrait of the deified Arsinoe. Double
cornucopia with royal ribbon*

*94–95 Eight-drachm coin: portrait of Ptolemy III Euergetes with ray
diadem, cornucopia and royal ribbon*

The king then had his courtiers called together to consult them about the matter. After ceremonial greetings the Viceroy of Kush said:

'It is said of the region of Akita that there has never been enough water there. There the people die of thirst. Every previous king wished to establish a well there, but without any success! This was already so in the days of King Sethos I. He had a well dug to a depth of 200ft [60m] – but in vain! No water came out of it. O King, ask your father Hapi [the Nile], the father of the gods, to bring water to the mountainous land!'

The king replied: 'It is true what you have said … but I wish to establish a well there …' He summoned the highest of the scribes and through him issued an order to the Viceroy of Kush to recruit workers for the building of the well. But the Viceroy complained: 'What am I to do? Am I to have the water of the underworld supplied to him?'

At the king's behest, the well was dug on the way to Akita, and the (no doubt extremely relieved) Viceroy

heavy labour involved in winning precious metals and valuable stones from the mountains of the desert. A map from around 1200 BC, one of the oldest maps in the world, does however show us what a gold-mining settlement and its facilities would have looked like.

The surviving fragments of the map, which is drawn on papyrus (96-97), are in the Egyptian museum in Turin. Presumably this papyrus roll, 16in (41cm) wide and originally several feet long, was laid, tightly rolled up, in the grave of an official of the mining administration. It has broken up into a dozen fragments, which still measure about 7ft (2.8m) when laid end to end, but the individual fragments do not follow on exactly from one another, and the extent of the gaps is unknown.

The fragment showing the gold mines (96) is the best preserved. It has mountains painted in red, which are identified in the annotations – written in the ancient Egyptian cursive script, the so-called hieratic – as the 'Mountains of Gold'. For the ancient

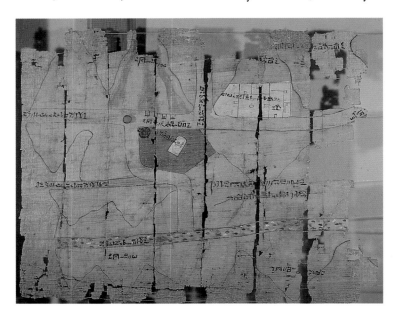

96 Map of the gold mines, Papyrus 1

97 Map of the gold mines, Papyrus 2

of Kush was able to report to his master: 'What Your Majesty has spoken with his own lips has come to pass: water came out of the well, which is only 20ft [6m] in depth, and it is 6½ft [2m] deep.'

Deliveries of gold from countries subjugated by the pharaoh, and in particular from Nubia (58), which brought regular tribute, are often represented in the tombs of officials of the New Kingdom, and temple inscriptions specify the quantities of gold the kings presented to the gods in thanks for their victories. No visual representation, however, has been found of the

Egyptians their country's head lay in the south, near the island of Elephantine, so the map has south at the top and north at the bottom, and the gold-mining region thus appears on the left – in the east.

On the succeeding fragments (97) the mountains are painted in black; according to the annotations they are of bechen-stone, dark green greywacke. The most important quarry for this stone is in the Wadi Hammamat, whose north-eastern end adjoins the gold mines of Fawachir. The wadi itself can be recognized in the stony path indicated towards the

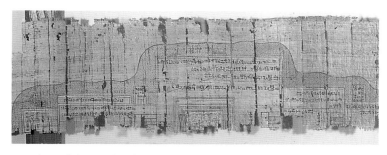

98 Plan of the tomb of Ramesses IV. In the annotations the burial chamber is called the 'house of gold'

bottom edge of the map, which continues at about the same height on all the fragments.

Near the centre of the fragments showing the gold mines a stela stands out against the background, a memorial stone with a semicircular upper edge and an inscription, erected by King Sethos I. On its left is a well; frequent use has turned the adjacent ground into fertile earth, which has been coloured black. Above this is the 'Village of the Gold-Workers'. A small reddish circle to the left of the village probably shows a dried-out well. The workers' settlement included a shrine, 'the chapel of Amun of the Pure Mountain'; and here some rituals for the gold they extracted were presumably performed. The mountain summit diagonally above bears the annotation 'the summit on which Amun rules'. Other mountains from which 'gold and silver' were extracted are also shown on the map. The parallel wadis run west – right – towards the Nile Valley, and east – left – towards the Red Sea. Further valleys are visible, with annotations whose geographical significance is unclear.

The mining region of Wadi Allaqi in Nubia is mentioned in an account of a journey by the Greek Agatharchidos of Knidos, which has survived from around 130 BC. It describes in detail the gold-mining

99 Mines in the Wadi Hammamat

methods and the harsh working and living conditions of the gold-workers of Ptolemaic times:

> In the vicinity of the Red Sea, on the borders of Egypt, there is a place where there are many big gold-mines. Gold is obtained from them by unremitting toil and at enormous expense. Aided by numerous labourers, the overseers of the mine hammer it out of the rocky ground, which is by nature black, but contains veins of radiant white quartz, whose bright colour surpasses in brilliance even the most gleaming things …
>
> The kings of Egypt send to the mines convicted criminals and prisoners of war, and also people who have been thrown into prison on false accusations, sometimes alone, sometimes with their wives and children, on the one hand to punish the convicts, and on the other hand to gain possession of great incomes by the exploitation of their labour. The convicts, who are very many in number, all have their feet shackled and must remain at work day and night without pause, being carefully guarded against any possible escape … there is no greater misfortune.

100 The temple constructed by Sethos I at Kanais

Tomb-robbery

For an ancient Egyptian, the destruction of his mummy or of the tomb and its furnishings meant the extinction of life in the hereafter. In orderly times, under strong pharaohs, it was only state supervision and the maintenance of a watchful guard on the royal necropolises – combined with every Egyptian's belief in his own afterlife, assured by burial-gifts befitting his rank – that protected the dead from being robbed of the treasures that were buried with them. As soon, however, as the state's grip on cemeteries loosened and

The Magic of Gold

To provide for their own burial, however, even kings sinned against the tombs of their predecessors. This is shown by the many costly stone vessels bearing the names of kings of the 2nd Dynasty found in the galleries below King Djoser's step-pyramid at Saqqara. Nor did Amenemhet I, the founder of the 12th Dynasty, show much reverence for his own predecessors. Some 500 years after the building of the mortuary-temple complexes of the kings of the 4th and early 5th Dynasties, which by the beginning of the Middle Kingdom were probably already falling into disrepair, he used blocks carved in relief and other architectural elements, some of them bearing the name of Cheops, as filling-material for his own pyramid at Lisht.

Tomb-robbery in Antiquity

It is difficult to establish any kind of date for the looting of the pyramids of the Old and Middle

101 Gilded wooden shrine, its gold statue stolen by robbers, from the tomb of Tutankhamun
102 A jewellery chest of Tutankhamun, ransacked by robbers
103 A piece of cloth and rings dropped by robbers in Tutankhamun's tomb
104 A column of the Abbot Papyrus with the report of the inquiry into royal burial sites

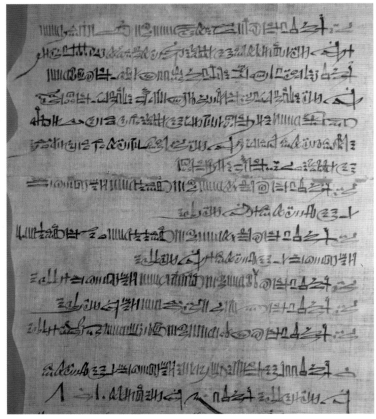

the guard on royal burial sites relaxed – for instance, when the royal capital was moved, or abandoned following the collapse of the state – tomb-robbers began to appear.

Looters and tomb-robbers were feared even in the Old Kingdom, as is shown by threatening inscriptions in burial chambers warning against damage to burial sites or the removal of offerings and tomb furnishings.

105 The plundered burial chamber and sarcophagus of Thutmosis III

Kingdoms. To penetrate into the natural rock beneath the pyramids and afterwards to break through the gigantic limestone blocks to gain access to the burial chambers would have required not only a detailed knowledge of the entrances to the hidden chambers, which differed from pyramid to pyramid, but also the work of a considerable number of stonemasons and labourers.

This last operation, however, would be conceivable only during a period in which state authority had collapsed totally – which in early Egyptian history occurred only at the end of the 6th Dynasty – and there exists a clue in the literature that might support this assumption. The premonitory words of a prophet who graphically described the situation at that time carry a warning: 'The one who is buried as a falcon [the king] lies on a bier; what the pyramid was hiding will become empty'. This somewhat obscure text appears in a description of the chaotic conditions that prevailed at the end of the Old Kingdom. Its reference can only be to the plundering of smaller pyramids, however; the larger pyramids at this date were still well secured.

Khaemwese, a son of Ramesses II who was made high priest in the old royal capital of Memphis around 1250 BC, devoted himself to the conservation of the dilapidated monuments of earlier times, among them the pyramid of King Unas from the end of the 5th Dynasty. There is, however, no record to show whether the burial chambers of the pyramids at Saqqara, Giza and elsewhere were still intact at that time, or were ever opened by Khaemwese.

The kings of the 26th Dynasty, which originated in Sais, took a similar interest in the constructions of the glorious past, and in their time the subterranean chambers of King Djoser's step-pyramid at Saqqara were opened and thoroughly examined for their 'archaeological' interest.

The Magic of Gold

Towards the end of the 18th Dynasty, at the apogee of pharaonic government, tomb-robbers were twice able to penetrate the tomb of King Tutankhamun soon after his burial. They made a great mess while rummaging through his treasures (102). They took jewellery away with them, leaving behind in a plundered chest a strip of cloth in which they had wrapped seven heavy gold rings (103). The break-in seems to have been discovered in time by the guards, and the robbers overpowered or driven away before they were able to enter the royal burial chamber itself, and the tomb was officially resealed.

The tomb-robbers' trade flourished after the end of the New Kingdom, by which time the royal capital had long since moved to Pi-Ramesses, the 'city of Ramesses', in the Eastern Delta. Thebes, the former capital, lived on only as a centre for the cult of the gods – mainly of the kingdom's tutelary deity, Amun – and as the traditional burial ground of the kings.

Weak government, mismanagement, the corruption of officials, the impoverishment of the population, widespread hunger and social unrest led to people 'helping themselves' to the treasures that lay in the tombs. A graphic picture is given by two papyri that record trials of tomb-robbers held in Thebes under Ramesses IX (104).

Following a report of thefts from the necropolis, the vizier Khaemwese sent a commission to investigate the tombs; it took official note of attempts to break into the tombs of the kings of the 17th Dynasty. The tomb of King Sebekemsaef II and his wife had been plundered; the suspected thieves were arrested and forced to confess under torture.

The quarry-worker Amunpanefer testified that, together with seven companions, he had regularly been robbing tombs for several years, and by digging tunnels they had penetrated the tomb of Sebekemsaef:

> We found the magnificent mummy of King Sebekemsaef II with gold jewellery on his breast and a golden mask over his face, and beside him a sickle-sword and the mummy of his illustrious wife … we took the gold and

106 Burial chamber of Taninenkhebu's mastaba at Saqqara
107 Saite period gallery discovered beneath the pyramid of Djoser
108 Sarcophagus in the Serapeum at Saqqara broken open
109 Tomb of Monthuemhet, mayor of Thebes and governor of the Kushites in Upper Egypt

110–111 Grand gallery and burial chamber of the pyramid of Cheops, lithograph around AD 1800

the amulets and the jewellery which were on them and we set fire to the coffins.

What is instructive in Amunpanefer's testimony is the incidental revelation that a great number of people in Thebes at this period were robbing graves. He himself had been released shortly after a first arrest – though only after he had paid a sizeable bribe to an official – and after this he was said to have gone on to rob further tombs.

A year later, it was noticed that the tomb of Queen Isis, wife of Ramesses III, in the Valley of the Queens, had been robbed and again around 1100 BC that the same had happened to the tomb of Ramesses VI. Soon after the turn of the millennium, these robberies led to the placing of mummies from plundered tombs in royal tombs that were still thought to be secure. Around 970 BC, when they had found no peace there either, Pinodjem II, the high priest of Thebes, took these mummies of kings, queens and princesses, which had already been moved several times for security reasons, together with what jewellery they still had, and reinterred them in a deep shaft, difficult to access, south of the Deir el-Bahari temple of Hatshepsut.

But in AD 1871 this hiding place, too, was discovered by Egyptian tomb-robbers, and the appearance of funerary papyri and *ushabtis* on the market provided a first clue to its existence. Family rows among the robbers led one of them to confess and to betray the location of the cache to the authorities, and the mummies were thus recovered from the rock tomb and taken into the care of the Cairo Museum in 1881.

Of the royal tombs of the 26th Dynasty, near the temple of the goddess Neith at Sais, which were visited and described by Herodotus, and of the tombs of their successors of the last indigenous dynasties, the 28th to the 30th, there survive only individual sarcophagi without precise details of provenance; and as early as the 4th century AD all trace had been lost of the tomb of Alexander the Great, and of those of the Ptolemies, his successors on the royal throne of Egypt, who had been buried in Alexandria.

Medieval and Modern Treasure-hunting

From what can be gathered from the meagre ancient records and the from the observations of modern archaeologists, the great pyramids and the tombs of dignitaries gathered around them were first systematically searched and exploited for treasure in the early centuries of Muslim rule in Egypt, under the authority of the state whose new capitals were at Fustat and later Cairo. According to Arabic sources, the pyramid of Cheops was opened in AD 830 by the authority of the Caliph el-Ma'mum, a son of Harun ar-Rashid, who had been sent to Egypt to suppress an uprising.

Under Ibn Tulun, ruler of Egypt from 863 to 884, the search for treasure and the plundering of pharaonic tombs was a state monopoly, supervised by the treasury. In the course of the millennia, enormous quantities of gold and precious stones had accumulated in the tombs of kings, queens, princes, princesses and higher dignitaries, and the recovery of this treasure was used to support the Egyptian currency. In the 12th century, Abd el-Latif el-Baghdadi speaks about organized treasure-hunters who 'dig everywhere for gold and in the process are destroying what was built by the pharaohs'. Financial records of the time note that a single such enterprise yielded 8,800lb (4,000kg) of gold, but unfortunately the records give no details of its origin.

It was in the early Muslim period that individual European travellers visited Egypt for the first time and viewed the pyramid of Giza, which in the Middle Ages was believed to be 'Joseph's granary'. Surviving travellers' descriptions of the pyramids from the 8th to the 17th century are so general that one cannot tell whether the burial chambers were accessible.

Treasure-hunting in Egypt never stopped, and it received a new, disastrous impetus after Napoleon's

Tomb-robbery

Egyptian campaign of 1798 to 1801. Mohammed Ali ruled Egypt from 1805 and strove to build a modern state on the European model. His efforts at technological innovation led to the arrival in the kingdom of European experts, among them a good number of adventurers. A new treasure-hunt began, which led to the removal of many monuments to Europe and to the establishment of the first collections of Egyptian antiquities at princely courts and in private hands. The physician Dr Giuseppe Ferlini of Bologna, who dismantled one of the pyramids at Meroe in 1837 and thus came upon the gold treasure of an Ethiopian queen, was probably the most successful hunter for gold.

Nor did the laws for the protection of antiquities, pushed through by Auguste Mariette in 1858 under Sai'id Pasha, halt the quest for treasure by Egypt's indigenous inhabitants. The search continues into our own time, with excavations carried out by trained archaeologists from all over the world, and with the approval of the Egyptian authorities. The archaeological activities of Mariette's day, however, were very little different from the tomb-robbing of earlier periods.

Conditions have long since changed, and every dig in Egypt is now intended to uncover new facts and to answer scientific questions – though spectacular finds are very rare. All objects found on Egyptian soil belong by law to the Egyptian authorities responsible for the management of antiquities, and only artefacts that have already been documented because of similar examples in Egyptian collections, may be given to the archaeologists who found them, and they are in turn duty bound to hand the finds to a public museum.

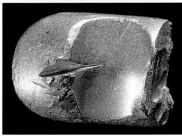

112–113 Signet ring broken by tomb-robbers

114 Gold statuette of the god Amun bearing the symbol of life and a harpesh, a curved sword. Perhaps a cult image or votive from the temple of Karnak. From the Carnarvon collection, bought by the Metropolitan Museum in 1926

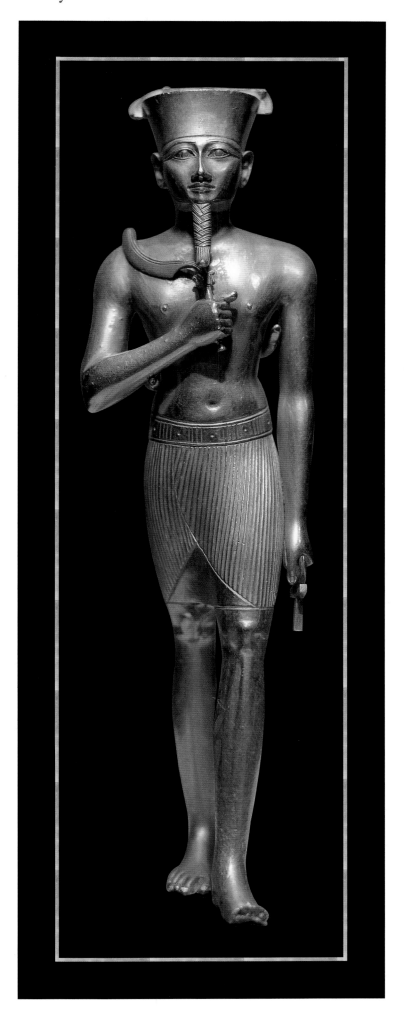

The Old Kingdom

From the time of the 1st and 2nd Dynasties the centre of Egyptian power lay in Upper Egypt, between the sites of Hierakonpolis and Thinis, near Abydos. The cultural and economic centre of gravity then shifted to Lower Egypt, because of trade between the cities of the Delta and lands far into the Near East. The political equality of the two parts of the country was brought about by King Djoser, the most important ruler of the 3rd Dynasty, whose reforms laid the basis for a powerful state, the Old Kingdom. The royal capital was moved to Memphis in Lower Egypt, where Menes, the founder of the kingdom, had earlier built the 'White Walls', the border fortress that watched over conquered Lower Egypt. For centuries Memphis remained the seat of government and the theological, intellectual and artistic centre for both parts of the country. Architects, artists and craftsmen were assigned to royal enterprises located in the capital, and Djoser completed the consolidation of the state with the construction of a hierarchy for the officials of his court. These officials made up a social stratum whose status found expression in a simple uniform with insignia that showed rank, and in the jewellery they wore.

115 Ornamental disc

116 The golden Horus-falcon of Hierakonpolis

Such insignia can all be seen in the painted reliefs and statuary of the tombs in the cemetery of the new royal capital at Saqqara, on the edge of the desert to the west of Memphis.

Titles, Insignia and Jewellery

The divinity of the king, which in the titularies of the first Egyptian kings had been indicated by his designation as 'Horus', the falcon of the sun and the heavens, now required a new formula. In later king-lists the founder of the Old Kingdom is designated as Djoser, 'the Magnificent', but in contemporary inscriptions his name is given as Horus Netjeri-khet, 'the Divine of Body'. Added to this name is the sign 'gold' with a solar disc above: 'gold sun' (118). Gold, the symbol of the eternally shining sun, raises the ruler above all earthly creatures, conferring on him divinity, brilliance and power, in life and in death. On the fragments of a relief from a shrine (55) which Netjeri-khet established at the holy city of Heliopolis, a god wears the same monogram on a necklace, and it is therefore likely that it was originally an emblem of divinity. This conception of the 'divinity' of the ruler's office, which is expressed in the immortality of gold, would always remain an element in the titularies of the pharaohs.

King Snefru, founder of the 4th Dynasty, expressed his claim to royal power in the new title 'Golden Horus'. Under Cheops, the builder of the largest of all the pyramids, kingship in the Old Kingdom reached the height of its power. His successor, Djedefre, was the first to add the title 'Son of Re' (the sun-god), his role as divine ruler being based on his status as a 'son of god'. The title 'Son of Re' would subsequently be borne by all Egyptian kings, until the end of the pharaonic period.

The Flesh of the Gods

As the son of the sun-god, the pharaoh was entitled to gold as the material of his flesh, for the idea expressed in a later text was current even in earlier times: Re said, 'My body is of gold, my bones are of silver, and my hair of pure lapis lazuli'. A tale preserved in the Westcar Papyrus tells of the birth of the first three successive kings of the 5th Dynasty. Their father was the sun-god, and their mother the wife of the high priest of his temple at Heliopolis. When the hour of birth came near, the sun-god sent goddesses as helpers, and of the birth of each of the three royal children it is said:

> the child [the future king] came out into her arms [the divine helper's] as a child one cubit long and with solid bones; his outward form was of gold, and the royal headcloth [*nemes*] of pure lapis lazuli.

There are innumerable examples from later pharaonic inscriptions of the 'lord of the two lands' being designated as 'the golden' and his appearance being compared or even equated with that of the sun-god: 'a mountain of gold that brightens all the lands, like that on the horizon [the rising sun-god]'.

The pharaoh might be divine, but both he and his subjects accepted that, being appointed by the gods, he could act only on their instructions and on the basis of divine command. What made him different from the gods was his mortality. He became a true god only after his death, by virtue of rituals of transformation and the magical effect of the signs of kingly rule, of his royal robes and gold jewellery. He took his place among the gods in the afterlife, in order to rule over and care for his deceased subjects. The massive construction of the tomb, provided with every possible measure of security, was intended to protect his mummified body, adorned with amulets and golden emblems of rule, and preserve it physically for all eternity.

The only pharaoh's tomb furnishings to have survived more or less intact are those of Tutankhamun; they give some idea of the extraordinary wealth of funerary objects and goldsmiths' work amassed to

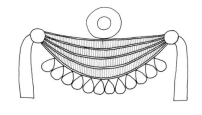

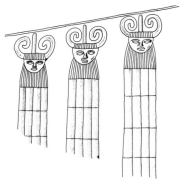

117 The Bat emblem worn on crossed chest bands was a sign of rank for palace officials

118 The sign 'gold sun'
119 The Bat emblem as belt hangings or pendants

ensure the power and rule of the king in the afterlife. We should not assume, however, that the extravagance of a period when the pharaohs ruled a conquered world-wide empire was also prevalent in earlier periods. In the Old Kingdom, gold was used more sparingly.

Jewellery and Magical Protection

As no specimens of royal dress or gold jewellery have survived from the Old Kingdom, our knowledge of them comes only from their visual representations. In a subterranean chamber of Djoser's mortuary complex a relief painting shows the king celebrating a festival, with the dual crown of Upper and Lower Egypt on his head and a bull's tail on his belt but without any jewellery. The belt with its pendants are also shown on a fragment of a statue of king Djoser (119), with the same emblems of Bat, the goddess of the heavens, as worn by the triumphant king of the Narmer Palette (37).

A single example of the Bat emblem, which may have originated as a pendant to a king's belt of the early period, has been found at Abydos (120). This small female head with its short fringe and cow's horns is of gold foil, which was presumably pressed into a mould and then chased with a sharp instrument. On the upper edges of the cow's ears the foil is reinforced by folding, the lower parts being chased, while the horns are made in a gutter-like form so as to take an inlay. For the bow, composed of three elements, narrow strips of foil have been soldered on to the outer edges, and the cells built up in this manner held coloured inlays.

The form of the belt pendants changed under Djoser's successors, and the Bat emblem, no longer used by the king, was worn by the highest palace officials as a sign of rank on bands crossed over the chest (117).

The amulets customarily worn in the Old Kingdom continued the traditions of prehistoric times. A fine example may be seen in the relief of Prince Kawab, a son of Cheops, in his daughter's tomb at Giza (127).

120 Emblem of Bat, goddess of the heavens

He wears a necklace of different amulets, on which the animal claws and two daisies are clearly recognizable. The heavy pendant over the chest is often found in statues from the Old Kingdom, though its significance is unknown. Daisies also appear on a bracelet that adorns the wrist of King Snefru (124) on a relief in the valley temple of the Bent Pyramid at Dahshur. The lightly bowed outer side with its raised border has two daisy flowers, and between them is the emblem of the god Min of Koptos, lord of the Eastern Desert and of the roads to the quarries and gold mines. Surviving traces of yellow, light blue and green show that this was a bracelet of gold inlaid with lapis lazuli or turquoise. The daisies could be a stylized descendant of the 'chief's flower' found on the gold knife-handle (36) and on the Narmer Palette. The emblem of the god Min might stand for Menes, the legendary founder of the kingdom of Egypt.

The most popular plant motifs, and those most often found in amulets and jewellery, are the flowers and buds of the lotus. The lotus is the symbol of eternal rebirth: at sunrise it emerges from the water as a closed bud, opens into a flower, and in the evening sinks back into the water. The scent of the lotus fills the dead with renewed life, as many representations in the tombs attest (128, 129). After the lotus, the papyrus is the most frequent plant motif, a symbol of greening, flourishing and regeneration.

Because of their magnificent appearance, beetles had been strung together with coloured stones to be worn as jewellery since early historic times. The best known of the beetle species indigenous to Egypt is the scarab beetle (*Scarabaeus sacer*). Also to be found are the splendid iridescent beetle (*Buprestidae*), the colourful beetle (*Cleridae*), the click beetle (*Elateridae*) and others. The click beetle may be unremarkable in colour, but it has a particular ability that gave it a special place in the magical thinking of the

Pages 62–63: 121 King Djoser's Step Pyramid and mortuary complex at Saqqara

Titles, Insignia and Jewellery

123 Egyptian with a wreath of
leaves in his hair and lotus
flowers around his neck

125 King Snefru with a bead
broad collar, headband and
horned crown

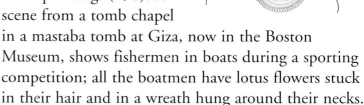

Egyptians. When lying on its back, it is able, by means of a spine on its thorax, to spring into the air and fall back on its feet. This is why as an amulet or jewellery motif it came to represent resurrection (49, 176). In the earlier hieroglyphic writing the click beetle probably signified 'life' (*ankh*).

From Headband to Circlet and Diadem

The circlet and the diadem have their origins in a woven band of linen, worn around the head by both men and women, and knotted or tied in a bow at the back to keep the hair in place. This band of fabric inspired circlets made of thin strips of gold foil, in which the bow at the back of the head often took the shape of two papyrus umbels that projected to the sides, and from which the two ends of the gold 'ribbon' would hang half-way down to the shoulders (128). From the Old Kingdom onwards the circlet was part of the king's costume and an item of festive jewellery for the men and women of the court. The earliest representation known to us of a headband with a wide bow is to be found in a relief portrait of King Snefru (125); over the simple linen band he wears a 'horned crown' from which rise tall feathers.

124 Wide bracelet
of King Snefru

Snefru is depicted in other reliefs wearing jewellery made of gold on his head (126). The royal cobra coils around the circlet, raising its extended hood and death-dealing head against all enemies. This was placed on the king's head at his coronation, during the 'festival of the diadem'.

Since the earliest days, the inhabitants of the Nile Valley had also worn wreaths of leaves about their

122 King Chephren with a Horus falcon positioned behind his
royal headcloth

heads (123), and for festive occasions they would stick fragrant lotus flowers in the headband, as can be seen in many tomb paintings (198). A scene from a tomb chapel in a mastaba tomb at Giza, now in the Boston Museum, shows fishermen in boats during a sporting competition; all the boatmen have lotus flowers stuck in their hair and in a wreath hung around their necks.

During the Old Kingdom this headband with its flower decoration inspired the design of the floral diadem of gold with a coloured inlay; and the highly stylized version of the wreath of flowers, the 'boatman's circlet', with which fishermen of the papyrus marshes adorned themselves at festivities, was worn by girls and women. In the statue of the princess Nofret (132) the stylization of the flowers, within the bounds of the narrow circlet, makes it clear that this was jeweller's work. The white ground suggests a silver circlet, with inlaid coloured flowers. A complete example of such a circlet has been preserved in the tomb of a princess of the Middle Kingdom in Dahshur (202).

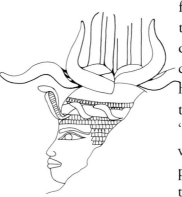

126 King Snefru wearing a
circlet with a uraeus coiled
around it

The diadems of the dead are distinguished by particular motifs – the crested ibis is the 'soul bird', symbol of the deceased's transfigured life in the hereafter. It is because the deceased has the nature of this bird that he will be able to ascend to the heavens after freeing himself from the wrappings of the mummy.

127 Prince Kawab with a
knot-amulet

The Old Kingdom

standing between them, and the papyrus umbels may be supplemented or replaced by lotus flowers.

Bead Collars

The bead collar was worn as jewellery and as magical protection by gods and kings, by men and women, until the end of the pharaonic period. After his victorious campaigns, Thutmosis III offered a bead collar to the god Amun-Re of Karnak; the hieroglyphic inscription calls such objects 'collars that protect the body of the god'.

Different versions are represented in the tomb reliefs and painted statues of the Old Kingdom. The broad collar made up of several strands of beads first appears with King Snefru, in the surviving fragments of reliefs from his valley temple (125). This visual evidence shows that the collars were built up in a complex manner from horizontal rows of tiny

129 Woman with floral diadem, collar and lotus flower

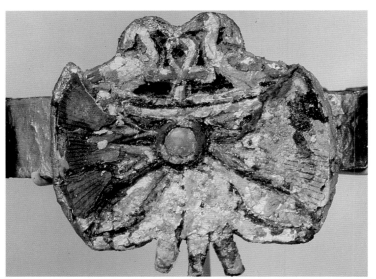

130 Ornamental frontal rosette from a funeral diadem

Resurrection occurs because of the magical power of the image, and its formalized design is an important element in the successful achievement of the magical transformation that is sought.

Several circlets of cheaper materials, made either of copper covered with gold leaf, or of stucco or painted wood (130), come from tombs in the cemetery of the royal tombs at Giza. The ornamental frontals here show crested ibises over papyrus umbels. This motif has minor variations: the birds may face each other or be turned outwards, with the sign of life (*ankh*) often

spherical or disc-shaped links that might be of gold, coloured stones or faience, between which were vertical rows of tubular beads. Only collars of faience beads have, however, been found. In pictorial representations, straight or zigzag bars are often introduced radially into the rows of beads to structure

131 Floral ornamentation from Nofret's circlet

132 Princess Nofret with a circlet and Broad bead Collar

The Old Kingdom

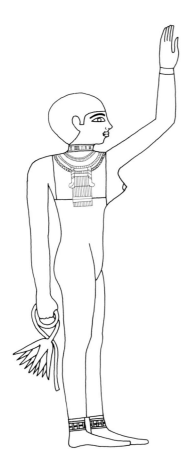

133 Girl with a bib-like bead pendant

or strengthen the collar. The number of rows and the arrangement of the beads vary. The lower margin can be made up of a row of droplet-shaped or elongated scarab-shaped beads, whose bottom edge is held in place with a row of tiny beads. An example is the collar of the court architect Imthepi from the cemetery at Giza (136), which has been preserved in its entirety. Even if the beetle bodies have been unnaturally elongated to give depth to the collar, here they are intended to recall the click beetle, and thus act as a magical aid to resurrection. Pendants in the shape of buds and leaves are also found. As is demonstrated in pictorial representations, the collar can be extended by a bib-like pendant made of coloured beads with a stiff edging (133, 135).

To keep the semicircular collar close to the neck, a kind of flat tassel was often hung from the clasp at the back as a kind of counterweight. It has an elongated form, broadening towards the bottom, and is also made up of tubular beads, the lower margin being formed by a row of droplet-shaped beads (134). Taking its name from the Egyptian word for 'life' (*menat*), this counterweight played a particular role in protecting the wearer's back. Later, a small representation of the *menat* was worn as an

amulet, and in the New Kingdom the ornament itself gained great importance (328–330).

The bead collar ends at the back of the neck with two gilded semicircular terminals with tiny holes drilled in the straight base, through which the linen threads were knotted. Towards the end of the Old Kingdom these terminals took the form of outward-turned falcons' heads (155).

Necklaces, Armlets and Anklets

Beaded necklaces made up of several rows and worn to fit closely round the neck are known from tomb reliefs of the 4th and 5th Dynasties, but no originals have been found; worn only by women, they were often accompanied by the broad beaded collar (133).

Armlets in the simple form of an outward-bulging hoop follow the pattern of prehistoric examples carved from ivory, horn and stone, and examples in gold, silver and copper have been recovered from tombs. Tomb reliefs show that several armlets were worn together, one above another, almost covering the entire forearm (129).

Anklets, too, were an inheritance from prehistoric times. They were worn only by women, and on both ankles. On the walls of mortuary temples and in officials' tombs they are often seen on women of the upper classes and on harem women and dancers (140). Worn as protection against all dangers emanating from the ground, anklets remained in fashion until the end of the Middle Kingdom. They have been found among the jewellery of female mummies, having disintegrated into individual beads and plaques.

135 Prince Bia with collar and bead bib

134 Mereruka's wife wears a bead collar with a counterweight at the back

136 Imthepi's bead Broad Collar
137 Jewellery chest from an Old Kingdom tomb in the necropolis of Gebelein

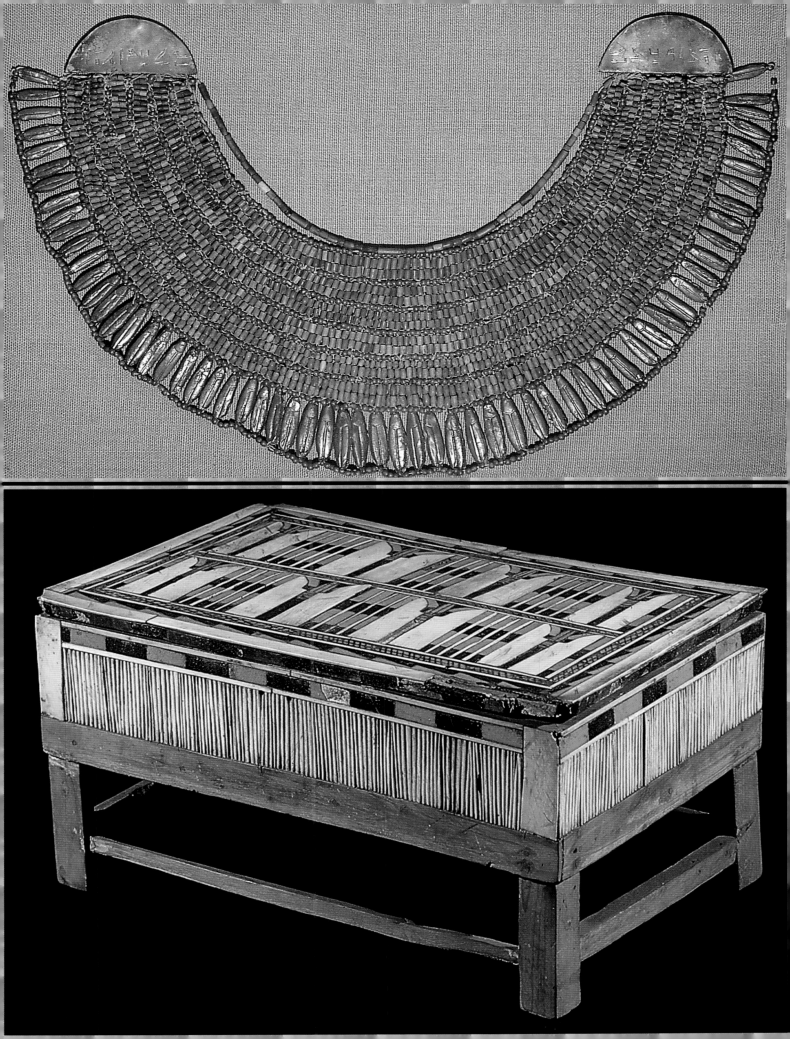

The Old Kingdom

Official and Honorary Insignia

Those appointed to a position in the royal administration were invested with the appropriate insignia of office and an official seal. Scenes of investiture are preserved on fragments of a relief from the mortuary temple of King

138 Official carrying a seal of office

139 A bead bib as a sign of rank

Sahure at Abusir (138,139). The officers wear a golden headband with a bow; one has been presented with a collar with a beaded bib, the other holds the seal of office – a cylinder seal – in his hand. This was

140 Women carrying offerings, with collars and bracelets
141 Female weavers being rewarded with collars

rolled over the clay sealing of an earthenware jar or chest while it was still damp, to authenticate it. Cylinder seals are of Mesopotamian origin, and several examples from the Old Kingdom are engraved with the royal name and the office-holder's title.

A cylinder seal, made of strong gold foil wrapped around a (presumably) wooden core and soldered and

engraved, has been found bearing the name 'Mykerinus' (142). The inscription reads as follows:

He who contents the heart of Horus and the Golden Horus. The supervisor of the gold-pourer, who does daily that which Mykerinus commands.

Also depicted in many officials' tombs is the presentation of rewards to deserving craftsmen. One of the most detailed of these scenes is to be found on the walls of the tomb chapel of an official named Akhtihotep (141). Woven linen is being delivered by women weavers, packed in boxes and presented to the lord of the tomb for approval. On the upper register of the section illustrated here, the rewards have been lined up on two chests, one above the other: bead broad collars, some of them with a bib, circlets and other gifts. On the left, a man accompanied by a scribe presents the weaver standing before him with a beaded belt and a bead collar. On the right of the lower register, a scribe records the jewellery lined up on the chest. To his left is a man who presents beaded jewellery and a collar to a weaver, while another is about to place an opened bead collar around a weaver's neck. On the far left of the scene, a weaver proudly leaves with the jewellery she has just received.

Goldworkers and Jewellers

The gold and precious stones brought back by royal expeditions were kept in the treasury at the royal capital. Here, too, were the workshops of goldworkers and jewellers who were entrusted with the manufacture of the royal regalia and the many symbols of sovereignty, jewellery for the royal family, insignia of rank for palace officers and retinue, and

Goldworkers and Jewellers

also decorations for a wider circle of deserving subjects. As the ancient Egyptians believed that the king would continue to rule in the afterlife as well, supported by his officials, his retinue had to be provided with tomb furnishings befitting their rank after death. For this purpose, craftsmen of the royal workshops were put at the disposal of officials, for whom they created funerary equipment in gold as well as statues for their tombs.

Goldworkers and jewellers had presumably been depicted in the mortuary temples at the pyramids of Cheops and Chephren, though nothing has survived. The oldest representation of such a workshop at a royal burial-site is from the rock tomb of Queen Meres-ankh III, a grand-daughter of Cheops. Another can be found on an incomplete relief block from the causeway leading to King Unas' pyramid at Saqqara (147, 149, 152). In the tombs of officials, this subject is most often found in those of the 5th Dynasty. These scenes, modelled on royal examples, are the essential source of our knowledge of the way the gold workshops operated.

142 Impression from a gold cylinder seal
143 Polishing stone
144 Bronze tweezers
145 Copper chisels

How the artists executed these paintings on the tomb walls is a matter of dispute. Egyptian artists were rigorously trained in the exact, freehand rendition of pictorial hieroglyphs. As well as these, a great number of stereotyped representations of human figures in various attitudes – standing, kneeling, sitting and even working – were prescribed; thanks to the Egyptian system of the canon of proportion they could easily be reproduced on any scale. New versions were constantly being introduced into tomb paintings in scenes taken from many areas of life.

The various distinct groups of goldworkers and jewellers are always arranged in each tomb according to the same scheme, in the same attitudes and performing the same work. The artists probably made use of a pattern on a papyrus roll, on which the composition was rendered as stick figures.

The artisans are depicted in small groups, illustrating succeeding stages of production, which gives us some insight into the organization of work with precious metals and into the social hierarchy within the trade (the latter extends from the ordinary semi-skilled assistants to the experienced supervisor who controlled the workers). Inscriptions are attached to each group, identifying the procedure in question, but also recording instructions by the supervisor and replies or other remarks by the workers – sometimes even their spontaneous exclamations or complaints about heat and thirst near the fire.

In these representations two different occupational groups can be distinguished: the goldworkers and the

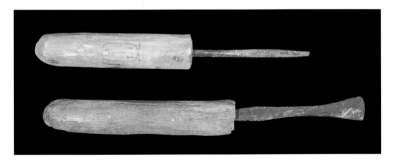

jewellers. The smelters, foil-beaters and gilders belonged to the group of goldworkers. All the finer work using gold, silver and precious stones was done by the jewellers, who are, however, seen only stringing bead Broad Collars. The collar, the hieroglyph for 'gold', stands in for all those specialized skills that could have been represented only with difficulty within the limits of the strict rules that governed Egyptian art. These include the manufacture of gold

146 Workshop scene from the tomb chapel of Ka-irer: on a set of scales in the form of a naked girl holding the pans suspended from her outstretched arms, two scribes check the weight, which is written down by a third scribe seated on the floor

wire or the embossing and chasing of gold and the cutting of precious stone to provide coloured inlays for jewellery.

The tools that these craftsmen had at their disposal were extremely primitive. In the pictures we see blow-pipes, which were used to help heat the fire to melt gold and to anneal metal that has become brittle through being worked, and flat and rounded stones, which were used to beat out gold foil and gold leaf. Surviving gold work shows traces of the use of other tools, such as copper chisels for cutting gold foil – there were no shears – and for incizing metal to take coloured inlays. Tweezer-shaped pliers of copper must also have already been in use at that time. The artistry of these craftsmen came from a talent for invention, along with skill, patience, experience and a sense of the unimportance of the time expended.

In none of the tomb reliefs is the complete sequence of the processes involved in the work reproduced. In those dating from the 4th Dynasty,

147 Metalworkers from a relief from the causeway to King Unas' pyramid. The inscriptions read (left to right): 'Beating electrum', 'Heating up silver' and 'Polishing'. Note the long blow-pipes used by the smelters in the centre

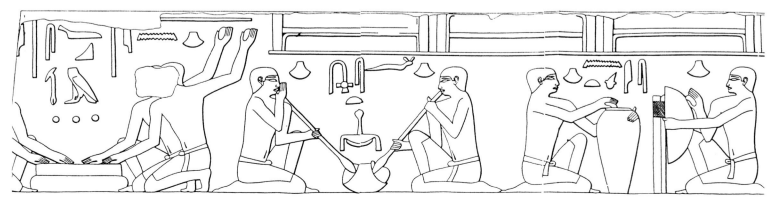

148 Workshop scene from the tomb chapel of Ka-irer: the crucible with the gold dust is brought to four smelters sitting on the floor.

They used long blow-pipes to concentrate the heat. On the right, is one of the two gold foil beaters

only the melting of gold and the beating of foil are represented. In tomb reliefs from the later Old Kingdom, the number of activities that are shown increases, and they are depicted in greater detail. In the overview provided here the individual phases of work are taken from different tombs of the 5th and 6th Dynasties and assembled in their logical sequence. As the earliest reliefs have lost their coloured paint and are often damaged as well, many in this book are shown in outline for the purposes of clarity.

In some tombs the weighing of the metal required for the day's work precedes the actual work processes. In the tomb chapel of Ka-irer (146), the lord of the tomb, seated on a bench with a stool at his feet, is shown supervising the process. A scribe with his scribe's palette beneath his arm hands him an opened papyrus roll on which, presumably, is recorded the amount of gold issued for processing and the work to be carried out. The scales are personified by a naked girl, her head turned sideways towards the lord of the

149 Metal workers from a relief on the causeway to King Unas' pyramid. The inscriptions read: 'Washing an electrum vessel',

'Sharpening the blade by annealing', and 'The scales are balanced'

150 Metalworkers and jewellers from the tomb of Ni-ankh-Khnum and Khnumhotep. The scenes shown are as follows: top, right to left: worker at the smelting fire and supervisor (the hieroglyph caption reads: 'The air becomes hot because of her brother [the heat rising from the fire]'); beating the cast metal; beating out a vessel (caption: 'Annealing a cup-shaped gold vessel'); 'Gilding a sceptre'; gilding decorations and terminals for belt pendants; gilding a staff of office; 'Production of circlets for funeral equipment'; bottom, right to left: 'Making the funerary collar'; 'Adjusting the collar'; 'Fastening the collar'; 'Washing the collar'; carpenters making tomb furniture

tomb. In each outstretched hand she holds a rope that passes over her shoulders, at the ends of which the scale pans hang at the same height, in balance. This representation of the scales as a girl could allude to Ma'at, the goddess of Truth, of justice, of right weight, or simply to the Egyptian word for 'scales', which is feminine in gender. Two scribes to the left and right of the scales carefully check the weight, which is written down by a third scribe seated on the floor. Other scenes of weighing show the use of a simple hand-held or free-standing balance (149, 155).

Precious metals and stones were under the strict control of the royal treasury. Just as the gold was weighed and the weight recorded before it was handed to the workers, so the jewellery made from it was weighed, in order to prevent embezzlement.

Smelting, Foil-beating and Gilding

Once the precious metal has been weighed, a man carries it in a crucible to the group of smelters (148). The smelting is an essential process, and is always shown with representations of gold workers. Four smelters sit facing one another in pairs at the open charcoal fire and with their blow-pipes heat up the embers, which were once shown in colour. To smelt the gold the fire has to be made hot enough to heat the crucible to the required temperature of around 1768°F (1000°C). The blow-pipes end in a nozzle of fire-resistant clay (*tuyère*), and are held with one hand while the other protects the face of the worker from the heat. A supervisor checks whether smelting has taken place (148, 150).

From the red-hot crucible, which he carries between two lumps of earth for insulation, one of the workers pours the molten gold out on a slab of stone to cool. One person, kneeling in front, uses a little stick to hold back the impurities that swim on the surface of the molten gold (153).

Once cool, the gold (or indeed electrum, or silver) is divided into portions with sharp-edged stone hammers (150) and beaten into foil by the next group of workers, the foil-beaters (148, 153). The foil-beaters were able to manufacture the thinnest of gold leaf, a fraction of a millimetre thick, by continuing to beat very thin foil, placed between animal hides.

With the smelting and the beating the rough work
is over. Now follows the skilled craft work. In these
particular images we see only the beating out on a tall
anvil of a vessel of gold foil (150) and the annealing
of a cup-shaped gold vessel that has become brittle
through too much beating. Finally, after being beaten
out, the finished vessels are polished (147).

The next scenes show the work of the gilders (150):
a wooden sceptre, a belt-buckle, a gold ornament for
an apron, a staff of office and finally a copper circlet
are covered with gold foil, which will stick to a
smooth surface under firm pressure, or may be
fastened with an adhesive substance. While the
jewellery worn in life was worked from solid gold, the
cheaper process of gilding non-precious metal (e.g.
copper) played an important role in producing
funerary jewellery.

Jewellers and their Techniques

The jewellers are depicted separately from the
goldworkers: they sit facing one another at low tables,
and together they hold up a finished collar that
symbolizes their manifold activity (150, 155). The
bead workers are often represented as dwarfs (154),

*151 Washing the collar (relief from the tomb of Ni-ankh-Khnum and
Khnumhotep)*
152 Smelting metal (relief from the Unas Causeway)

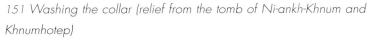

153–154 gold workers and jewellers on a relief in the tomb of the vizier Mereruka: smelting; pouring the metal; foil-beating; knotting a necklace (with the inscription 'It is very beautiful, friend'); work on a deep choker with a bib pendant and the inscription 'Get on with your work, slowcoach'; knotting a collar

whose dainty hands and agile fingers made them well suited for the complicated knotting of collars made of rows of tiny beads.

In the tomb of Pepi-ankh at Meir the twisting of thread for the beads is also depicted, and here and there are representations of the very last process, when the finished bead collar is rinsed over a large basin (150) so that the thread is tightened by wetting and the collar gains its firm, final form.

Representations of workshops from the late Old Kingdom also show finished jewellery, and in these are shapes that are not known from original finds or from other representations. In the tomb of the vizier Mereruka at Saqqara (154, 155), lined up on low tables, are 'boatman's circlets' with papyrus umbels and hanging 'ribbons', and there are also bead collars with wide pendant bibs, whose terminals take the form of falcons' heads. Almost certainly only the

Horus-king would originally have been entitled to use these as funerary jewellery, and their presence here shows how, with the weakening of kingship towards the end of the Old Kingdom and the new belief in the resurrection as Osiris for everyone, the pharaoh's privileges in terms of robes and insignia of power were claimed by a wider public, at least in visual representation.

The jewellers' techniques developed continuously during the Old Kingdom, thanks to growing royal commissions and the organized supply of gold and precious stones. However, the workshop representations offer very little information about craft techniques or skills. Our knowledge of these

155 Weighing the metal (and noting the weight) and knotting a bead collar with falcon-head terminals, from a relief in the tomb of Mereruka

relies for the most part on modern experiments aimed at recreating the methods of manufacture by the examination of surviving artefacts.

High-carat gold is very soft and highly ductile, but also more easily scratched. It melts at 1920°F (1065° C). Gold from the mountains of the Egyptian and Nubian deserts usually contains some silver. Because of this, and the presence of a small amount of copper, *elektron* – as the Greeks called it, after its

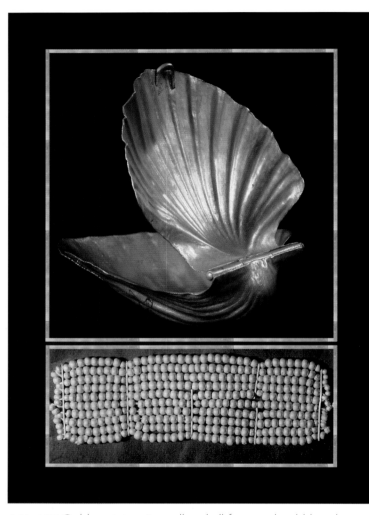

156–157 Gold container in scallop-shell form and gold bead bracelet from the pyramid of Sekhemkhet

amber colour – is harder, and this natural alloy was most commonly used in ancient Egypt for the production of jewellery for wearing. It has a melting point of 1768°F (1000°C).

The soldering of gold and electrum has been found in objects dating from as early as about 3000 BC; this was done over the fire using blow-pipes and soldering metals that melt at low temperature. Lead and tin were not used; silver was found used as a soldering agent on Queen Hetep-heres' sleeping tent. To solder pure gold, gold containing a high proportion of silver

(electrum) was used. The soldering of gold or electrum, which is almost always invisible, was probably carried out with the help of copper oxide, which was applied to the areas to be soldered with natron and glue. The gold wire that is already found in the jewellery of a queen of the 1st Dynasty (45) was made from very narrow strips of gold foil which were presumably pulled back and forth through the hole in an elongated stone bead.

At first, as can be seen from the bracelets of Queen Hetep-heres (163), coloured stone inlays were glued with resin into recesses gouged into the metal. Only from the later Old Kingdom has cloisonné work occasionally been found, on smaller jewels. For this, narrow gold strips were soldered by their edges on to a gold foil base; these cells served as a setting for inlays of precious stone. Finds from the royal tombs of Ur show that the cloisonné technique was already known in Mesopotamia by about 2300 BC.

Old Kingdom Jewellery Finds

Only a few important finds of jewellery have been discovered originating from the time of the pyramid-builders. Two were made in the royal cemetery at Saqqara, and two more in Giza, one being the almost complete funerary treasure of Queen Hetep-heres.

158 Entrance to the burial chamber of the unfinished step pyramid of King Sekhemkhet

Old Kingdom Jewellery Finds

Jewellery from the Step Pyramid of Sekhemkhet
Not far from King Djoser's step pyramid in Saqqara, his successor built his own funeral complex, whose step pyramid, however, remained unfinished. The king's empty sarcophagus, of golden yellow calcite (alabaster), stands in the corridor leading to the burial chamber. Here in 1950 archaeologists of the Egyptian Department of Antiquities discovered a treasure that presumably belonged to a lady of the court who had

eyelets on the opposite side to close it. It was perhaps used as a container for cosmetics, eye make-up or ointment. With the shell was also found a pair of gold tweezers, which were presumably used to remove unwanted hair.

The jewellery beneath the rubble was arranged in order, probably having been stored in a box whose wooden parts had decayed; only remnants of its gold panelling remained. Tomb-robbers had probably

159 Gold ewer and basin of Queen Hetep-heres

been buried in the king's still unfinished tomb. This find consisted of twenty-one simple gold bracelets of different diameters, and also carnelian and faience beads, hundreds of hollow spherical beads of gold, as well as two complete and a few broken gold plaques with small drill-holes, through which the threads on which the beads were strung were passed. It was possible to reconstruct a ten-row bead bracelet from the hollow beads and plaques (157).

The most important piece was a large, double shell of beaten gold (156), a reproduction of the scallop shell (*pecten*). The shell opens on a hinge and has two

hidden the box and then forgotten it, for the burial to which it relates has not yet been found.

The Funerary Treasure of Queen Hetep-heres
A very significant find from the Old Kingdom – a tomb complete except for the missing mummy – was made by a happy accident. In 1925–26 the American archaeologist George A. Reisner was directing an excavation on the eastern side of the Cheops pyramid. While setting up his camera, a photographer with the expedition noticed that his tripod was sinking into the apparently rocky ground. Investigation revealed a

The Giza Find

The Great Pyramid of Giza is among the Seven Wonders of the Ancient World. During the Islamic Middle Ages the tombs of the pharaohs and others arranged about them had been systematically robbed and stripped of gold treasure. One hoard, however, escaped the tomb-robbers: the funerary finery of Queen Hetep-heres.

It was only chance that led to the discovery of this treasure, the most significant burial find of the Old Kingdom. While setting up his camera, the photographer of an American expedition carrying out an excavation on the eastern side of the pyramid of Cheops noticed that the tripod was sinking into what

seemed to be rocky ground. He had discovered the shaft leading to a burial chamber that was intact.

When the 70-ft (25-m) deep shaft was excavated and the bricked-up entrance at the bottom opened, the archaeologists glimpsed a scene of extraordinary disorder. Inside the low rock chamber on the left there stood a sealed sarcophagus. On top of it and strewn about the floor were broken funerary objects, parts of chests and other furniture, and among the chaos, large gold pieces. When this jumble was cleared the archaeologists had an exciting prospect before them: the opening of the sarcophagus. It was sealed, and so should still have held its precious contents, the

Above: the location of the shaft of Queen Hetep-heres' tomb on the eastern side of the pyramid of Cheops; on the left is the pyramid of Chephren.

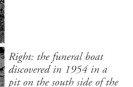

Right: the funeral boat discovered in 1954 in a pit on the south side of the pyramid of Cheops.

Left: the interior of the queen's burial chamber as it was being cleared; the sarcophagus can be seen to the left in three of the pictures.

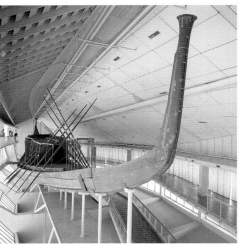

mummy of the queen, with her jewellery provided for all eternity. But when the sarcophagus was carefully opened, before a group of invited dignitaries, it was found to be empty. The mystery of the absence of the queen's mummy has only been solved by further investigation of the site in more recent years.

---

layer of gravel and mortar beneath a thin covering of sand, hiding the entrance to a shaft cut into the rock.

Further excavation uncovered a short flight of steps and then a deep shaft, which ended at the bricked-up door to a previously undiscovered burial chamber. The removal of these bricks disclosed a scene of confusion. Inside the low rock chamber on the left stood a large, sealed sarcophagus of alabaster, and on top of and around it on the floor of the whole chamber lay broken funerary objects, parts of chests and other furniture, and among these were large pieces of gleaming gold. An alcove in the wall of the burial chamber contained a square canopic chest with four compartments inside, in which the dead woman's internal organs had been placed.

This chaotic jumble was cleared out with the greatest of care, fragment by fragment, with the exact

context of each piece removed being punctiliously recorded. The wooden furniture buried with the queen had been covered with gold foil or leaf and decorated with inlays of coloured faience. The wood had been reduced to dust, but the gold and faience panels had survived allowing the original form to be deduced and so making possible the precise reproduction of the chests and furniture, and even of the queen's canopied tent.

The inscriptions embossed on the gold foil told the archaeologists how significant a find they had discovered: it was the funerary equipment of Queen Hetep-heres, wife of Snefru, the founder of the 4th Dynasty, and the mother of his successor Cheops, the builder of the largest of all the pyramids.

When the chamber had been emptied, the archaeologists prepared for the most exciting moment.

Old Kingdom Jewellery Finds

From what had been found so far, they confidently expected that the sealed sarcophagus had preserved intact its precious contents, the mummy of the queen and its jewellery. On 3 March 1927, before an illustrious group of invited guests, the heavy lid of the sarcophagus was slowly raised. A first glimpse through the crack between lid and side brought deep disappointment – the sarcophagus was empty.

The strangeness of the whole discovery – the richest funerary equipment of a queen and queen mother of the powerful 4th Dynasty discovered in incomprehensible chaos, the surviving gold panels, the canopic chest with its contents, yet an empty sarcophagus, and finally the absence of any superstructure, such as a queen's pyramid – all this demanded an explanation.

160 The chair of Queen Hetep-heres; the poles behind are part of her canopied tent

In his attempt to solve the puzzle, Reisner came up with the following reconstruction of events: the Queen had originally been buried near her husband's pyramid at Dahshur, but because of the lack of supervision of the royal cemetery after the capital had been moved, tomb-robbers had stolen the valuable funerary jewellery and destroyed the mummy. On the orders of Cheops, the funerary equipment had had a secret second burial immediately in front of his pyramid, without the stolen mummy and without a pyramid of its own.

The results of further, more recent investigations have shown that this hypothesis has become untenable, for in the vicinity of the shaft there are traces in the rock of a small pyramid that had evidently been laid out but not built. The tomb at Giza had thus, in fact, been conceived as the final resting place of the queen. Cheops must subsequently

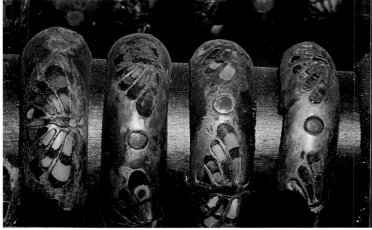

161 Terminal cap of a carrying-pole on the sedan chair

have changed the plans for his royal cemetery to provide three smaller pyramids for his royal wives, which were built in a row on the eastern side of his pyramid. The pyramid intended for the queen mother would have stood in the way of this plan. On the other hand, Cheops would not have wished to be completely deprived in the afterlife of the company of his mother, whose burial chamber had been aligned on his own in the Great Pyramid. Hetep-heres' mummy was moved to Dahshur for burial near the pyramid of her husband, Snefru; the funerary furnishings and canopic chest, however, remained at Giza. In order for the mummy to be transferred, the sarcophagus had to be opened in the narrow burial chamber and it was then that the equipment and furniture would have been scattered about.

Although the Queen's mummy and the rich jewellery intended to guarantee her passage to the world of the gods were missing, her personal jewellery, twenty silver bracelets (162) which, according to a small relief, she wore stacked on both her forearms, was kept in a jewellery box with panels of gold foil. Embossed in the foil is the hieroglyphic inscription: 'Mother of the King of Upper and Lower Egypt, Hetep-heres – box with bracelets'.

The inside of the box contained two removable tapered wooden shafts, on which the silver bracelets were placed in order of decreasing diameter. Each of these bracelets was decorated with four butterflies, inlaid in turquoise, lapis lazuli and carnelian.

162 Jewellery box of Queen Hetep-heres

163 Silver bracelets of Queen Hetep-heres

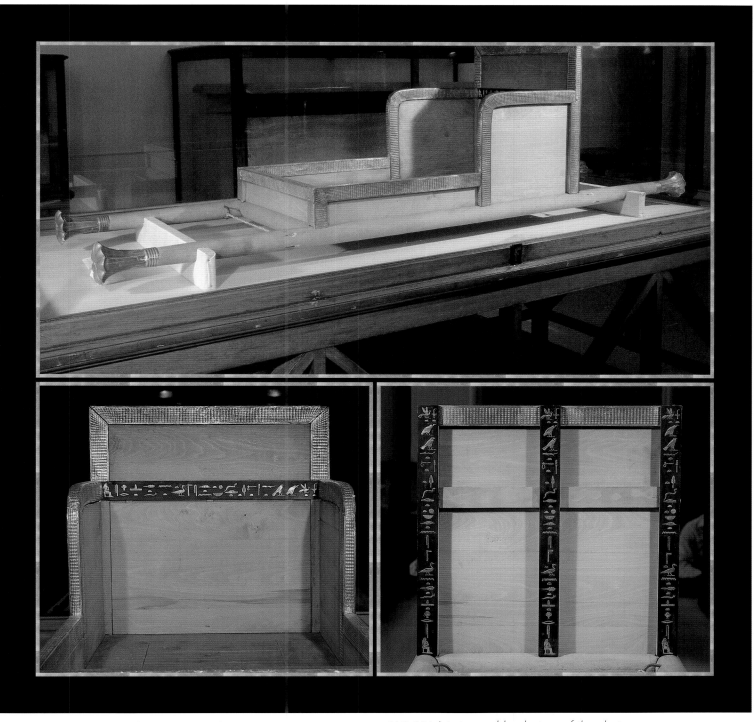

164 (top): Sedan chair of Queen Hetep-heres

165–166 Interior and back view of the chair

The poles of the queen's bed canopy lay dismantled on top of the sarcophagus. The burial chamber was not large enough to erect it. Thanks to its clear construction, however, the frame of the canopy, covered in gold foil, could be reconstructed at the Cairo Museum with the modern replacement of the wooden parts (167).

The inner surfaces of the two thick posts at the canopy entrance bear hieroglyphic inscriptions in a master's hand, beaten and chased in the gold foil. They give the name and royal titles of Snefru, and the titulary expressing the ruler's conception of his divinity, closely tied to the nature of gold:

> The Horus, Neb-Ma'at [lord of the divine order], the great god, endowed with life, permanence and might, King of Upper and Lower Egypt, lord of both lands, Golden Horus Snefru, lord of the Hepet [the tiller of the Ship of State], Golden Horus, first among the gods eternally (172).

The bed canopy and the inscribed chests that held the curtains were presents from Snefru to his wife. The back of the ebony backrest of the Queen's

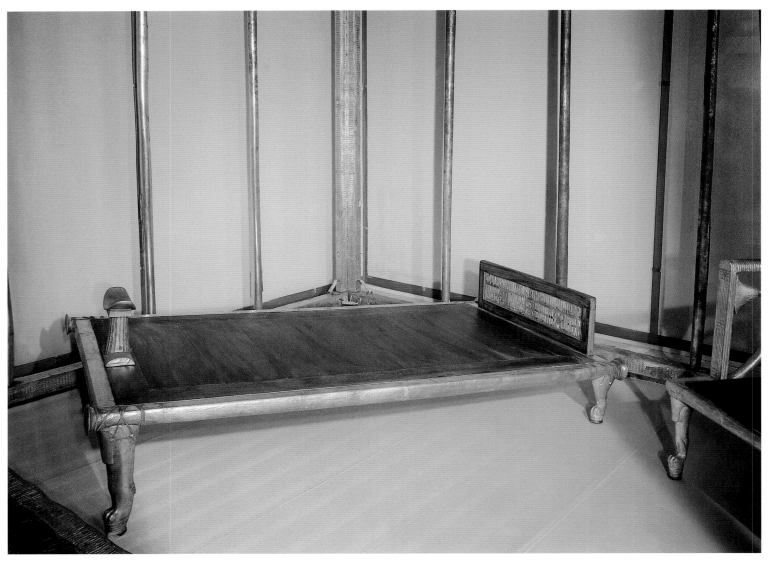

167 Structure with poles of the bed canopy and the bed of Queen Hetep-heres

carrying-chair (164–166) is inlaid with a hieroglyphic inscription in gold: 'Mother of the King of Upper and Lower Egypt, companion of Horus, head of the slaughterers of the acacia house [the funerary sacrifices for the king were prepared in the acacia house], whose every word is obeyed, the divine daughter by birth of Hetep-heres'. The inscription relates that Cheops presented the carrying-chair as part of his mother's funerary equipment.

The ewer and basin of beaten gold (159) were found in a large chest covered with gold foil, as were other vessels and a razor with a gold handle and a copper blade. Also in this chest was the smaller box containing the silver bracelets (162).

The reconstruction of the furniture from the tomb took several years. The Egyptian Museum in Cairo holds not only the bed canopy and the carrying-chair, but also the bedstead (167) and another chair (160);

they are among the most magnificent pieces in the museum's collection. If the funerary equipment of a queen was so heavily laden with precious gold, how much more sumptuously were the famous rulers, the builders of the great pyramids, laid to rest?

Queen Hetep-heres' furniture has an abundance of decorative motifs in the insignia of royalty, protective emblems of the gods and symbols of life and rebirth.

The triangular posts at the back of the bed canopy (168) are held together with copper bolts, whose gilded heads are made in the form of a click beetle. By its ability to get back on its feet unaided when lying on its back, this beetle guarantees the resurrection of the dead.

The butterflies on the Queen's silver bracelets, inlaid in lapis lazuli, turquoise and carnelian (163), and separated by discs of carnelian, may symbolize the sun and promise light, life and freedom of

Old Kingdom Jewellery Finds

168 *Detail of a corner post of the bed canopy (left)*

169 *The hieroglyphs 'permanence' and 'life', along with a floral motif below (right)*

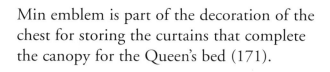

movement in the hereafter.

The gilt legs of the chairs and bed are made in the form of lions' legs; the front legs are distinguished from the back legs by the presence of the lower part of the mane. Symbolically, the Queen was intended to take her rest upon an animal that embodied divine power, which would protect her and help in her rebirth. The raised head-board ensures that the deceased is lying in an inclined position that may signify the very first moments of the body's resurrection.

The back and front of the backrest to one of the chairs (170) are richly decorated in faience. The panel is adorned with emblems of the goddess Neith, and the strips of wood at the edges bear a repeated pattern of stylized falcon feathers, interrupted by a floral motif. This is composed of two highly stylized lotus flowers, open towards the side, and between them at top and bottom, two buds.

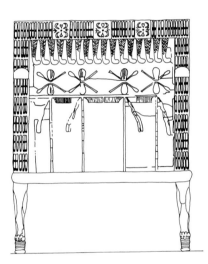

170 *Decoration on the back of one of Hetep-heres' chairs*

This mix of lotus flowers and buds, in many variations, became a permanent feature of the Egyptian art of jewellery, and apparently a kind of amulet: this motif appears alongside the hieroglyphs for 'permanence' and 'life' in a shrine at the mortuary temple of King Sahure (169). Also found is the emblem of Min of Koptos, the old god of war, already seen on the bracelet of King Snefru (124). The

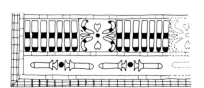

171 *Decoration on the curtain-chests*

Min emblem is part of the decoration of the chest for storing the curtains that complete the canopy for the Queen's bed (171).

The Bead Belt of Ptah-shepses

In a cache at the valley temple of the pyramid complex of King Unas, archaeologists discovered the sarcophagus of Prince Ptah-shepses. This had already been robbed, and the interior had filled with water, which had completely destroyed the mummy. They did, however, make a valuable find, a beaded belt (175) that demonstrates the artistry and feeling for colour of the ancient jewellers. Some of the belt had fallen apart, but the beads were carefully restrung, following the pattern that had survived. The belt is made of a thin strip of gold foil whose outer side is covered in a geometric arrangement of beads of carnelian and gilded steatite. The beads are strung on gold threads, which are in turn anchored in small gold tubes soldered all along the upper and lower edges of the gold foil in lengths of approximately ½in (1.5 cm). The pattern consists of an overlapping row of squares, set on their corners, with a cruciform bead at the centre of each square. It looks very much like the pattern on the belt depicted in the triumphant image of King Narmer (38). A drawing of a reconstruction (174) shows the complexity of the bead pattern.

The two ends of the beaded belt are covered and held fast by semicircular caps of solid gold. The elongated closure with its slightly sloping sides is made of doubled gold foil. Grooves have been incised in the outer surface and inlaid with carnelian and obsidian (173). The two sitting figures facing each other represent the owner of the belt, identified by the hieroglyphs as Prince,

172 *Post at bed canopy entrance, with hieroglyphs embossed in gold foil*

son of the King, Ptah-shepses. In his hand the prince holds a ceremonial staff, and on his forehead the *uraeus* flicks out its tongue. A falcon flies towards him, wings protectively outstretched, holding the ring of 'eternity' in its claws.

Plates have been soldered on to the inward-folded edges at both ends of the closure. The semicircular caps at the ends of the belt itself were pushed under these and tied together with gold threads behind the closure. In the middle of the belt, the beaded work is interrupted by a gold plate, in which a slit allowed the attachment of the bull's tail that always formed part of the royal regalia.

Jewellery from an Unidentified Female Mummy

In 1931 a collection of jewellery was discovered in the intact tomb of an unidentified woman at Giza. The superstructure, with its tomb chapel that had been associated with the burial chamber, had fallen victim to the later tomb of a high palace official, and the name and rank of the dead woman remain unknown. The mummy found in this untouched tomb was adorned with a golden circlet and a necklace of beetle-shaped links, together with necklaces of faience and gold beads, and bracelets and anklets of gold and copper. The necklaces and other bead jewellery were still partly held together by gold thread and had partly disintegrated into scattered beads.

The fifty beetles that make up the necklace (176) were made by pressing gold foil into a mould, the wings being chased. They represent the click beetle, noted above in an amulet and funerary offering in the early dynastic tombs of Nag ed-Deir (168), and also on the bed canopy of Queen Hetep-heres (149).

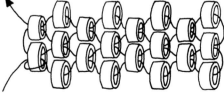

173–175 Bead belt of Ptah-shepses, its closure, and a reconstruction of the stringing of the beads

The circlet (177) is a copper band covered with gold foil, perforated at both its rounded ends so that it can be tied with a string, allowing adjustment to fit the head. On the band are three ornamental discs in embossed and chased gold, attached by copper pins, which pass through tubes of gold. The point of attachment is hidden by a small carnelian.

The middle disc bears a simplified form of the flower motif found on the furniture of Queen Hetep-heres (171). Around the small, round carnelian and its gold setting at the centre are four lotus flowers arranged as a quatrefoil; the pistil is shown projecting from the calyx, and between each of the flowers is a lotus bud. While this flower motif is a symbol of life, the decorative discs on each side symbolize the state of the deceased after her transfiguration. Papyrus umbels grow out from both sides of the carnelian, and upon these, as if upon a nest, sit two crested ibises whose long curving beaks merge with the upper corners of the umbels, so completing the disc.

The Golden Falcon's Head from Hierakonpolis

In 1897–98 the archaeologist J. E. Quibell unearthed a unique find in the Horus temple at Hierakonpolis. In a carefully prepared cache under the paving of the central chapel he discovered the golden head of a statue of the Horus falcon (116), together with the

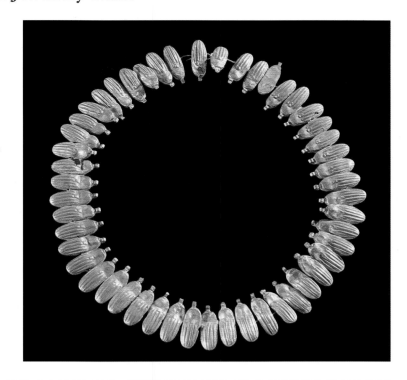

176 Necklace with gold beetles

177 Funerary diadem with ornamental discs

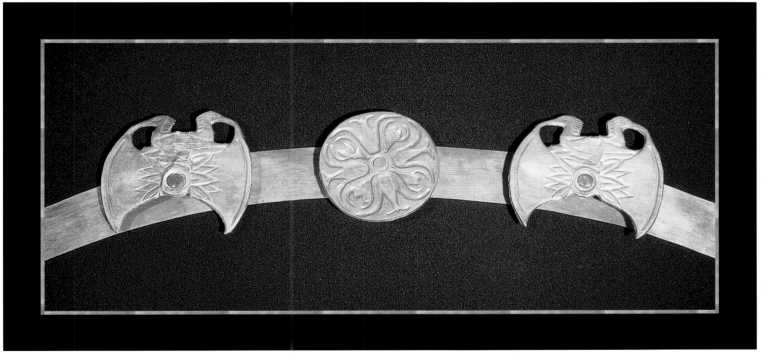

remains of its wooden body. This was a cult image that had been ritually laid to rest when Thutmosis III rebuilt the temple in the New Kingdom. The falcon head is a marvel of the Egyptian gold-beater's art. The head and base of the neck are of beaten gold, worked from the inside outwards, and then presumably filled with resin and the details worked on the outside with a punch and chasing tool. Only the beak was made separately and soldered on. The eyes are formed by the curved ends of an obsidian rod which passes through the head, while the eyelids are represented by the rings that hold this in place. The modelling of the falcon's head is true to nature, but at the same time endows it with divinity.

Small, square holes and the signs of hammer-blows and green copper oxide at the bottom edge of the gold foil show that the head was nailed on to a wooden body, which has since decayed. The falcon's plumage was rendered by small plates of beaten copper nailed on to the wooden core. The gold circlet with its *uraeus* and tall feathers are later additions.

The same hiding place also yielded offerings that all originated from the 6th Dynasty, and were constructed in a variety of materials.

The Middle Kingdom

Absolutist forms of state bear within themselves the seeds of their own dissolution. After the elevation of the kings of the 3rd and 4th Dynasties to divinity, and the development of a creative administration that built the great pyramids and laid down the foundations of Egyptian art, many areas of the state showed signs of decline. The pyramids of the 5th Dynasty were more modest. Originally the highest offices of state had been in the hands of royal princes, but they were now occupied by a rising class of professional officials. To meet their requirements, these officials were granted lands and labourers. As a result the state's wealth was diminished, not only by these transfers of land but also by the endowment of shrines to local gods, which were increasingly exempted from taxes. Administrative posts in Middle and Upper Egypt became hereditary, until the government there no longer depended on the king. The struggle of princely governors for greater power and autonomy led to the dissolution of the state.

178 Amenemhet IV sacrifices to the god Atum
179 Hand mirror with Hathor head from the tomb of Princess Sit-Hathor-Yunit

180 Princess Ashait with a necklace of round beads

The decline of the Old Kingdom and the associated rivalries and internal feuds finally led to the partition of the Kingdom of Egypt. Lower and Middle Egypt, and parts of Upper Egypt as far as Abydos, were ruled by a dynasty from Herakleopolis, while the south of the country was governed by the hereditary princes of Thebes.

The short reign of the Herakleopolites (9th and 10th Dynasties) was a period of intellectual reassessment of the past, in which the thought and teaching of Egyptians were marked by a profound awareness of the catastrophic end of the Old Kingdom and a sense of decline:

Bead necklaces are around the slave women's necks, while the once aristocratic ladies go through the land complaining: 'Oh, if only we had some food!'

This pessimism also raised questions about the point of having costly funerary equipment: eternal life could not be gained by material means. Osiris, ruler of the kingdom of the dead, whose cult had spread since the end of the Old Kingdom, demanded that one followed Ma'at, the righteous path, and every upright mortal was welcome in the hereafter. So the cult of Osiris led to a 'democratization' – to the conviction that it was only an individual's moral qualities that could guarantee access to eternal life.

These changes led to the collapse of the hierarchic order and to social chaos. The pyramids were plundered and the mortuary temples destroyed.

Around 2040 BC, Mentuhotep Nebhepetre of Thebes, the founder of the 11th Dynasty, vanquished the Herakleopolites and their allies, the provincial princes of Middle Egypt, and restored unity and internal order to the kingdom. Thebes in Upper Egypt became the royal capital. The re-establishment of unity and orderly administration and the flow of royal commissions rapidly led to a new flourishing of the arts. Artists from Memphis, acquainted with royal models and still familiar with the basic rules and styles of the past, were called to Thebes for the construction of Mentuhotep's monumental funerary complex in the basin of Deir el-Bahari.

The testimony of an artist, Iri-iru-sen, who had a memorial stele erected for him in Abydos, survives from the period around 2020 BC. The inscription is proud in its praise of his abilities: he had a masterly knowledge of all materials and techniques. Nothing more than this is said, but it is characteristic of the Egyptian artist that his fundamental knowledge is of a ritual nature: 'I know the secret of the divine words'.

Such divine words were recorded and preserved in the 'House of Life'. It was here, too, that the models for statues, reliefs and wall-paintings, and for royal and funerary jewellery, were developed, in accordance with theological conceptions and the rules of Egyptian art and writing. It was here that pictures and signs were endowed with their magical properties. The testimony continues:

I know the order of the festive ceremonies [that is, the rituals that bring 'life' to the works created by artists and craftsmen], I have made use of every magical power.

The Middle Kingdom

These are the words of a self-confident craftsman who was also familiar with the rituals prescribed for the creation of life; the inscription also proves the existence during the 11th Dynasty of independent craft businesses.

Mentuhotep Nebhepetre might have reunified the kingdom, but neither he nor his two successors were able to prevent the renewal of the princes' struggle to promote their private interests. Ameni, the vizier of Mentuhotep IV, the last of the line, re-established order, and under the name of Amenemhet I became founder and first king of the glittering 12th Dynasty. Step by step, he reduced and finally broke the powers of the provincial princes.

Amenemhet transferred the capital back north to the city of Memphis, the centre of ancient culture and the link between Upper and Lower Egypt, or 'balance of both lands'. The renaissance of the kingdom extended to every field, for the restoration of kingship not only required visible expression in buildings, statues, reliefs, inscriptions and jewellery, but also encouraged the arts to new heights of creative power in their expression of Ma'at, or righteous order.

Reliefs and hieroglyphic characters show a clear affinity with those of the 6th Dynasty, but in the 12th Dynasty the style underwent further refinement, and hieroglyphs and relief figures achieved their canonical form in terms of proportion, outline and detail. Figures constructed according to strict rules stand against a flat background almost completely covered by monumental hieroglyphs.

181 Princess Kawit at her toilette

We now need to consider the royal reliefs of this period, because jewellery of the 12th Dynasty begins to acquire pictorial and hieroglyphic motifs whose design and symbolism are closely related to the standards of expression developed in relief work. The vividness and wealth of meaning of certain characters, and their integration as pictorial elements in an overall composition – thus endowing it with new formal and expressive possibilities – made hieroglyphs an essential feature of royal jewellery. The right to be adorned with gold when dead was now no longer

182 Frieze of household objects painted inside a coffin

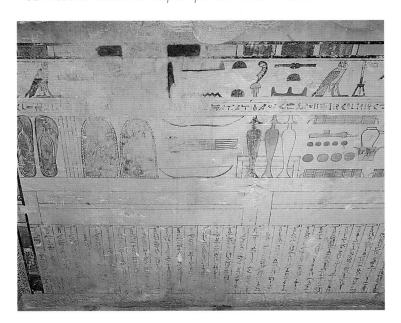

183 Jewellery represented by paintings inside a coffin

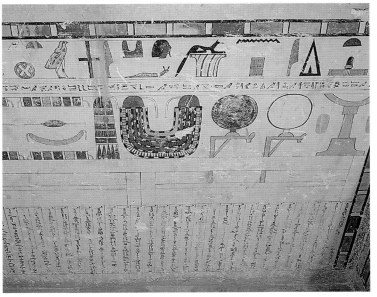

The Middle Kingdom

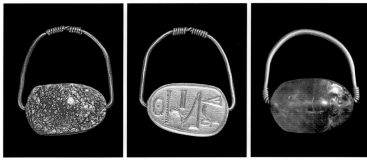

184–185 Rings of Amenemhet III, with carnelian scarabs
186 Ring, with scarab of amethyst

restricted to the king, but the collapse of the Old Kingdom and the rise in the practice of tomb-robbing that accompanied the decline raised doubts about how effective such costly funerary equipment might be. The custom emerged of decorating the inside of the coffin (182–183) with representations of royal emblems and with excerpts from the 'Coffin Texts', which promised 'eternal permanence through gold', emerged. Alongside elements of the royal regalia, objects to meet personal needs, such as cloth, jewellery, hand mirrors, head-rests and washbasins, were also represented, as were utensils for the prescribed funerary rituals, such as oil jars and the instrument for the 'opening of the mouth', which endowed the mummy with new life. Thanks to the magical power of the image, these items would be at the disposal of the deceased for use in the hereafter.

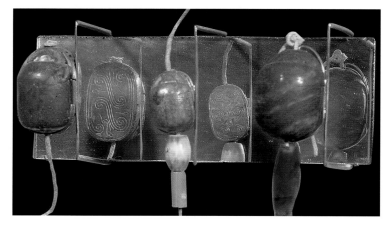

The art of the Egyptian goldsmith reached its zenith during the Middle Kingdom, as fresh artistic ideas were met by a new abundance of gold and precious stones, while the repertoire of forms and techniques was extended by ideas from the Near East and the Aegean.

New Forms

The scarab or dung beetle replaced the click beetle as an amulet, inheriting its role as the symbol of 'resurrection and life'. 'May you live [*ankh*] like the *ankh*-scarab', it says in the Pyramid Texts of the Old Kingdom. *Khepre*, the scarab's name in Egyptian, stands for 'life in the hereafter'. In its early beetle form it is found as an amulet from the end of the Old Kingdom, but in the Middle Kingdom increasingly the belly was flattened and decorated with inscriptions or other ornament to heighten its magical power. Such amulets were also used as seals. The three scarabs of Wah, the master of a prince's household, are among the earliest examples of this new type of amulet (187–188).

Cylinder Amulets and Fish Amulets

Cylinder amulets, which have been found only in women's tombs, have no predecessors in earlier times. They appear during the 12th Dynasty, together with other exotic jewellery using new decorative techniques, and are otherwise found only in the early 18th Dynasty, among the funerary offerings for secondary wives from Palestine or Syria. They are therefore certainly a product of foreign influence.

These cylinders, 1–2½in (3–7cm) in length, are made of gold foil, and are often reinforced on the inside by a copper tube. Both ends are closed off with gold caps.

An eyelet or small loop on one cap allows the cylinder to be worn as a pendant. The exterior may be decorated all around with rows of small, warty protrusions, or with zigzag motifs in granular technique (191-193). In another type, rings of semi-precious stone and gold foil are lined up on a copper cylinder. How these amulets were worn remains

187 A scarab of Wah, with gold inlay
188 Wah's scarabs, two of silver with gold inlay, one of lapis lazuli
189 Gilded cartonnage mummy mask

The Middle Kingdom

unclear, as no actual representations have been found in tomb reliefs or on the statues of the important women of the royal court. There is no evidence to support the suggestion that the hollow space inside held a piece of rolled-up papyrus with a magical spell; there is no doubt, however, of its character as an amulet.

Fish amulets, too, were exclusively feminine. As an emblem of Hathor and symbol of rebirth they were worn by very young girls. Neither original examples nor representations survive from the Old Kingdom. The Westcar Papyrus, however, preserves a story from the 4th Dynasty in which a fish amulet made of turquoise plays a role, the stone having come from the Sinai, where the goddess Hathor reigned:

> For his diversion King Snefru had himself rowed over a lake in the palace garden by a crowd of pretty girls. The girls moved the oars up and down and His Majesty's heart was glad as he saw them row in this way.
>
> Then the side lock of hair of a girl became caught in the rudder – the fish pendant of turquoise that was hanging from it dropped into the water. She fell silent and stopped rowing, and the others did the same. Snefru promised to replace the lost jewel but the girl wished to have her fish amulet back again at all costs. She did indeed get it back, because with the help of a magician,

the waters were parted and the jewel rescued from the depths of the lake.

Fish amulets, however, are frequently found dating from early in the 2nd millennium BC, in both surviving examples and representations of young girls (190), who wear them as pendants on a necklace or in their hair. The catfish (*Synodontos batensoda*) and the Nile perch (*Tilapia nilotica*), two species of fish of special mythological significance, make their appearance as amulets. The catfish swims on its back, and is thus, like the click beetle, which can right itself when lying on its back, a symbol of resurrection. The Nile perch incubates its eggs in its mouth, from which its offspring then emerge fully developed, and is thus a guarantor of constantly renewed life. As a symbol of self-reproduction it is often shown together with the lotus plant, another symbol of rebirth.

A number of such symbols are found on a girdle or necklace from the tomb of a Theban girl (194). Eight scallop shells of electrum are joined together by doubled rows of beads made of electrum, amethyst, lapis lazuli, turquoise and carnelian. From the beads hang two catfish and two locks of hair fashioned from electrum. The cloisonné pendant in the middle takes the form of a papyrus umbel, itself made up of three lotus flowers – a fusion of 'revival' and 'freshness and youth'. At the bottom hangs the hieroglyph for the god Heh, symbol of 'millions of years'.

Pectorals

In the Old Kingdom a trapeziform bib was worn as an extension and terminal for the bead broad collar. This is the precursor of the pectoral in its classic form, which makes an unexpected appearance around the middle of the 12th Dynasty in a series of

191 Four cylinder amulets of Mereret   192 Two amulets of unknown origin   193 Four amulets of a wife of Thutmosis III

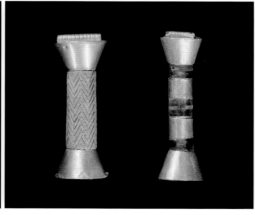

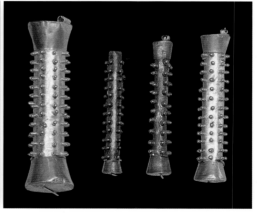

194 Necklace or girdle from the tomb of a Theban girl

masterpieces of the goldsmiths' art, and is then found until the end of the pharaonic period.

As far as one can tell from finds in tombs and visual representations, pectorals were worn only by women during the Middle Kingdom. There are two black granite statues of Queen Nofret, wife of Sesostris II, on which a pectoral, incized in the stone, is shown hanging from beaded bands over the chest. These two statues, created around 1890 BC, were carried off to Tanis in the Delta in the 21st Dynasty, around 1050 BC. On one (195–196), the trapeziform pectoral, which tapers outwards towards the bottom, is divided into upper and lower zones with complementary motifs. The upper part has the throne name of Sesostris II in a cartouche, flanked by two *uraei*, the one on the left wearing the crown of Upper Egypt, and the one on the right that of Lower Egypt – these are the two guardian goddesses. In the lower, the two watchful Horus eyes hover over two young falcons who sit on the sign for 'Gold', between which stands the character for 'permanence'. The bottom edge is made up of a row of teardrop-shaped beads.

The Middle Kingdom

There survives another representation of a pectoral from the reign of Sesostris II, in a painted relief from the tomb of the nome (local) governor Djehuti-hotep at el-Bersheh (198). It shows the female members of the family in a long, festive procession. The prince's daughters wear sumptuous lotus diadems on their 'Hathor' hair, and also beaded bracelets and a trapeziform pectoral. This hangs from broad bands of beads held together at intervals by bars. Enough paint remains to allow the motifs to be discerned: a red solar disc flanked by two *uraei* with the Lower Egyptian crown.

This design is different from that which appears on the surviving pectorals of the royal family (219–220, 233, 234). With their varying motifs these pectorals are a propagandistic demonstration of the sovereign nature and duties of kingship. They combine hieroglyphic and figurative elements in accomplished works of art, and as amulets they possessed magical powers. The design for every piece came from the 'House of Life'.

The magnificent effect of the pectorals comes from their closed composition, which lends an inner monumentality to the small format, from the brilliant colours of the stone and glass inlays, and from the delicate framing of the motifs by the narrow gold bars used for the setting. In the 12th Dynasty this type of jewellery reached a peak that was never to be attained again.

197 Pectoral with emblem of the goddess Bat between Horus-Harmachis and Seth in the form of mythical creatures

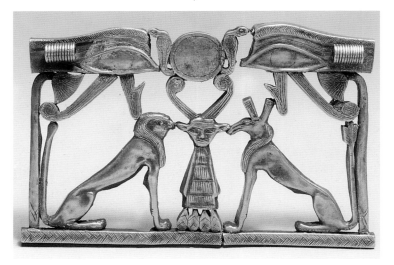

Queen Nofret wears her hair in the style of the goddess Hathor and her priestesses, the abundant tresses being bound with bands, and the ends curling snail-like around a piece of jewellery. On her brow a *uraeus* rears up, its body snaking up towards her parting. The other statue shows the queen with the same coiffure. The pectoral, of simplified design, shows the throne name of Sesostris II in the middle, in a cartouche, crowned with horns and tall ostrich feathers; above this is a pair of magical eyes, and on both sides of the royal cartouche the guardian goddess Nekhbet of Upper Egypt appears in the form of a vulture.

198 *The daughters of the governor Djehuti-hotep with lotus diadems and trapeziform pectorals*

New Techniques

The motifs found in the superb pectorals of the Middle Kingdom may be purely Egyptian, but the technique used in their manufacture was hardly invented in the valley of the Nile. It appears so suddenly and in such perfection that one can only conclude that it came from itinerant foreign craftsmen who offered their services to the royal workshops and introduced new techniques into Egyptian goldsmiths' work.

Cloisonné

The Egyptian jewellers had been masters at inlaying metal with coloured stone since the time of the Old Kingdom, and the bracelets of Hetep-heres (163) and the belt of Ptah-shepses (173) are early examples of the art. The metal was gouged out with a chisel to fit the inlays precisely, and the cut stone was then cemented in place. Pectorals and jewelled pendants of the 12th Dynasty utilized many complex techniques that can all be considered types of cloisonné. The little amulet in the form of the emblem of the goddess Bat (120), with its cow's horns and bow under the chin, may represent a transitional stage.

The Egyptian jewellers probably proceeded in the following way: they cut out the required shape for the jewellery from thin gold foil, then laid it on a smooth and elastic bed of resin and wax, to which it stuck. The outlines were then cut into the ductile gold with a sharp stylus, and the surface between these lines was then beaten back into negative relief using a blunt modelling tool of hardwood or ivory.

When this beating, or repoussé, had been done, there followed the most difficult aspect of the work. Thin gold strips, about 1⁄16in (2 or 3mm) in width, had to be cut and bent to correspond exactly to the outlines, then fastened by their edges with solder, a mixture of copper oxide, natron and glue. When the work was heated to 1530°F (850°C) the copper oxide turned to copper and attached the gold strips firmly to the foil base.

Once the whole composition had been outlined with soldered strips, inlays of precious stone or coloured glass were shaped to fit and cemented in place within the outline.

The inlay now gave the piece such solidity that the gold background between the motifs could be cut out using the sharp corner of a tempered copper chisel. On the raised reverse the detail of the motifs was engraved with a burin. Finally, the outer edges were polished with a fine-grained stone.

This method was ideal for pectorals tightly packed with figures and hieroglyphic characters; those with larger gaps between motifs were probably made up by soldering individual pieces together.

Granulation

The high art of invisibly attaching tiny gold balls to a smooth gold background to produce geometrical patterns was not an Egyptian invention. As can be seen in jewellery from the royal tombs of Ur, this technique had been mastered in Mesopotamia by around 2500 BC. It presumably became known in the Nile Valley from the Sumerian gold jewellery imported via Byblos. In Egypt, granulation appears for the first time during the Middle Kingdom on jewellery of distinctly un-Egyptian appearance from the tombs of the king's daughters Khnumet and Mereret at Dahshur (191, 214). The ancient Egyptians probably used a method that is still employed today by jewellers in Luxor (ancient Thebes). The gold granules are obtained by slowly dripping molten gold into a wooden bowl, from a height of about 3ft (1m). Under constant stirring it breaks up into countless tiny balls, which are then sieved several times and sorted into exactly identical sizes. These little balls are then rolled in soot and heated up to just below their melting point, so that their surface takes up the carbon from the soot. This is done with a flame controlled through the use of a blow-pipe. After the

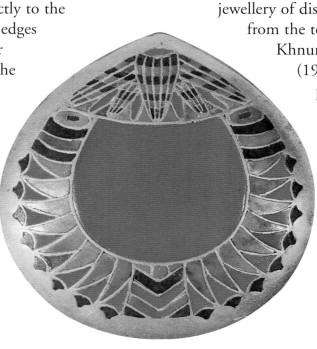

199 Pendant in the form of a shell with a butterfly and lotus flower in cloisonné work

200 Pendant in the form of a shell

201 Pectoral of Sesostris II, detail enlarged 7 times

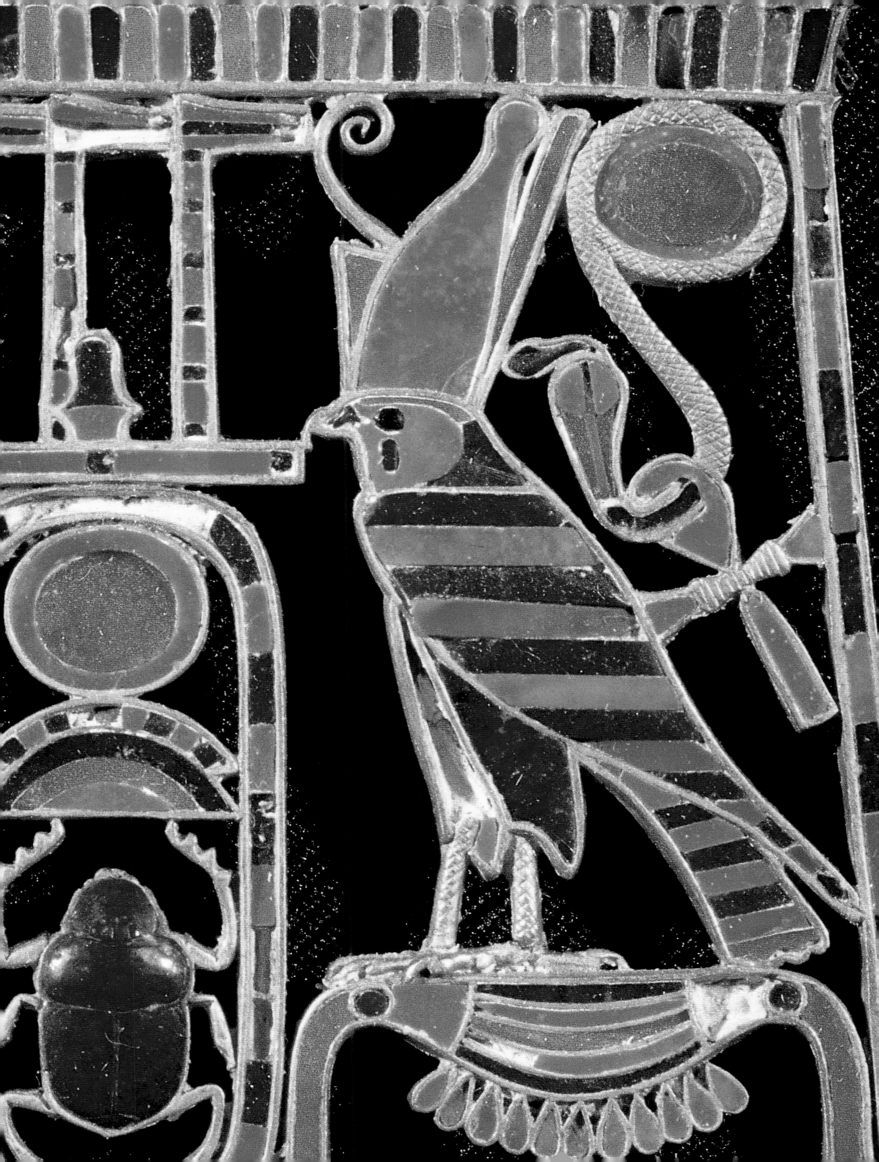

Finds from Pyramid Complexes

The pharaohs of the powerful 12th Dynasty did not build their pyramids of solid stone but instead employed rubble and sun-dried bricks made out of Nile mud. A limestone casing was then put over this core of mixed material, which in many constructions was intended to stabilize a star-shaped internal stone skeleton.

The burial chambers were secured at the greatest expense. In the Old Kingdom their entrances were always orientated towards the north, towards the Pole Star. To keep tomb-robbers at bay, entrances were now constructed facing different directions and sealed

Top: The weathered pyramid of Amenemhet III at Dahshur is entirely constructed of brick.

Left: Snefru's mortuary temple at Dahshur. On the left horizon the 'black' pyramid of Amenemhet III rises from the desert.

Right: The mortuary complex of Mentuhotep II, in the Deir al-Bahari basin

Left: The Hawara pyramid, in which Amenemhet III was buried, and the pyramid of Sesostris II at Illahun.

with huge quartzite blocks. All these pre-emptive measures, however, failed to save a single royal pyramid from being plundered.

Members of the royal family – royal wives and princesses – would be buried within the temenos walls of the pyramid complex. A few of these burials, hidden in deep shafts, were undiscovered by the tomb-robbers of antiquity and remained secure until they were found in recent times.

In 1894–95 Jacques de Morgan discovered near the pyramids of Amenemhet III and Sesostris III in Dahshur the tombs of four princesses, with their accoutrements of exquisite jewellery. In 1914, at the pyramid complex of Sesostris II at Illahun (Lahun), Flinders

Petrie found treasures belonging to Princess Sit-Hathor-Yunit, which had escaped the tomb-robbers. In the flooded burial chamber of Sesostris' pyramid he found a royal *uraeus*, presumably coming from the king's mummy. Further jewellery finds followed at Hawara, Lisht and Dahshur.

---

gold foil base has been similarly treated, it is painted with resin and the little balls are arranged on it in geometrical patterns.

The absorbed carbon reduces the melting point at the surface from 1918°F to about 1620°F (1064° to about 900°C). When the piece is heated, the gold base and the granules fuse only at tiny, hidden points of contact, and the balls preserve their spherical form because the gold core does not melt. The foil and the granules must have exactly the same gold content, so they have exactly the same melting point.

In the ancient world, the Egyptians, Etruscans, Greeks and Romans all brought the art of granulation to its zenith. The technique was later lost, and was rediscovered by jewellers only at the beginning of the 20th century.

Inlaid Metal Work

Investigators took an X-ray of the mummy of Wah, the master of the household to Mektire (the crown prince, treasurer and chancellor), who had been buried around 2020 BC in his master's rock-cut tomb at Thebes. Beneath the wrappings of the mummy, they discovered a broad beaded collar and three large scarabs: one of the scarabs was of lapis lazuli, and the other two had been cast in parts of solid silver and soldered together (188). The metal is 90 per cent pure, the earliest example of such a high quality to be found in Egypt, and it was probably an import or a tribute from Syria. The elegant spiral motifs engraved on the flat underside surface suggest some Cretan influence. On the right wing of the larger of the scarabs is the hieroglyphic inscription 'chancellor

Mektire', and on the left, 'property administrator Wah'; both are inlaid in gold.

This is the earliest example of inlaid metal to be found in Egypt. In Mesopotamia, however, inlaid metalwork can be seen in finds from the royal tombs of Ur dating from 2500 BC. This technique, too, probably arrived in the Nile Valley with itinerant foreign jewellers.

In inlaid metalwork, one metal is inlaid into grooves incized into metal of another colour. The required decoration is incized with a chisel in such a way that the groove is undercut (wider at the bottom than at the top on both sides). This technique creates a thin upper edge to the groove that can easily be bent upwards with a chisel and then hammered back down after the gold or silver inlay, in the form of wire or small pieces cut to the correct shape, has been put in place. This hammering also beats the inlay flush with the surface.

Middle Kingdom Jewellery Finds

Nothing survives of the royal jewellery of the 11th Dynasty – the tombs of its kings were all plundered. Only the tombs of secondary wives who had been buried in deep shaft tombs within the area of Mentuhotep Nebhepetre's mortuary temple escaped the tomb-robbers. The jewellery they contained was quite plain – necklaces with beads of silver and gold, semi-precious stones and faience. In the tomb of Princess Mujet a skein of large, spherical, hollow beads in gold was found, presumably for wearing in the hair, together with a second skein with beads of carnelian, feldspar and blue glass, and a third composed of round gold disks strung on a leather thong. Spherical beads were particularly popular at this time. Just as in the Old Kingdom, two hemispheres were produced by pressing thin gold or silver-foil into moulds, and these were then soldered together.

202 Stylized floral crown of Princess Khnumet

The Middle Kingdom

The pyramids of the powerful 12th Dynasty were no longer constructed of solid stone, but built from rubble and brick and clad with an outer covering of limestone. Enormous efforts were made to ensure the security of the burial chambers. To mislead the tomb-robbers, tomb entrances were no longer consistently orientated towards the Pole Star to the north, but opened in different directions, and access was blocked by enormous quartzite blocks. None of these measures, however, succeeded in saving any of the royal pyramids from being robbed. Only one precious piece of jewellery escaped – the golden *uraeus* from the headcloth of Sesostris II (229).

The walled pyramid complexes also provided a last resting-place for the closest members of the royal family – royal wives and princesses – in deep vaults, some of which remained undiscovered by tomb-robbers. The rich finds of jewellery from the princesses' graves at Dahshur and Illahun (Lahun) give some idea for the first time of the wealth of provision that was made for the afterlife. Among them are some of the noblest and most inventive creations of the Egyptian goldsmith's art. Gold jewellery of equal perfection has also been found in non-royal tombs. This has usually been women's jewellery: floral diadems, bracelets and anklets, belts and rings. Some pieces from the princesses' graves have suggested that they might have been inherited from the king himself, such as, for example, a costly dagger, a diadem with a *uraeus*, and pectorals showing royal emblems and the slaughter of the enemy.

Dahshur

In 1894–95, near the pyramids of Amenemhet II and Sesostris III at Dahshur, about 14 miles (25km) south of Giza, the French archaeologist Jacques de Morgan uncovered the tombs of the royal family. Within the walls of the enclosed complexes he discovered four burials that had escaped the tomb-robbers and remained intact: the tombs of princesses Khnumet and Ita at the 'white' pyramid of Amenemhet II, and

203 Falcon's head from Khnumet's collar

those of Sit-Hathor and Mereret at the 'black' pyramid of Sesostris III.

More interested in finding treasure than in archaeological investigation, de Morgan did not make an exact record either of the relations between the many beads and other elements, or of the precise locations in which they were found. So there was no proper provenance for the finds when they were handed to the Cairo Museum, and they could only be reconstructed by reference to the jewellery of the same period found at Illahun.

Princess Khnumet, a daughter of Amenemhet II, was particularly richly provided with jewellery, among which was included two crowns and a large falcon collar, together with necklaces, pendants, belts, bracelets and anklets.

One of the two crowns (202) is made up of eight repeated groups of highly stylized flower motifs similar to those adorning the circlet of the princess Nofret (132). At the centre of each group is a rosette with petals made of tiny turquoises, lapis lazuli and obsidian, radiating from a disc of red carnelian. On both sides, the open bells of lily-like flowers are turned towards the rosette. This ornamental group is repeated eight times, each group separated from the others by a similar rosette, from which the lily-like flower springs upwards. The group above the brow is spanned by a gold vulture, its wings stretched out in a flattened arch, its talons holding the ring of eternity. During the Old Kingdom, the vulture was found as the head-dress of the goddess Nekhbet of Nekhen; as the guardian goddess, she protects the wearer of the diadem.

The flowers and rosettes of the diadem were made

204 Construction of the falcon's head terminals from Princess Khnumet's bead collar
205 Gold falcon-collar of Princess Khnumet
206 Naturalistic floral crown of Princess Khnumet

The Middle Kingdom

individually from gold foil and soldered together after the precious stone had been inlaid. The body of the vulture had been cast, its wings beaten from gold foil, with the details brought out by engraving, while the eyes were inlaid in obsidian. At the back of the crown, a small tube was soldered on the inside, which held a stylized palm tree in gold. Khnumet's second crown (206) is a diadem of completely different design. Around this feather-light garland, a tangle of gold threads strewn with tiny flowers and fruits, are six crosses each made of four papyrus umbels in cloisonné work with turquoise and carnelian inlay. The delicate gold flowers, soldered to points where the gold threads cross, are also inlaid in the same materials, and polished and cemented into place.

This floral diadem has no relationship to any Egyptian diadem of earlier or later date, and it was

207 Anklet with bird claws

probably designed and created by craftsmen from Crete. Many Cretan influences are found in the jewellery of the princesses Khnumet and Mereret.

The falcon collar (205) is made up of strings of spherical and disc-shaped gold beads, a row of vertically threaded oval beads and four rows of gold hieroglyphs inlaid in lapis lazuli, turquoise, green feldspar and carnelian. The hieroglyphs for 'health', 'life' and 'permanence' alternate in each row. The beads and hieroglyphs have been reassembled in accordance with the approximate positions in which they were found on the chest. The gold falcon's-head collar terminals are masterpieces of design and technique. They are inlaid with lapis lazuli and carnelian, with garnet for the eyes. The heads have been soldered together from separate elements; the soldering is visible, allowing the method of assembly to be analysed by modern experts (204).

208–209 Charm bracelets of Princess Khnumet

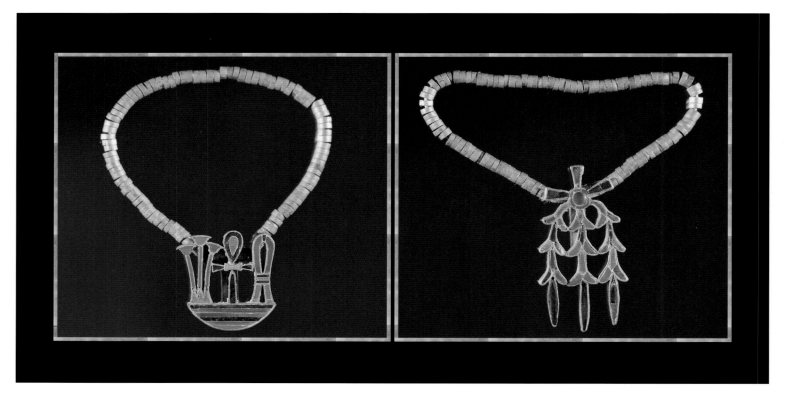

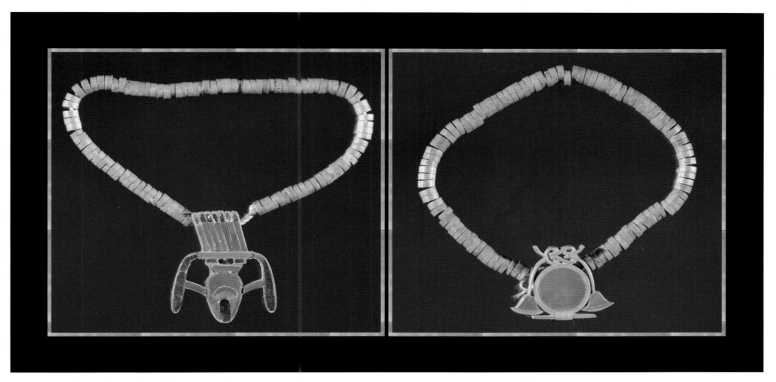

210–211 Charm bracelets of Princess Khnumet

The stringing of the falcon necklace (212) had also come apart. In the present reconstruction, all the individual pieces that were found together have been arranged symmetrically about the centre of the necklace: the grouped hieroglyphs for 'life' and 'contentment', found only once in the middle, are succeeded on left and right by a jackal-headed god; a vulture and an *uraeus*, the two major elements of the king's titulary, each on a basket; a Bat emblem; a *wedjat* eye; a tall pitcher with a handle (of ambiguous significance); the characters for 'permanence', 'life' and 'union'; and a bee (the title of the king of Lower Egypt). It is not possible to read these characters as a coherent statement.

The falcon heads at both ends of the necklace, each fitted with a soldered eyelet through which a ribbon could be threaded to close it, are inlaid in turquoise and lapis lazuli. Detail is provided by the gold strips that hold the inlay. Two small tubes have been soldered on to the straight bottom edge of each of the falcon's heads, from which are hung the two strands of gold beads. The lower margin of the necklace is made up of the customary drop-shaped beads, which are here inlaid in turquoise, carnelian and lapis lazuli.

In another necklace (213), there are two rows of gold, turquoise and lapis lazuli beads linked together by spacers composed of pairs of tubular beads that are made out of turquoise and lapis lazuli. Here, too, the outer margin is composed of teardrop-shaped beads that are decorated in cloisonné.

Hieroglyphs of turquoise, lapis lazuli and carnelian inlays set in gold were intended to bring the wearer every kind of good fortune: 'rebirth' (209), 'a joyful heart' (210), 'eternal youth' (211), 'every protection and life around me' (208). These have been restrung in modern times with beads found at the same location. How these good-luck pendants were worn, around the neck or on the wrist, however, is unclear.

The hieroglyph 'protection' (*sah*), inlaid in dark blue lapis lazuli and mounted between gold bars, was used on a bracelet clasp (215). Its significance derives from the bundle of reeds bound in the same form, which was worn diagonally over the chest and shoulder to keep a swimmer above water, like a lifebelt. At the top of the hieroglyph is a further protective sign, a panther's head in gold, a motif that often appears on the necklaces, bracelets and belts of the 12th dynasty (71, 215). On the reverse of the hieroglyph the gold is chased in life-like detail, the panther's head being replaced by a hatched gold band. The gold bars at the sides were each provided with a slot into which a T-shaped tenon could be slid, while sixteen tiny holes on the outer edges held the ends of the strands of beads.

Pages 106–107: 212–213 Necklaces of Princess Khnumet

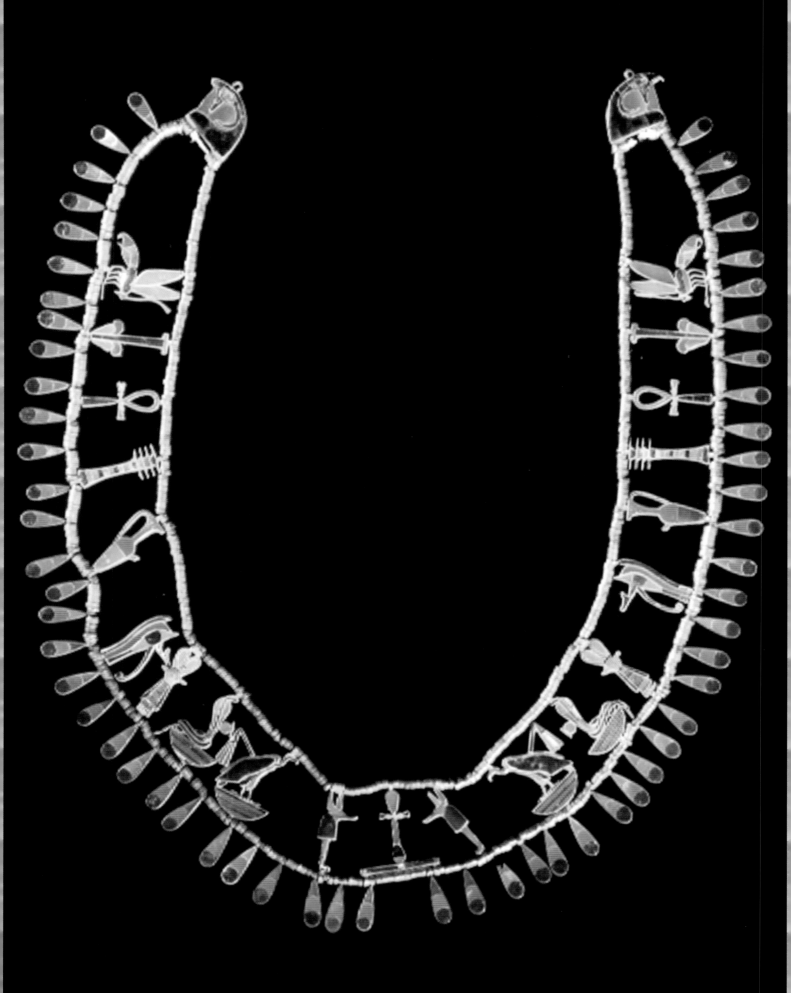

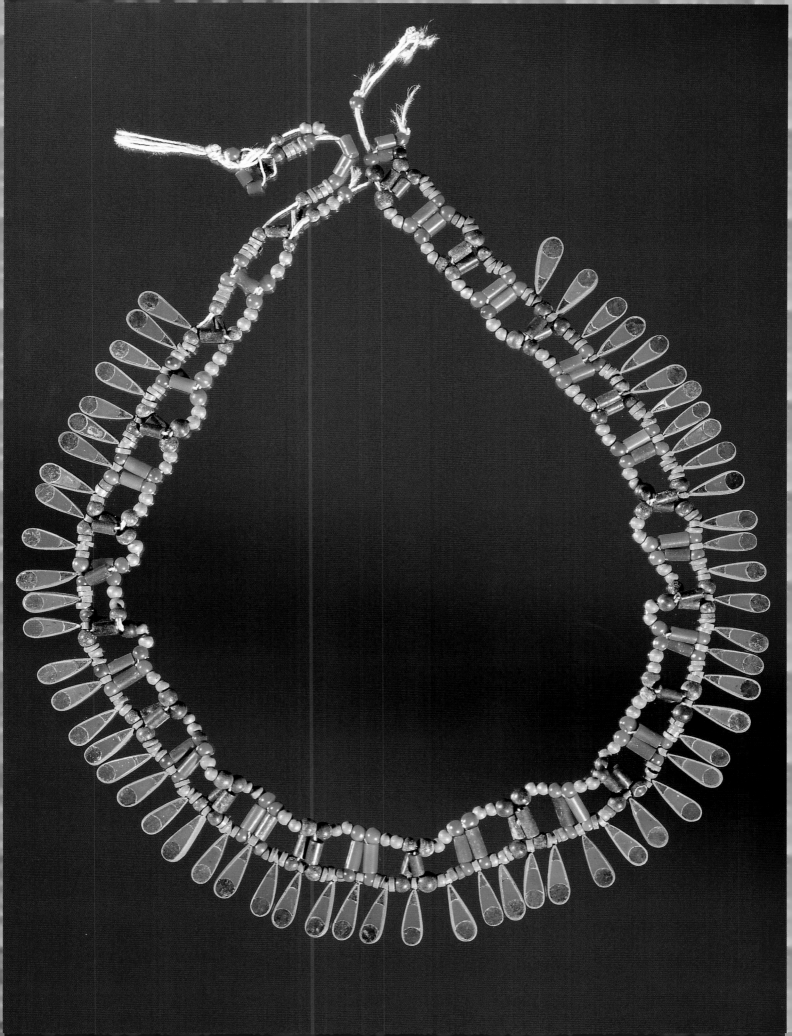

Middle kingdom Jewellery Finds

The girdle of gold, lapis lazuli, turquoise and carnelian beads in the form of acacia seeds (216) also played a protective role. From prehistoric times, girdles made of such seeds had been worn under the clothing to protect the lower abdomen from illness and the danger of miscarriage. Most of these are continuous, that is to say, they have no fastening but are put on by being pulled over the head and shoulders.

In the anklet with bird's claws (207), the setting is of granulated gold wire, while the surface is decorated with a pattern of coloured scales made of tiny, precisely cut inlays of turquoise, carnelian and lapis lazuli, set in gold cells. The claws are each suspended by an eyelet from a short string of gold beads with a knot-amulet

215 Bracelet clasp

dancer in the tomb of provincial governor Uah-ka at Qau. She also wears a hairband of beads, a necklace with a *menat*, and various items on her wrists and upper arms that are difficult to parallel in surviving jewellery.

Amongst the jewellery of Princess Khnumet from Dahshur were a few pieces that are different in form and technique from any other Egyptian jewellery previously known, and which indicate Aegean influence. This is granulated jewellery (214). In one of these pieces (top centre) two delicately worked circular pendants are linked by a small gold chain. The outer circle, itself set with eight half-circles, encloses a hollow square with inward-curving sides. The individual narrow strips of gold have other strips

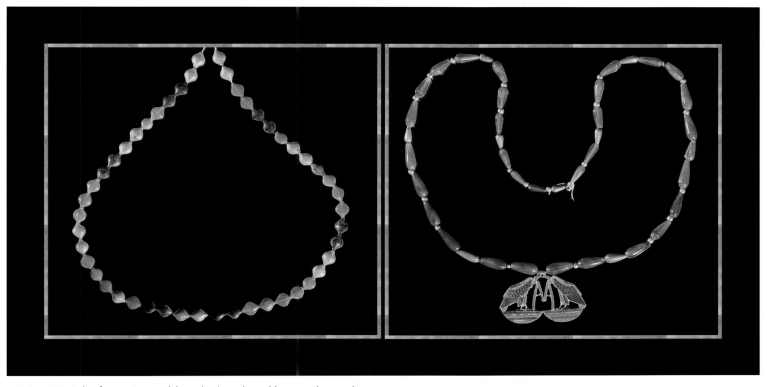

216–217 Belt of acacia-seed beads, bead necklace with pendant

fastening. The two knots are of beaten gold foil, in two halves that can be locked together by a removable pin. In the magical literature, knot amulets are said to protect the body against poisonous snakes and other creeping things.

Anklets with bird's-claw amulets, which had been worn since prehistoric times, also appear in contemporary wall paintings, for example on a female

214 Granulated jewellery of Princess Khnumet

soldered to their edges, the space between them being filled with rows of small gold balls. Between the two discs hangs a round medallion in a gold setting. The composition of multi-coloured glass mosaic depicts a recumbent black and white cow, which is enclosed in a circle of brown and white dots. A lens of rock crystal is laid over the mosaic. Three star-shaped pendants hang from the medallion by short, fine chains. They are of the same open-work construction as the two round pendants and are decorated in the same way with granulation; the edges of the circles, however, are set with eight points, forming a star pattern.

Another chain (214) is formed of intertwined links of doubled gold wire, from which hang flies or bees cut out from gold foil, arranged in groups of three. On yet another short, fine chain (214) the pendant is a butterfly of granulated gold foil. This motif has already been seen in the inlaid decoration of the silver bracelets of Queen Hetep-heres (163), but Princess Khnumet's butterfly has a different outline. The outer edges, the contour of the body and the structure of the wing-covers are emphasized with soldered fine gold wire. On the reverse is a device to attach the two chains.

The last is a chain of interlaced gold wire from which hang two starfish and on either side a row of five shells in high relief (214). Gold wire has been soldered around the edge of the circular central section of the starfish, and the space within filled with granulation. For the shells, gold foil was pressed into moulds, and the outer surface chased to reproduce the natural ribbing.

Ita, a daughter of Amenemhet II, was buried near her father's pyramid at Dahshur. In her coffin an unusual and precious item was found – a dagger (218), together with the remains of a belt. The crescent-shaped pommel is 2¾in (7cm) wide and made of lapis lazuli, probably the largest piece ever worked in Egypt. The short hilt is a tube of beaten gold, oval in cross-section and slightly drawn in towards the middle. Exactly fitted to the curve of the hilt are circular discs of lapis lazuli and green feldspar; they are cemented in horizontal and vertical rows, with each roundel being inlaid with a diagonal cross of thin gold. The small curvilinear squares that are formed in the spaces between the roundels are carefully inlaid with polished carnelian.

The shoulder is cast of solid gold, and fastened to the bronze blade by three gold rivets. The concave lines of its two edges give the blade itself great elegance. The ferrule of

solid gold and the tip of the blade were also found beside the dagger.

The large pommel in lapis lazuli and the sturdy hilt of gold are otherwise unknown in Egyptian daggers of the period, while the hilt, with its flower pattern, is unique in Egypt in type and technique. This weapon was presumably made for Princess Ita by goldsmiths of foreign origin. The shape of the blade suggests Byblos, while the pattern on the handle is reminiscent of the Cretan carpet-patterns on the ceiling frescos with which, in the time of Sesostris I, the provincial governors' tombs at Assiut were decorated in imitation of 'feasting tents'. A stone sphinx bearing the name of Ita and set up at Quadana near Homs, Syria, suggests that the princess was of Syrian origin. The tomb of Princess Sit-Hathor, a daughter of Sesostris II and sister of Sesostris III, who was buried near her brother's pyramid, contained a pectoral bearing the name of Sesostris II (219). As in later pectorals, the composition is set in a frame, representing a divine shrine with its angled outside walls, the upper edge being made of a hollow moulding. Two falcons, each with the double crown of Upper and Lower Egypt, stand upon the hieroglyph 'gold', giving the title 'Golden Horus'. The solar discs inlaid in carnelian with the *uraei* and the *ankh*, the sign of life, symbolize the protective powers of kingship. A group of hieroglyphs and the throne name of Sesostris II, Kha-kheper-Re, occupy the central section. The composition of this pectoral is to be read as a rebus: 'Pleased are the gods with Kha-kheper-Re'. With its generous bands of dark and light blue colour, the inlay on both falcons is more festive than in the example from Illahun,

218 Dagger of Princess Ita

219 Pectoral with the name of Sesostris II

Pages 112–113: 220 Pectoral with the throne name of Sesostris III

which bears the name of the same king (233). The relief and the chasing on the reverse are of similar detail and precision.

Mereret, too, was probably also a daughter of Sesostris II, and wife of her brother Sesostris III. She lived into the reign of her nephew Amenemhet III and was buried near her brother-husband's pyramid at Dahshur, close to the tomb of Sit-Hathor. Buried with Mereret were two pectorals, one with the name of Sesostris III, the other with that of Amenemhet III.

On the pectoral with the name of Sesostris III (220) is a motif that can be traced back to the Old Kingdom: the king is represented as a griffin, a composite creature with a lion's body and the head of a falcon, trampling down the enemies of Egypt with its paws. The motif is doubled, as if by reflection. The falcon's head is crowned by a double horn diadem from which rise two tall feathers, and over its brow is the *uraeus*; the lion's body has the colourful feathers of the falcon. The raised forepaw strikes at a Libyan, who pleads for mercy, while the hind paw tramples on a dark-skinned Nubian. In the middle, the royal cartouche with the throne name of Sesostris III, Kha-kau-Re, rests on the outstretched forepaws of the two griffins. Above this, the vulture-goddess Nekhbet of Upper Egypt, her wings outstretched, holds rings of eternity in her talons. This composition is set within a shrine, whose upper moulding is supported by two lotus flowers on slim stems, from each of which springs a second flower that both fills a gap and helps support the end of the lion's tail.

The pectoral with the name of Amenemhet III (234), which is also symmetrically composed and surrounded by a frame in the shape of a shrine, shows another version of the theme 'the pharaoh ritually destroying Egypt's enemies'. The king is seen wearing a robe fastened over one shoulder and an apron of beads. Boldly stepping forward, he holds a

vanquished Near Eastern Bedouin by the hair, so as to bludgeon him with his club, which is fitted with an axe blade. The victim, who has fallen to his knees, holds out his dagger and curved sword (*harpesh*), the characteristic weapons of the nomads, and offers them to the pharaoh in supplication. Above this ritual event hovers the vulture-goddess, described as mistress of the heavens and ruler of the two lands. With her outspread wings she bestows 'life' and 'permanence' on the king's arm. In the centre of the composition is the royal titulary, the beneficient god, master of all lands, who strikes down all foreigners, flanked by the throne name of Amenemhet III, Ny-ma'at-Re. Behind the king the hieroglyph 'life', provided with human arms, fans the breath of life towards him.

With this multitude of pictorial and hieroglyphic elements, not enough empty space is left to separate clearly the individual motifs from one another, and the composition is dominated by its colours, the red carnelian especially. For the first time in a pectoral, pieces of faience with coloured glazes have been used instead of semi-precious stones; they have decayed and taken on a brownish tint. The chasing of the figures and hieroglyphs on the reverse no longer has the precision of the older examples and, despite its ingenious workmanship, this splendid piece from the close of the 12th Dynasty shows that the art of the Egyptian goldsmith had passed that peak that it would never again attain.

Among Mereret's jewellery there was also a necklace with pendants and an amulet. Eighteen round stones of carnelian, turquoise and lapis lazuli, held by crossed strips of gold, hang from a string of tiny gold beads by short gold tubes fitted with eyelets. In the middle is a pendant amulet with three hieroglyphs: flanked on either side by the sign for 'protection', the 'life' sign stands on a basket which signifies 'everything, of everybody'.

Illahun (Lahun)

Sesostris II, the fourth ruler of the 12th Dynasty, built his pyramid at the entrance to the Fayum oasis. Presumably he was the first to build a dam there to regulate the flow of water to the oasis from this arm of the Nile. The ancient Egyptian word *lahun* means 'mouth of the canal'.

221–222 Crown of Princess Sit-Hathor-Yunit

The Middle Kingdom

The pyramid complex of Illahun (Lahun) was first explored in 1888–89, by the famous English archaeologist W. M. Flinders Petrie. In 1914, during his second campaign, he discovered four more burial shafts while clearing the southern court. Three of these were empty, while tomb-robbers had broken into the granite sarcophagus in the fourth and the mummy had been completely destroyed. The alabaster canopic jars with the internal organs, however, still stood in the burial chamber and an inscription on them gave the name of the tomb's owner: royal daughter Sit-Hathor-Yunit. Translated, this name means 'Daughter of Hathor of Dendera'.

The shaft and burial chamber of the princess's tomb had been dug in the lifetime of her father, Sesostris II, and had stood open for some 40 years before her death. Rainfall had washed clay and sand into the empty tomb, and when the princess was buried there,

Brunton worked for a whole week, even sleeping in the tomb, until he had carefully freed all the beads and other items from the solid mud layer, using a scalpel and a long hat pin. So as to be able to reconstruct the jewellery later on, the location of every single piece had to be recorded in drawings.

Gaston Maspero, the director of the Egyptian Museum in Cairo, allowed Petrie to keep the Illahun (Lahun) jewellery, with the exception of the crown, the mirror and the princess's second pectoral, as his museum already possessed similar pieces of the same period from Dahshur. In 1916 Petrie sold the jewellery to the Metropolitan Museum of Art in New York, to meet the high costs of excavation. Here the pieces were magnificently restored and reassembled.

What was most important about this new find was the fact that with Brunton's sketches, all the beads and gold that belonged together could be reunited.

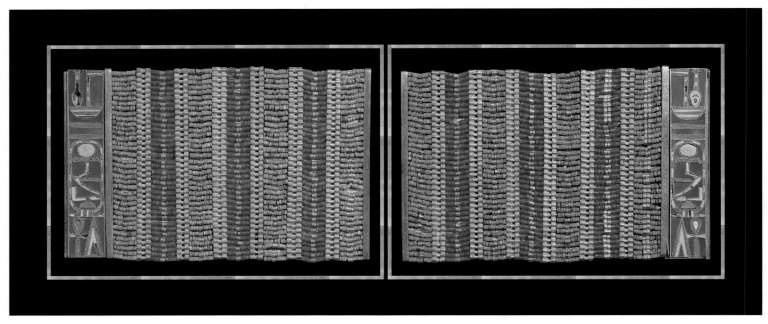

223–224 Pair of bracelets with the name of Amenemhet III

it seems only minimal efforts were made to clear it out. After the tomb was robbed in the period of chaos that followed the collapse of the Middle Kingdom, the shaft again stood open, and water, clay and rubble were able to enter and accumulate on the floor.

It did not seem a very promising tomb. The archaeologists had already explored everything, except for the alcove in the antechamber. Then, when they were scraping away, little tubes of gold appeared in the hardened mud filling the alcove. To maintain secrecy, Petrie allowed only his assistant Guy Brunton and a young Egyptian back into the antechamber.

These newly reconstructed pieces then provided a model for the reconstruction of the jewellery from Dahshur, which had also been found scattered. Both finds belong to the same period, and were probably produced in the same royal workshops.

Sit-Hathor-Yunit, a daughter of Sesostris II and a younger sister of Sesostris III, was possibly also the

225 Girdle with gold cowrie shells
226–227 A pair of anklets with bird's claw and 'Hercules' knot-amulet clasp
228 Girdle with golden double leopards' heads

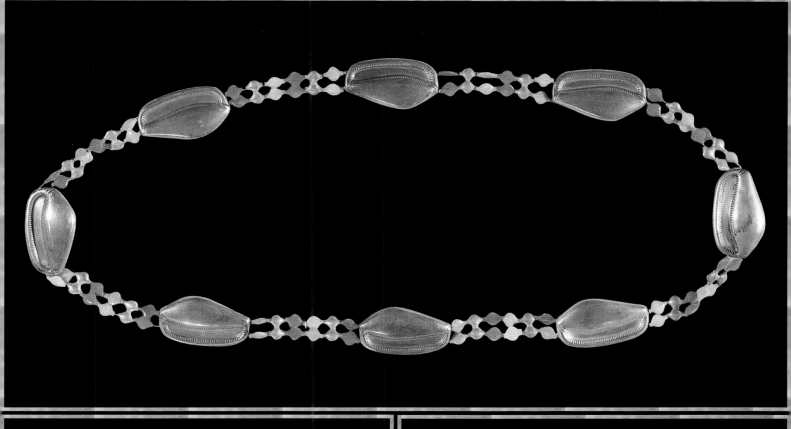

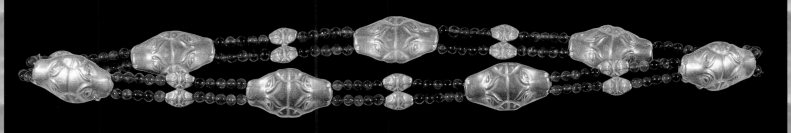

The Middle Kingdom

younger sister of Sit-Hathor, who had been buried near her brother's pyramid at Dahshur. Sit-Hathor-Yunit survived her father and brother, and died early in the reign of her nephew Amenemhet III. Her jewellery, which shows evidence that it was actually worn during her life, suggests a very slim, small woman with fine wrists and ankles.

The crown (222) had been stored in a chest, along with a wig. Its feathers and pendant ribbons had been detached and lay across the circlet. The wig had completely broken up because of water that had entered the chest.

The circlet is of beaten gold foil, the fifteen evenly spaced rosettes attached by rivets. The ornamentation of the rosettes – a cruciform arrangement of lotus flowers, with lily flowers in the angles – is based on Old Kingdom models, with gold strips soldered to the base and lapis lazuli, carnelian and faience (now white, but originally blue and green) inlaid in the cells.

The upright *uraeus* on the front of the diadem is removable, slotting on to a T-shaped bar. The snake's body is of perforated gold foil with soldered strips of gold, the cells so formed being inlaid with lapis lazuli, carnelian and green (now white) faience. Its head is of

229 Uraeus of Sesostris II, probably from a mummiform coffin

carved lapis lazuli, mounted on a protruding tongue of gold foil that forms the lower jaw. The eyes, of red garnet, are set in gold rings.

Opposite the *uraeus*, on the inside of the circlet, a tube with a papyrus umbel is soldered. This tube holds a pair of feathers, an emblem of the goddess Hathor, who bestows love and beauty. Double ribbons of thin gold foil hang down on both sides and also beneath the feathers at the rear, attached to rosettes; these are very flexible and respond to even the slightest head movement of the crown's wearer.

Under the diadem, a large number of tubes of very thin gold foil were discovered. In the reconstruction of the crown exhibited at the Metropolitan Museum of Art (221), these have been drawn over the outer braids of a shoulder-length wig.

Like the other pectoral from Dahshur that bore the same royal name (219), the pectoral with the name of Sesostris II from the tomb of Princess Sit-Hathor-Yunit at Illahun (233) is one the most accomplished achievements of the Egyptian goldsmiths' art. The unframed composition is built up on a narrow base whose several individual cells are inlaid with wavy red lines on a turquoise background, representing the 'primeval waters'. Two falcons facing each other form the outer border at the sides. Perched

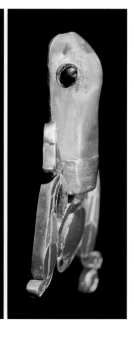

230–232 Amulet with snake's head and solar disc and two uraei above lotus flowers

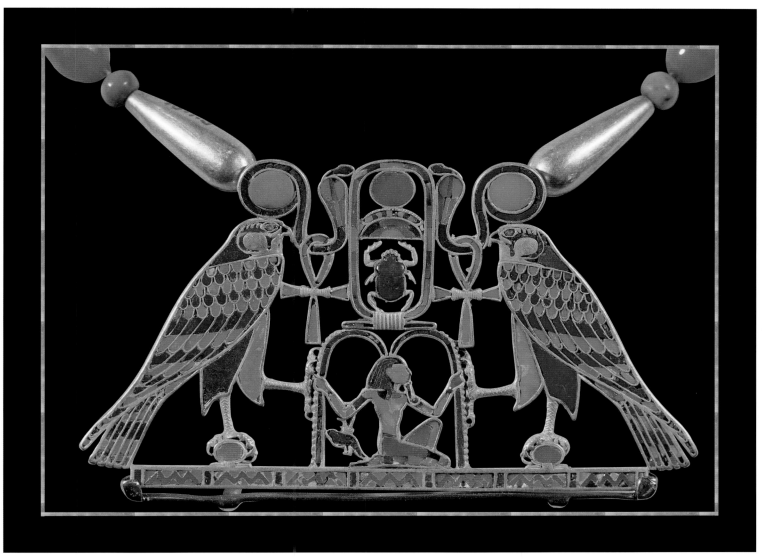

233 Pectoral with the throne name of Sesostris II

on one leg, the claws of which hold the symbol of eternity in their grasp, they stand above the 'primeval waters', symbolizing the ordering power of Egyptian kingship emerging from the chaos. The other, extended, leg rests against the hieroglyphic sign 'a hundred thousand years': a seated man (the god Heh) holds a notched palm rib, the sign for 'years', at the end of each outstretched arm; over his right elbow hangs a ribbon with a tadpole, the hieroglyph for 'a hundred thousand'. The throne name of Sesostris II, Kha-Kheper-Re, rests on the incurved ends of the ribs. The royal cartouche is flanked by protecting *uraei*, from whose bodies hangs the *ankh* 'life' sign. The snakes' tails are wound about the solar discs of inlaid turquoise that each Horus falcon bears on its head as the emblem of the sun-god. The artful composition of the pectoral is to be read as a rebus: 'May the sun-god give Sesostris II a hundred thousand years of life'.

The perfection of the inlay calls for particular admiration. The precision in the positioning of the soldered gold strip is matched by the exact cutting of the tiny stones to fit the cells, and this perfection is matched on the reverse by the execution of the repoussé and the chasing of the details. Short tubular eyelets are soldered to the back of the solar discs to take a chain. Another pectoral, which carries the name of Amenemhet III, copies the composition of this example. The differences, however, are not restricted to the fact that a different royal name figures in the cartouche. Instead of the light gold used for the bold outline and finer details, here apparently a gold of high silver content was used, and the alternation of light blue and dark blue has been replaced to gloomy effect by inlays of dark red carnelian, lapis lazuli and faience, the latter now

Pages 120–121: 234 Pectoral with the name of Amenemhet III

decomposed. It is coarser, too, in execution; neither the gold cell-work on the front nor the repoussé and chasing on the back are as precise as in the older example. Even taking into account the bad state of preservation, the decline in the art of jewellery towards the end of the 12th Dynasty is unmistakable.

Two girdles, one with double leopards' heads (228), the other with gold cowrie shells, were also found at Illahun (Lahun). The leopard's head has already been encountered as a protective amulet in the jewellery of Princesses Khnumet (215) and Mereret (71). Each of the hollow double-headed beads is composed of two identical halves of gold foil pressed into a mould, soldered along their edges. Perforated twice at each end, they are linked by short double rows of tiny amethyst beads. Enclosed within each head are small

turquoise, carnelian and gold beads, divided by six bars that are made up of pairs of gold beads joined by tiny gold tubes and soldered on to a narrow strip of gold foil. The ends of the threads are fastened to hollow end pieces, on to whose outer edges a T-shaped bar is soldered. Over these slides the grooved clasp bearing the titles and name of Amenemhet III. The formerly coloured faience of the cloisonné hieroglyphs, inlaid against a background of carnelian, has now faded.

A pair of anklets with bird's claws and gold knot-clasps (226–227) complete the jewellery of Princess Sit-Hathor-Yunit. The bird's claw is carved in obsidian, the upper part being set in grooved gold foil, soldered to two rows of three gold beads each. It hangs from a double string of dark-purple amethyst

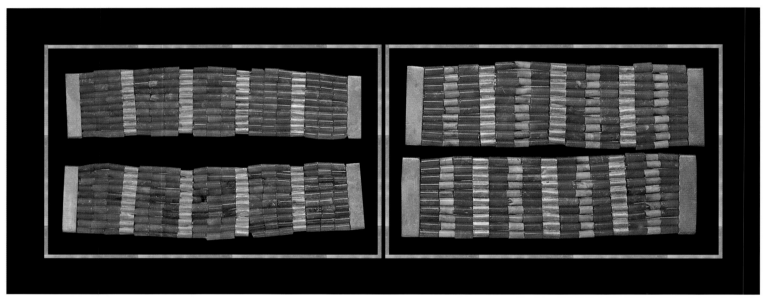

235–236 Paired bracelets and anklets of Princess Neferuptah

stones which rattle. The clasp is formed of a double leopard's head worked in two halves; each half is closed with a gold plate, and one is provided with a slot, the other with a slot and tongue to act as a clasp.

The eight cowrie shells of the second girdle (225) were also formed in moulds, the halves being soldered together lengthways. These, too, have double perforations and are connected by short double rows of tiny acacia-seed beads of turquoise, gold and carnelian, the gold beads being soldered together. Inside the shells are a few grains of a copper/silver alloy to make a rattle. The clasp is made in the same way as that in the leopard-head girdle.

The name of Amenemhet III appears on a pair of bracelets (223–224), each made up of 37 strands of

beads. The clasp is a knot amulet of beaten gold, formed in two identical halves that may be locked together by a removable pin.

A hand mirror of polished silver, with an obsidian handle in the form of a papyrus stalk surmounted by the head of the goddess Hathor, with its human face and cow's ears (179), is one of the most exquisite examples of the jeweller's art. In its use of this motif, this sumptuously fashioned object for personal use plays on the princess's name, 'daughter of Hathor of Dendera', and recalls the words of a hymn to the goddess of beauty, joy and love:

Your face's beauty gleams and glows, you are perfect.
Before your beautiful face, one becomes drunk. Gold!
Hathor!

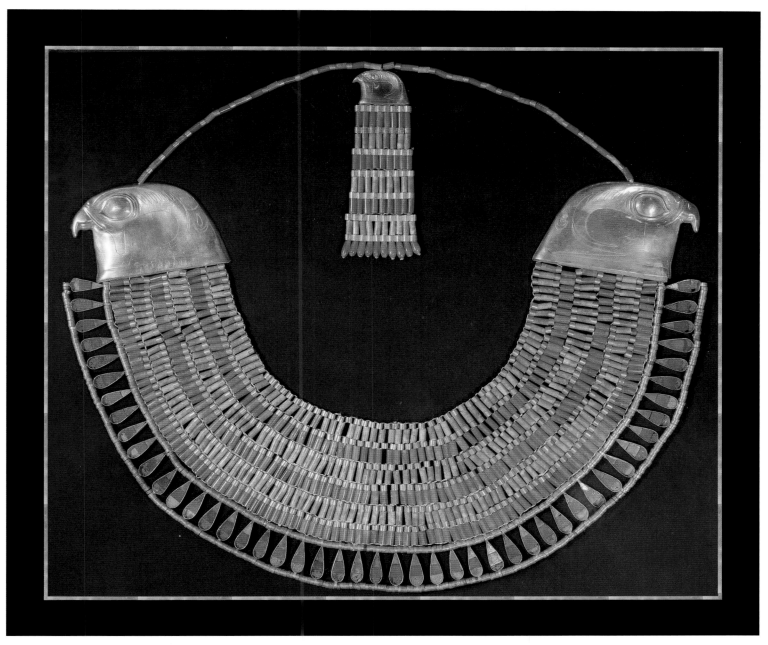

237 Collar of Princess Neferuptah

The head beneath the wide-open papyrus umbel is double-sided, cast in two identical parts that are soldered together at the edges. The eyebrows are inlaid in lapis lazuli, which has fallen out in parts. The quartz eyeballs have pupils of rock crystal edged in silver. The head is connected to the handle by a collar-like arrangement of four bands of gold inlaid with carnelian, lapis lazuli and quartz.

The obsidian handle emerges from a lotus flower in cloisonné. Four gold bands covered with granulation run from the flower to the collar. They are ornamental, yet at the same time they make the smooth polished handle much easier to grasp. This mirror-handle is the only known example of obsidian with inlays.

The magnificent hand mirror lay in a cosmetics box, one of five chests made of ebony imported from the Sudan; it also contained obsidian ointment pots, two bronze razors with gold handles, and two stones for grinding cosmetics. The chest itself had decayed, but the reconstruction includes its surviving parts: the slender golden hieroglyphs for 'permanence' in flat niches, the ivory inlay on the sides, the gold settings of the feet and the jewellery of the gently vaulted lid – four emblems of the goddess Hathor, made of gold with inlays of carnelian and faience, and three ivory plaques with the names and titles of Amenemhet III.

In the course of his thorough investigation of the pyramid in 1920, Petrie found in the rubbish in the burial chamber a few very fine carnelian and feldspar

238 Gold diadem of Senebtisi

Falcons' heads of beaten gold foil adorn the bead collar (237) in which alternating rows of tubular beads in green feldspar and carnelian are separated by rows of smaller gold beads. The lower margin is composed of droplet-shaped beads with feldspar and carnelian inlaid within gold strips, with a strand of small gold beads at top and bottom. The *menat*, which hung down the back as a counterweight to the heavy collar, was constructed on the same principle.

The fly-whisk, scourge or flagellum had been one of the king's insignias of majesty since the earliest dynastic period. The example found in Neferuptah's tomb has a wooden handle covered in gold leaf, which has broken off, and three strands made up of small conical beads of brownish, corroded faience, three long faience tubes and thirteen annular faience and carnelian beads with gold edging. Such whisks have also been found in other women's tombs. They were part of the insignia of the royal and divine majesty of Osiris, god of the dead, taken over by mortals when the hope of becoming Osiris was extended to all. Here, however, it is more probably a highly decorative fly-whisk, presumably intended to chase away evil influences as well as flies.

beads and a gold *uraeus* (229), which the robbers may have dropped. The *uraeus* was made of thick beaten gold foil. The thin gold strip for the cells and the raised central rib of the underside was soldered on and inlaid with coloured semi-precious stones, the head of lapis lazuli was attached, and the surviving eye of dark red garnet was set in gold. The snake's body coils upwards. It was presumably attached to the royal headdress of the mummiform coffin; reinforcing rings are soldered into the hollow back of the coils.

Hawara

During an excavation by the Egyptian Antiquities Service in 1956, the tomb of Neferuptah, a daughter of Amenemhet III, was found under a dilapidated brick pyramid, not far from the king's own pyramid at Hawara. In this, the last tomb of a princess of the 12th Dynasty, were found bracelets and anklets (235–236), a bead collar (237) and also a fly-whisk. The solid, simplified style of the jewellery evidences a decline from the refinement and formal richness displayed in the jewellery of the earlier princesses.

239 Pendant from Byblos

Lisht

During the Middle Kingdom even women who did not belong to the royal family were buried with rich jewellery. One such was Senebtisi, a noble lady from the family of the vizier Senusret, who was buried at Lisht towards the end of the 12th Dynasty, not far from the pyramid of Amenemhet I. The tomb was excavated by an expedition from the Metropolitan Museum of Art, New York, in 1906–07. Though the tomb had been robbed, some remaining jewellery was discovered between the bandages of the mummy: a diadem of gold wire and daisies of gold foil that adorned the hair of the wig, three collars, one beaded belt with pendants, bracelets, anklets, amulets, and a gilded fly-whisk.

Senebtisi's diadem (238) is made of gold wire, loosely woven in three elastic rows of intertwined loops, held together at the back of the head by thin gold wire. The rosettes, which are made of moulded gold foil, 98 in total, some with 16 and some with 18 petals, were bound into the hair. A pendant of gold wire falls over the forehead, in its form alluding to the *uraeus*, to which this lady was certainly not entitled.

The falcon-headed collar that Senebtisi was given as a funerary offering was also originally a royal attribute. The falcon's-head clasp on one of her three bead collars is made of gold foil beaten into a mould, with a filling of plaster. The eye is a carnelian, and the feathers of the head are schematically rendered in blue faience. The rows of vertically orientated tubular beads, which reduce in length towards the clasps, are composed from top to bottom of gold, blue-green

Further Jewellery Finds
A unique amulet, the only one of its kind so far discovered, combines a snake's head, a solar disc and two *uraei* resting on lotus flowers to powerful magical effect, and must certainly come from a royal burial (230–232). There are rock crystal, gold, lapis lazuli, turquoise, carnelian and obsidian. This piece, of unknown provenance, shows no traces of wear.

A pectoral now in Boston (240) shows the two guardian goddesses, the snake-like Wadjet of Buto, together with Nekhbet in the form of a vulture with outspread wings, the sign for 'protection' in her talons, just as she has been seen in reliefs since the Old Kingdom, presiding over ritual acts by the king. The base was cut out of silver-foil, and narrow strips

faience, carnelian, dark-blue faience, gold and blue-green faience. The bottom edge is made up of droplet-shaped gold pendants, which are hung between rows of tiny horizontal beads of blue-green faience, carnelian and gold.

240 Pectoral from a royal coffin

of electrum soldered on to this, precisely cut inlays of carnelian being cemented into the cells. The remaining coloured inlays are now much decayed, and it must therefore remain a matter of speculation whether the marbling of the colours is the result of early experiments with molten glass. Pins on the back suggest that this pectoral was fixed on to a mummiform wooden coffin. The king who was buried in this coffin probably would have belonged to the 13th Dynasty, when the Middle Kingdom approached its end.

The belt, which consists of forty rows of glazed, disc-shaped faience beads coloured in dark green, light green and black, arranged in a zig-zag pattern, bears on the clasp the name of Senebtisi, in blue faience inlaid on a gilded wooden core. Twenty-two strands of beads hang down from faience emblems on the belt. Some of these are lotuses, some papyrus – the heraldic plants of Upper and Lower Egypt. At the back is attached a representation of a bull's tail, in beads over a wooden core. It may be inferred from the many beads of the same type found in women's tombs that such belts were very common during the Middle Kingdom, and were probably also worn in life. The bull's tail does, however, seem to have had a ritual significance, and bead belts with a bull's tail can be traced back to the predynastic period as part of the pharaoh's regalia (37).

In the days of the powerful 12th Dynasty there were close ties with Byblos, and the rulers and shrines of the Phoenician port were given rich presents by the pharaohs. Evidence for this comes from the many precious objects from Egypt that Pierre Montet found in 1924 at the royal necropolis of Byblos, among them a pectoral with the name of Amenemhet III (239). The princes of this commercial metropolis adorned themselves with insignia of pharaonic kingship, for which their goldsmiths borrowed motifs and techniques from Egyptian models.

The New Kingdom

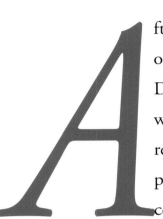

241 Gilded mummy mask
of the lady Thuya
242 War-chariot of
Tutankhamun, front detail

After the brilliant 12th Dynasty, the later history of the Middle Kingdom under the 13th Dynasty recalls the end of the Old Kingdom, with a rapid succession of rulers whose short reigns did not allow the re-establishment of political stability. This led to a weakening of central authority, to insecurity at the borders and to a noticeable decline in artistic standards. The southern border retreated to Elephantine, at the First Cataract, and an independent principality was established in Nubia. In the north, too, in Syria and Palestine, Egypt lost its position of power. The fortified border in the Eastern Delta became permeable, and was no longer sufficient to prevent the constant incursion of nomadic tribes of Semitic origin. As these intruders from Asia made themselves largely independent of central government, and at the same time were ruled over by various minor kings in the Delta, the last kings of the 13th Dynasty saw their sphere of influence reduced to Upper Egypt. In the first half of the 17th century BC the vanguard of a general migratory movement in the Middle East reached the Nile Valley. Its leaders were called *hekau-chasut* ('rulers of foreign lands') by the Egyptians, which was rendered as 'Hyksos' by the writers of antiquity.

The New Kingdom

With their energetic policies, and their superior weaponry and methods of combat, they were able to seize the leadership of the tribes of Syria and Palestine and then go on to subjugate the Delta, founding their own dynasty at Avaris around 1650 BC. The Hyksos kings laid claim to power over the whole of Egypt, though they left independent under-kings in parts.

Like so many conquerors after them, the Hyksos took over virtually all the forms of Egyptian culture. Their innovations included the horse-drawn war-chariot and improvements in weapons technology, while the metal-workers' repertoire was broadened to include the niello technique. In this technique, a mixture of silver, copper, lead, sulphur and borax is fused to produce a blackish (Latin *nigellum*) material against which gold or silver inlay stands out distinctively. The technique has been documented in Byblos around 1800 BC – earlier than anywhere else – and was probably invented there. A sickle-sword from Shechem (243) probably comes from a workshop in this port on the Phoenician coast. Its bronze blade is inlaid with a rib of copper, which is coated with niello and inlaid with gold wire. Sickle-shaped swords

243 Blade of a sickle-shaped sword (harpesh)

with the same form and using the same inlay technique have been found in three of the princely tombs at Byblos.

Among the finds of jewellery that bear the stamp of the Near East, the most notable is a gold headdress with a stag's head flanked by two gazelles' heads on each side (244). Although the goldsmith who made it clearly had no precise idea of what a stag was, this frontal found in the Eastern Delta can only be assigned to the culture of the Near East, and must have belonged to a foreign princess. The deer is not found among Egyptian fauna, despite a few representations in ancient Egyptian hunting scenes. The rosettes riveted on the band, which have notably

sharp-edged petals, also have a foreign look. The gazelles' heads, not found in diadems before this, were not adopted as a motif in Egyptian jewellery and wall paintings until the 18th Dynasty (343).

After the end of the 13th Dynasty, whose rule in its last years was restricted to Upper Egypt and forced to pay tribute to the Hyksos kings, a Theban house took on the royal title, so founding the 17th Dynasty. Its short-lived rulers made no great mark, and were only ever of local significance. Their tombs, crowned by small brick pyramids, lie near the Dra-abu'l-Nag'a in the northern part of the vast Theban necropolis. It was here in 1909 that Flinders Petrie discovered the rock tomb of a woman and child of the royal family; it contained jewellery (now in Edinburgh) that provides evidence for the continuation of the Egyptian tradition, albeit at a more modest level.

Seqenenre Ta'a II, ruler of Thebes around 1560 BC, rose against the Hyksos king Apophis and met his death in the process, as is shown by the wounds on his mummy (now in the Cairo Museum). His son Kamose determinedly carried on the struggle. When he died, after a short reign, he was succeeded by his brother Ahmose, who triumphed in bringing the foreign domination of Egypt to a definitive end, reuniting the country and securing its borders through campaigns in Palestine and Nubia. Significant evidence from this period of struggle against the Hyksos has survived in the funerary treasure of Queen Ahhotep.

The Jewellery of Queen Ahhotep

Ahhotep was the sister-wife of Seqenenre Ta'a II 'the brave', and mother of kings Kamose and Ahmose. Kamose had a stele erected at the temple of Karnak to commemorate a victory, on which her merits are spelled out. She had distinguished herself during the years of war by her prudence and courage and the moral support she had afforded him:

> Praise the mistress of the land, princess of the coast of the Mediterranean island-dwellers, whose name is great through every foreign land; who gave counsel to the

people, royal wife, sister of the ruler, king's daughter, king's mother, illustrious and knowledgeable one who cared for Egypt. She looked after and protected its soldiers. She brought back its refugees, gathering together its emigrants. She pacified the south land by driving out her opponents. The royal wife Ahhotep, may she live!

Discovery and Features of Ahhotep's treasure

In 1854, Prince Napoleon, a nephew of the French emperor, announced his intention to visit the viceroy of Egypt. The latter instructed Auguste Mariette, the French archaeologist in his service, to excavate some ancient treasure as a present for his high-ranking visitor. Mariette decided on the Dra-abu'l-Nag'a in western Thebes. Only a few days after the start of the dig his workers came upon a painted wooden coffin in the rubble. The mummy inside had decayed but the funerary gifts had survived – a dagger, together with two small lions moulded in gold foil, and a royal cartouche in the form of a little box with inlays of

224–246 Frontal with stag's head and gazelles' heads

lapis lazuli and gold which, like the lions, had probably been sewn on to a leather wrist-protector, and which bore the name of King Ahmose. It was clear from the inscription, however, that it was Ahmose's brother and predecessor Kamose who had been laid to rest in the coffin. Although the French prince did not go to Egypt after all, he was given the finds, which are today in the Louvre.

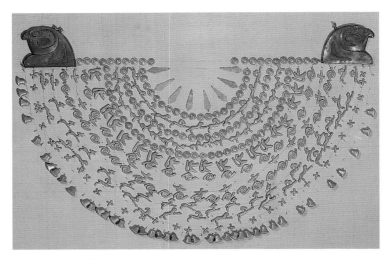

247 Broad collar of Queen Ahhotep

and violence, and presented it himself to the Khedive, who was so enthused by the find that he decided to build a museum for the antiquities already uncovered.

Queen Ahhotep's jewellery, and the ceremonial weapons with which she was provided, belong to a transitional period. The tradition of the Middle Kingdom still survives in certain bracelets (253–256) and a pectoral (268). Other pieces, however, show the adoption of new forms and techniques that had arrived in Egypt with the Hyksos kings. The falcons' heads on the beaded collar (247), the battle-axe (272) and the dagger (275) are the earliest niello work to have been found in Egypt.

Connections with the Minoan culture of Crete, implied by the mention of the Mediterranean islands on Kamose's stele, appear in animals represented at a 'flying gallop' (247, 275), and in the griffin motif on

Mariette, who in the meantime had been appointed the first head of the Egyptian Antiquities Service by the viceroy, had to leave his assistant to continue the excavations, and when the latter died not long after, work was continued by gangs of fellahin under a foreman, but without any scholarly supervision. They soon came upon the coffin of the famous Queen Ahhotep; it contained the mummy, still wrapped in its bandages, and precious funerary ornaments.

The governor of Qena heard of this discovery and quickly had the coffin brought to his palace. There the bandages were removed from the mummy, which was robbed of its jewellery and then burnt; from what is known of royal burials of the period, it would seem that at least one diadem disappeared along the way.

The governor now made his way to Cairo by boat, in order to present his booty to the khedive in person. Mariette, informed of the find and its confiscation, boarded a steamer and intercepted the governor's boat in mid-Nile. He recovered the jewellery by threats

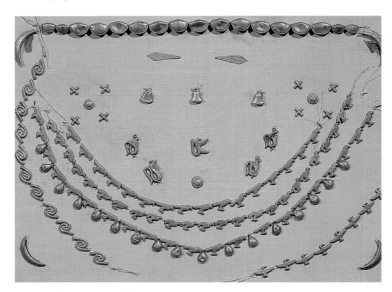

249 Gold cowrie shells, links and amulets

the battle-axe (272); the dagger from the queen's coffin (275) also shows clear Aegean influence in its form and technique.

The Queen's Personal Jewellery

It is particularly regrettable that the circumstances of the find had not allowed records to be made that would have given clues to the assembly of the different elements of the bead broad collar with falcons' heads (247). A considerable number of these, found scattered over the mummy's breast and body, are missing from the reconstruction, and there is still

248 Jewellery from Ahhotep's treasure

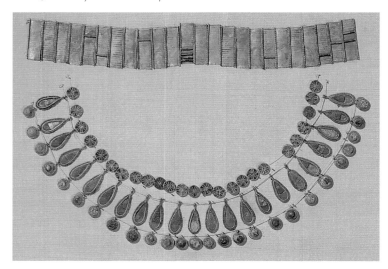

250–252 Rigid bracelet with the vulture of Nekhbet of Queen Ahhotep

controversy about the original arrangement, as no other collar of a similar type has yet been found.

The different elements were all beaten from thin gold foil. There are simple ornaments – round bosses, little crosses, spirals, and emblems of gods and goddesses – representations of Seth as a mythical creature, winged *uraei* and flying birds; and there are

inserted at the wrong place during the reconstruction – at the neck; close inspection reveals that they have an eyelet at both top and bottom, suggesting that these alone originally acted as links between the adjacent strands of beads.

The falcons' heads at the collar ends are soldered together from several parts, the curve of the cheek,

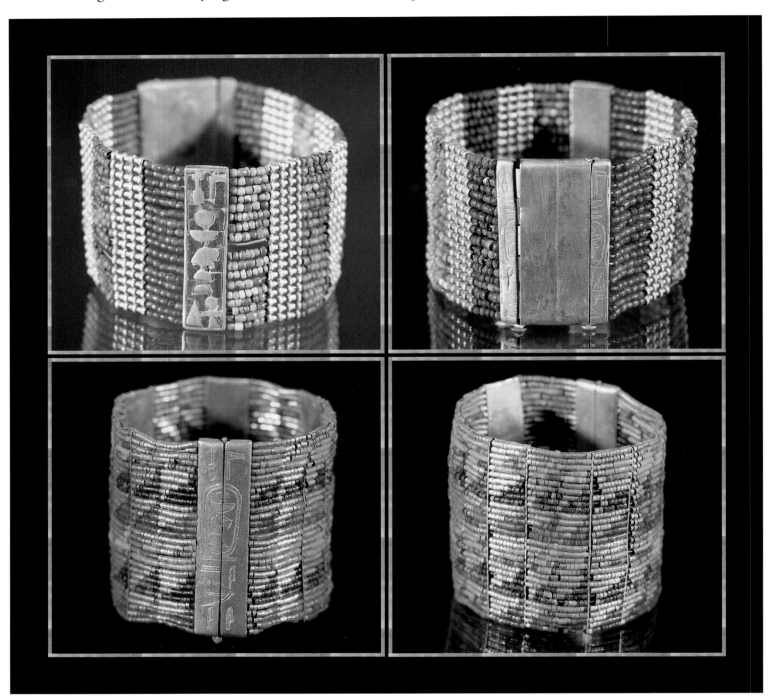

253–256 Beaded bracelets of Queen Ahhotep

lions, gazelles and ibexes at a 'flying gallop', after the Aegean model.

Strangely enough, all these items were perforated only at the sides, so they were not connected to the rows above or below. The leaves, it now appears, were

the stripe under the eye and the line of the jaw being made of a compact mass of niello embedded in a relatively deeply-incised base. In the straight bottom edge of the falcons' heads are ten holes through which to fasten the threads of the beads.

The Jewellery of Queen Ahhotep

The long gold chain with a scarab pendant (262–263) is a masterpiece of the goldsmith's art, an extraordinarily even six-fold braid fitted with end-pieces each in the form of a goose's neck and head in gold, with an eyelet. Each has a tiny royal cartouche, one with Ahmose's birth name, the other with his throne name, Neb-pekhti-Re. At over 6½ft (2m), this chain would have had to be wound several times around the neck for the scarab to lie on the breast.

As an amulet, the scarab signified 'becoming', 'being capable of change', and is itself another outstanding example of the goldsmith's craft. The body is made up of two pieces of gold foil soldered

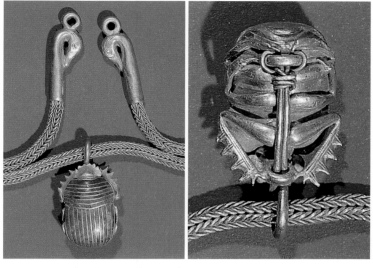

262–263 Gold chain with scarab pendant

Upper Egyptian guardian goddess Nekhbet, is constructed of two rigid semicircular parts. These are linked by two hinges, one of which can be opened by removing a pin. The feathered body of the vulture goddess is rendered in lapis lazuli, carnelian and green glass, inlaid in gold cells. In her talons she holds the ring of eternity, inlaid in carnelian, the royal protective symbol. The inner part of the bracelet is composed of two parallel hollow semicircular elements, rounded on the outside and set with closely spaced turquoises, whose inside is sealed with soldered strips of gold foil. Between these is inserted a carnelian in a gold setting, from either side of which springs a fine gold stem that terminates in a turquoise bud mounted in gold.

A bead bracelet (253–254) has Ahmose's throne name twice. It is composed of eighteen strands of

257 Simple bracelet of Queen Ahhotep

together. Underneath, the belly and legs of the beetle are faithfully rendered in repoussé, while the upper domed part has soldered strips of gold, horizontal on the prothorax, and vertical on the wing-covers. Lapis lazuli inlay is cemented in the cells so formed. The beetle's gold head is soldered on, as are the forelegs and the ring set between them, through which passes the loop of gold wire that attaches the pendant to the chain. The two ends of the loop pass over the belly and are knotted to a further ring.

The bracelet (250–252) in the form of a vulture with protective wings outspread, representing the

258–260 Gold bracelets of Queen Ahhotep

261 Bracelet of the type awarded as a decoration

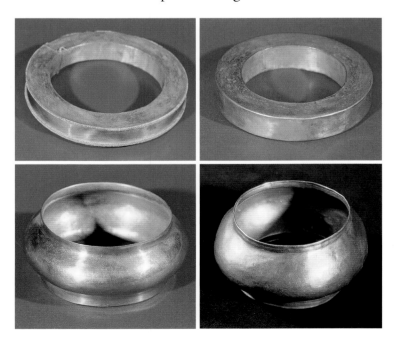

264–267 *Rigid bracelet showing the coronation of King Ahmose*

beads strung on gold wire to form nine vertical bands, of blue lapis lazuli, green turquoise and red carnelian, separated by seven bands of gold, each of these being formed of rows of four gold beads, joined with a fine gold tube and soldered together vertically – a technique developed during the Middle Kingdom. On the front of the bracelet is the inscription: 'The perfect god, Neb-pekhti-Re, given life'. The gold hieroglyphs are soldered on to a gold plate within a narrow frame, and pieces of lapis lazuli are cemented in to fill the gaps. Later on, a connector was inserted between the two parts of the clasp, and the single inscription engraved on the two end pieces were thus divided. It reads: 'The perfect god, Lord of the Two Lands, Neb-pekhti-Re, given life forever'.

On another beaded bracelet from the tomb of Queen Ahhotep (255–256), the thirty-one strands of beads are arranged in small squares each made of one triangle of colour and another of gold. Triangles of the same colour – turquoise, lapis lazuli, carnelian – each with its complementary triangle of gold beads, form horizontal rows. To hold the rows of beads more firmly, and give greater precision to the pattern, plates of gold foil with a narrower bar soldered in the middle are inserted at a regular distance apart, visible on the outside as thin strips and on the inside as

268 Pectoral showing the purification of King Ahmose

broader bands. The fastening is composed of narrow tubes, through which a pin is inserted. On the end pieces is engraved the following inscription: 'The perfect god, Neb-pekhti-Re, beloved of Amun'.

The flat-sided bracelet is of unusual form (258). Gold foil was folded to form a rectangular channel, then beaten into a circle and the outside closed by soldering on a strip of gold foil. The soldered edges were decorated with notched and braided wire. Its inner diameter indicates that the bracelet was worn on the forearm.

Numerous visual representations show that jewellery of the same type as the bulging bracelet (260) was worn by men on both wrists; it was one of the decorations awarded by the king. Finally, there is a gold bracelet (257) of the same simple form as that used since prehistoric times for bracelets of ivory and other materials. Its outer side was beaten from folded gold foil, the smooth inner side being formed by a soldered strip of the same material.

Jewellery and Weapons Offered by Ahmose
Alongside Ahhotep's personal jewellery, treasures were found that were given to her for use in the afterlife by Ahmose, the second of her sons to occupy the pharaoh's throne. Among these were a pectoral (268),

The New Kingdom

with the same frame as the pectorals of the Middle Kingdom and a torus moulding for its upper edge, but the figurative representation takes up a new theme: the 'ritual purification' performed at the king's coronation and on its anniversary. The lower edge is formed of a strip of gold foil decorated with stylized ripples of water – the primeval waters from which the world was created. On the water is a boat on which stand three figures: in the middle, the king, on his right, the god Amun-Re, with his crown of tall feathers, and on his left, the falcon-headed god Re-Harakhte, with a red solar disc on his head. From slender ritual vessels (*hes* vases) the gods pour water over the king, which flows down before and behind him in a light blue zigzag pattern. In the upper corners, falcons spread their wings protectively over the ritual scene. The names of the gods and Ahmose's own two names and title are also given within the pictorial space. Compared to the pectorals of the 12th Dynasty, the motifs seem crowded together, and the clarity of composition has been lost. However, as in these earlier examples, all the details of the beaten relief on the reverse have been carefully chased.

An image of Ahmose is also found on a bracelet (264–267) made up of two semi-cylindrical plates of gold foil connected by hinges; the outer surface is decorated with figures and inscriptions and inlaid with lapis lazuli. The relief-like repoussé motifs with chased detail make up one single scene: King Ahmose's coronation by the earth-god Geb, the primeval ruler of the earth. In the centre, the enthroned god is shown twice, on the right wearing the Double Crown, and on the left the crown of Lower Egypt. King Ahmose also appears twice, with a curled wig and *uraeus* on his head; he kneels with his back to the deity, who holds him by the upper arm and places his other hand protectively on his shoulder. This main picture is flanked by vertical inscriptions; that on the right reads, 'The perfect god, ruler of the two lands, Neb-pekhti-Re, given life', and that on the left, 'Re's own son, Ahmose, living like Re'.

The king directs his gaze upon the two groups of figures on the other half of the bracelet. They are the falcon-headed 'souls of Hierakonpolis' and the jackal-headed 'souls of Buto' who, as the representatives of the coronation cities of Upper and Lower Egypt, greet the new-crowned king with 'gestures of jubilation', one fist raised and the other held before the breast. Above them are blessings: 'We give you all joy. We give you all life and health eternally.'

Another bracelet (269–271) has the royal cartouche on the front, with the inlaid inscription 'Son of Re,

269–271 Wrist-guard of King Ahmose, worn for archery

272 Battle-axe of Ahmose

Ahmose, who lives always and eternally', flanked by two sphinxes, symbols of the Semitic god of vengeance, Hurun. The sphinxes and the royal cartouche are of beaten gold foil, soldered on to a thick, hollow plait of gold. The royal cartouche is raised as if upon a little box between the heads of the fully three-dimensional sphinxes. The back half of the bracelet is made of a band of gold, from which protrudes a long narrow tongue. Both band and tongue are inlaid with semi-precious stones, the former with the protective signs for 'life' and 'permanence', the latter with a herring-bone pattern. When the coffin was opened, this bracelet was found over the mummy's head and was at first thought to be a 'little crown'; it was then believed to be a decorative armlet presumably worn on the upper arm, the protruding tongue being supposedly intended to 'stabilize' the weight of the heavy figurative jewellery. If worn like this, however, the inscription and the sphinxes that flank it would be lying on their sides, and thus dishonouring the royal name. This unique bracelet can only be sensibly explained as a guard for the wrist of the left hand that holds the bow. Worn in this way, the royal cartouche stands upright. Pulled over a leather cuff, the bracelet with its tongue would then protect the forearm against the blow of the bowstring as it sprang back.

Given Queen Ahhotep's role in the war of liberation, so highly praised by Kamose, it is no surprise that magnificent weapons were placed in her coffin, together with the 'Order of the Gold Flies' (274). This was a decoration for outstanding warriors, flies being symbols of indefatigable attack. Three large examples hang from a gold chain braided in the same way as the long chain (262). Their outline was cut from gold foil, the heads with their bulbous eyes and the stylized, perforated body being beaten out of gold foil and soldered on.

Ahmose's battle-axe is famous (272). Its shape is derived from the simple weapons employed by the Hyksos warriors: the blade of forged copper is set into a groove in the slightly bowed handle and fastened with leather straps. In this royal version the cedar-wood handle is covered with gold leaf and provided on the back with an inlay of gold foil, in which Ahmose's name, together with his full royal title, is

273 Blade of Ahmose's battle-axe

inlaid. The gaps we see held golden rings, which have not been preserved.

On each side, the blade of forged copper is divided into three zones. On one side (273), these are covered with gold leaf and inlaid with lapis lazuli, carnelian and turquoise or light-green glass. In the upper section, a seated man (the god Heh) is depicted. He holds a knotched palm branch, the hieroglyph for 'millions of years', in each of his outstretched hands; beneath this, there are the two guardian goddesses with the emblematic plants of Upper and Lower Egypt, the vulture over the lotus, the *uraeus* over the papyrus; the section nearest the blade edge has a sphinx, which holds the head of an enemy in its raised paw. Like the two sphinxes on the wrist-guard (270), it presumably represents Hurun, the Semitic god of vengeance.

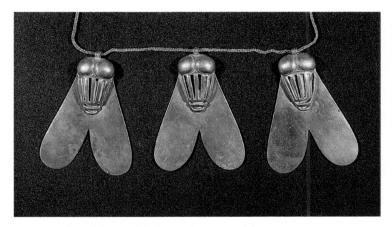

274 'Order of the Gold Flies' of Queen Ahhotep

On the other side of the blade (272) only the upper section is gilded, and bears an inscription in coloured inlay, some of which has now fallen out: 'The perfect god, Neb-pekhti-Re, son of Re, Ahmose'. In the two lower sections, the copper blade is coated in niello, with figures and hieroglyphs inlaid in electrum. In the centre, the King, stepping out boldly, seizes a Nubian, who falls to his knees, and symbolically overcomes him with a blow of the fist to the head. The section nearest the edge is occupied by a griffin. The form of this mythical animal emerged in Crete, and probably came to Egypt via the Near East. In later Semitic sources, the griffin is a symbol of 'the mightiest power' and of 'the avenger', and so of the god Hurun. The accompanying hieroglyphic inscription identifies it with the Theban god of war, Montu.

275 Dagger from Queen Ahhotep's tomb

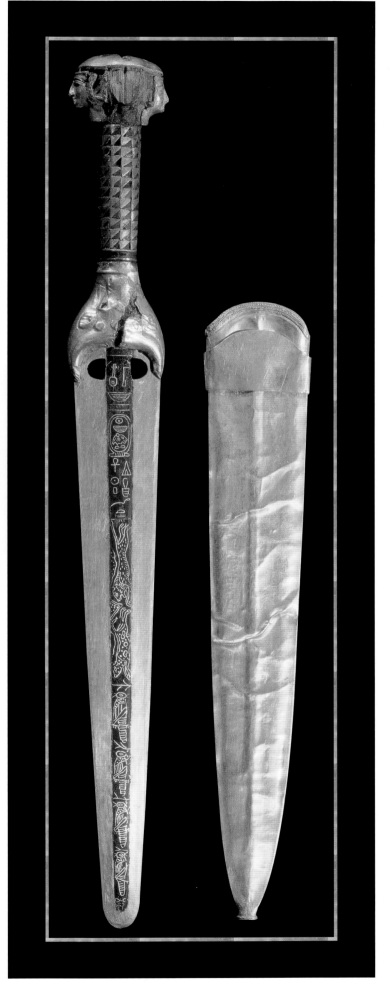

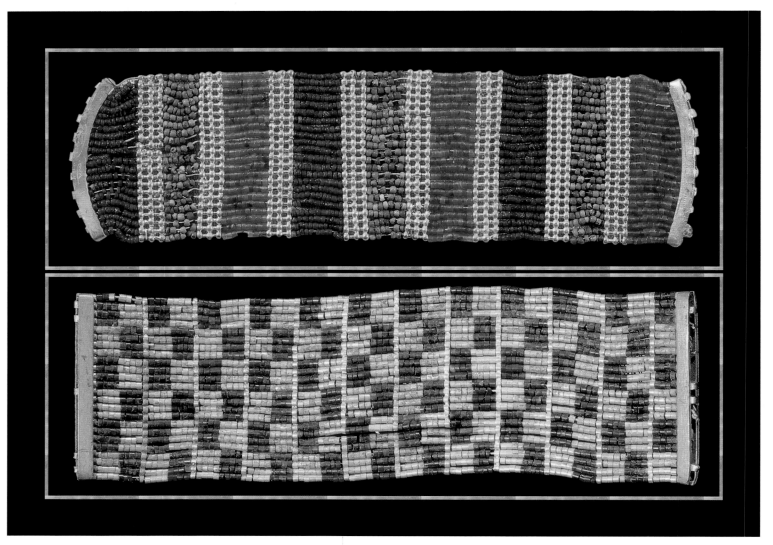

276–277 Bead bracelet with the names of two queens and a bead bracelet with gold stiffeners

As mentioned, the dagger (275) is Aegean in form and technique. A pommel made of women's heads facing in different directions crowns a cylindrical handle inlaid in electrum, carnelian and lapis lazuli. The hilt on both sides is in the form of a bull's head, the semicircle of the horns enclosing the top of the blade. This motif is derived from Mycenaean models. On both sides, in the centre of the blade from hilt to tip, instead of a groove, there is a slightly tapered niello strip. This has the name and title of King Ahmose inlaid in fine gold wire, with depictions of animals: a lion chases a bull, both at the 'flying gallop', and four locusts are in grass. The lion stands for the king, the bull for his victim; the locusts symbolize the host of soldiers who follow the king.

Related Finds
In 1910, pieces of jewellery appeared on the market that evidently came from the funerary treasure of

Queen Ahhotep, among them a beaded bracelet (277), which now belongs to the Miho Museum in Japan. Tiny annular beads of gold and lapis lazuli have been arranged in a chessboard-like pattern, in squares of four beads by four. The twenty-four rows are held together by eleven gold bars, which are flat on the inside and worked on the outside to match the beads; they are perforated for the passage of threads of beaten gold foil. On the end-pieces are eyelets that interlock and may be fastened together with a pin.

Closely related to the jewellery from the coffin of Queen Ahhotep are a pair of bead bracelets (280–281) and also another bracelet (278–279), on loan to the Pelizaeus Museum in Hildesheim; they probably come from a royal tomb in West Thebes. The same is true of a bead bracelet with the names of two queens (276), which with its matching counterpart was worn on the wrist. Alternating bands of beads of lapis lazuli, turquoise and carnelian are

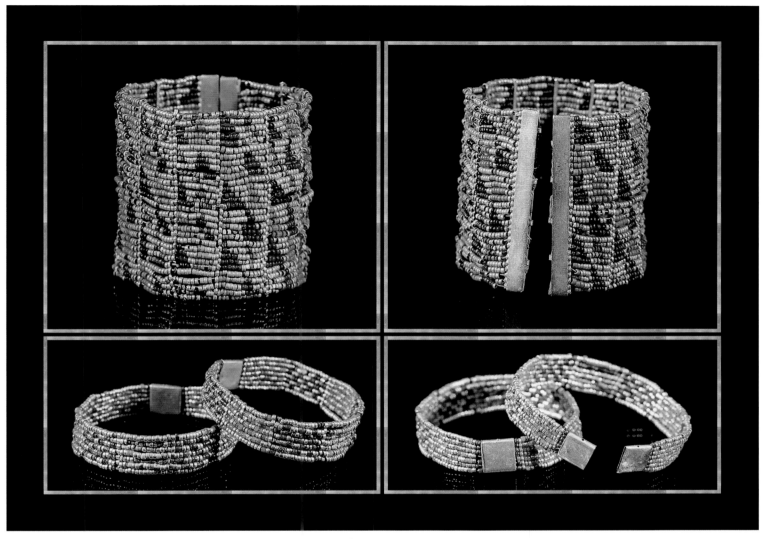

278–281 *Broad bead cuffs and a matching pair of narrow bead bracelets*

separated by bands of gold, the sequence being repeated three times. The eight bands of gold consist of rows of three beads lined up on a fine tube through which the gold thread passes; these rows are soldered to each other. The gold end-pieces (now buckled) were held together by a pin. An inscription is incised on the outside of the two halves of the clasp: 'The god's-wife Ahmose-Nefertari, beloved of Amun'. Another on the inside reads: 'The god's-wife Sit-Amun, beloved of Amun'. Ahmose-Nefertari was the wife of King Ahmose; Sit-Amun was her daughter.

Valuable belongings were passed on through the generations. The tomb of Psusennes I in the royal necropolis at Tanis held a multitude of precious metal vessels, among them a gold pitcher for holy water with the throne name of Ahmose, which was already 500 years old at the time of Psusennes' burial. This slender vessel is soldered together from individual parts of beaten gold foil. The broad rim curves down on the outside and is so formed on the inside that it fits the short neck to which it is soldered. The body and base of the vessel merge into each other, being separated only by an engraved line over the soldering. Here the pitcher is at its narrowest, and this is where it was held. A curved spout juts out from the rim. Right under the join are two rows of inscription engraved in a rectangle: 'The perfect god Neb-pekhti-Re, justified, beloved of Osiris, Lord of Abydos'. Representations on temple and tomb walls show pitchers of this type (*hes* vases) being used in rituals of purification and renewal, as well as for offerings of water; they were clearly standard ritual equipment.

Gold in Abundance

Under the 18th Dynasty, founded by Ahmose, the pharaoh's empire expanded far beyond the borders of Egypt. The Middle Eastern coast, Palestine, Syria as far as the upper Euphrates, and Nubia as far as today's

The New Kingdom

Sudan, were all conquered; incredible riches flowed into Egypt as booty and regular tribute payments.

On the walls of the tombs of high-ranking administrators we see how the gold revenues were precisely weighed and recorded at the treasury, using fixed units of weight – the *deben* (282–284).

In thanks for his victories, Thutmosis III, the great conqueror and organizer of the Egyptian empire, offered Amun-Re, tutelary deity of the kingdom, precious collars and vessels made of the gold from the subjugated territories. In the inner sanctuary at the temple of Karnak, his offering is immortalized in the description: 'Adornment which guarantees the protection of the limbs of the god' (289). Half a century after the bold conquests of Thutmosis III, the pharaoh Amenophis III was addressed as the gold mountain that shines over the whole world, like the god of the heavens.

This abundance of gold also served the ends of foreign policy. Gifts of gold would keep allies quiet and reduce the burden of constant wars. During the Amarna period a Middle Eastern prince, Tushratta of Mitanni, made it very clear to the pharaoh:

> Pure gold lies around in Egypt like dust on the roads. I would like you to send me the same amount as your father did before.

Military Decorations

The Egyptian empire was the greatest power in the Middle East. As a triumphant hero, the king was supported by a military élite of officers personally close to him who, alongside the civil officials, played a leading role in state and society. In their tombs, outstanding officers make reference to decorations for bravery bestowed by the pharaoh. Such decorations existed in the form of gold flies, the symbol of indefatigable attack, and gold lions symbolizing strength and courage on the battlefield (286–288).

Great deeds were also honoured by gifts of weapons and golden utensils from the hand of the king. From Thutmosis III, General Djehuti received a golden bowl (290–291). The outside of the rim bears the hieroglyphic inscription:

282–284 Weighing and recording gold tribute: wall-paintings from the Punt relief in the temple of Queen Hatshepsut and from two Theban tombs

285 Thutmosis III wearing a war-helmet, the khepresh

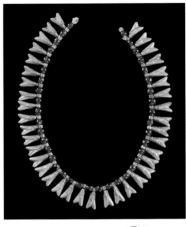
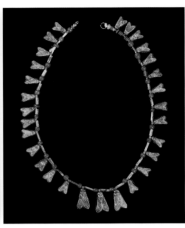

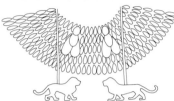

286–287 Necklace with gold flies

288 'Lions and flies': decoration belonging to General Dedi

with chased details, like the fish. The Nile perch (*Tilapia nilotica*) is a symbol of resurrection, and the papyrus umbels may be read as a reference to the Theban goddess of the dead.

Gold of Favour

Not only officers, but also high officials of the empire were awarded decorations by the pharaoh in recognition of their merits. They were given chains of annular gold beads and other jewellery, and those who had been awarded this 'gold of honour' would record the fact in their tombs. Khaemhet, the chief supervisor of the royal granaries in Upper and Lower Egypt under Amenophis III, has the honour placed around his neck by a representative of the King (297).

Ay, a holder of the highest offices under Akhnaten, accompanied by his wife, Ti, whose hands are held up in praise, receives his decoration from the hands of the royal couple, making a humble bow (293).

The very fact that Sennufer was allowed to erect his statue (294) in the temple of Karnak was a special mark of esteem to this favourite of Amenophis II, who held the offices of 'Mayor of Thebes' and 'Supervisor of the storehouses and gardens of Amun'. He also enjoyed a distinction not shared with anyone else, as far as we know. The statue shows him wearing not only the collar (a mark of honour) but also a 'double heart'. Sennufer had himself depicted with the white and yellow double-heart amulet (292) in several places on the walls of his magnificent tomb. In some cases, it is adorned with the name of Amenophis II, and the accompanying inscriptions explain its significance:

Given as a sign of the King's favour, by the King of Upper and Lower Egypt, Men-kheper-Re, to the prince and earl, father of the god, beloved of the god, companion of the king in all foreign lands and on the islands in the middle of the sea, who fills the storerooms with lapis lazuli, silver and gold, governor of the foreign lands, commander of the army, praised by the perfect god, whose rank is granted by the Lord of the Two Lands, the king's scribe, Djehuti the justified one.

The bottom of the bowl is decorated with plant and animal symbols. Daisy petals are engraved around the boss in the middle, and this flower is surrounded by a zigzag line that suggests the water in which the Nile perch swim round in a circle. The edge of the decoration consists of a crown of papyrus umbels, linked together by shallow curves, beaten in relief

289 Offerings to Amun, tutelary deity of the kingdom, given by Thutmosis III. Relief at the temple of Karnak

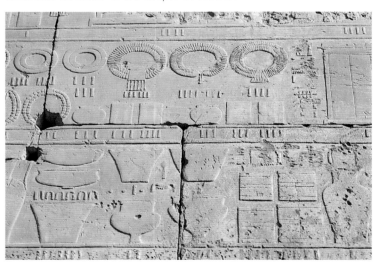

> To the beloved of the King, to whom two hearts of silver and gold were given… tied about his neck before the whole land… he [the pharaoh] knew that I was most excellent… greater was what he [the pharaoh] did to me than what had been done to others…

This unique distinction was probably intended to express symbolically that Sennufer 'possessed' the heart of his king.

Among such royal marks of honour are a pair of bulging gold bracelets that Sennufer wears on his wrists (292). Jewellery of this type is often depicted, and original examples have also been preserved (260–261); one was found in Queen Ahhotep's coffin.

290–291 Gold bowl of General Djehuti

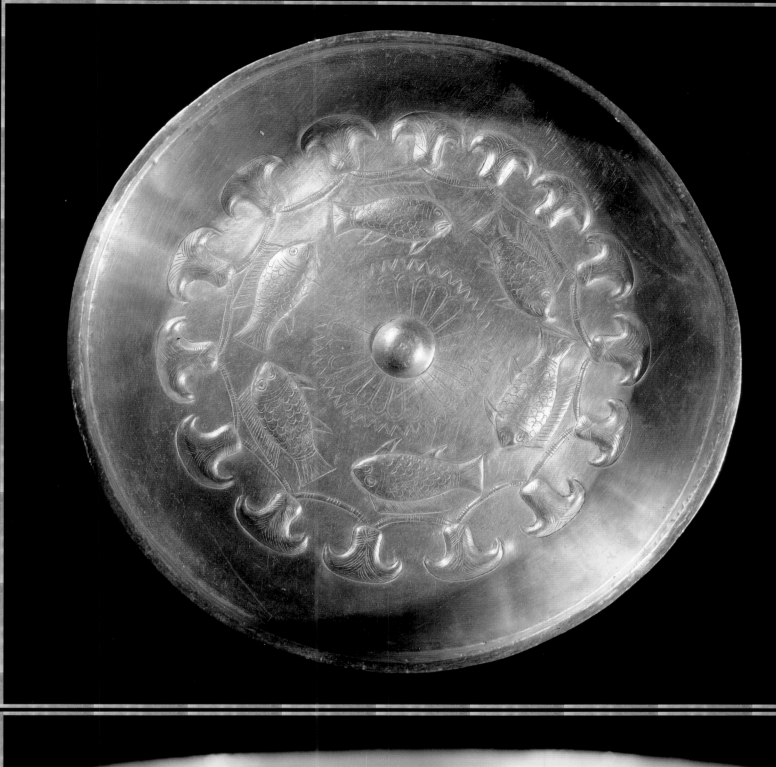

Gold in Abundance

Tombs and Funerary Jewellery

The precious jewellery and fine objects that have survived were mainly funerary offerings. The jewellery buried with the mummy would often have been worn during life, but in purely funerary jewellery the motifs relate to resurrection. The significance of the emblems of the gods, and indeed of the materials used – gold and coloured inlays – is explained in the instructions and maxims contained in the Book of the Dead, which from the 18th Dynasty onward was put into the deceased's coffin as a guide to the afterlife.

At the beginning of the New Kingdom, a large scarab placed over the mummy's heart became an important feature. Its mysterious reproductive behaviour of the dung beetle (*Ateuchus sacer*) led to its

293 The award of the 'gold of honour' to Ay, with his wife Ti

294 Sennufer with wife and daughter

use as a symbol of 'becoming' and 'constant renewal'. On the flat underside of the scarab was engraved a chapter from the Book of the Dead, which implored the heart, the seat of the conscience, not to testify against the deceased at the judgement
of the dead:

> My heart of my mother, my heart of my mother, my heart
> of my changing forms – do not rise up as a witness against
> me, do not face me in the court of justice, do not incline
> against me before the master of the scales!

A particularly beautiful example is the heart scarab from General Djehuti's tomb (295–296). The beetle of green stone set in gold hangs from a long gold chain. The passage above is engraved on its underside, while the prothorax bears the name and title of the owner: 'Governor of the mountain regions and inhabitants of the northern foreign lands, Djehuti'.

292 Sennufer with the 'gold of honour': the collar of lenticular gold beads, the double heart and gold bracelets

The funerary equipment of the young King Tutankhamun, preserved in its entirety, shows how sumptuous funerary jewellery must have been. In the New Kingdom, the burial chamber was given the name 'house of gold', as can be seen in the papyrus fragment with the plan of the rock-cut tomb of Ramesses IV (98), which gives Egyptian terms for the individual chambers of the tomb. The burial chamber also held the sarcophagus, with its gilded coffins.

The kings of the New Kingdom no longer built pyramids, but were laid to rest in rock-cut tombs. For a burial site they chose a remote valley in the hills to the west of Thebes, which was presided over by a natural pyramid in the form of a mountain. The ease with which the entrance to the valley could be closed off and kept under surveillance against robbers seemed to provide the best possible security. The temples for the permanent cult of the dead were erected far from the royal tombs at the edge of the cultivated land. Of those mortuary temples that

The New Kingdom

295–296 Heart scarab of General Djehuti

survive, Queen Hatshepsut's is the most impressive. Its terraced construction rises from the bottom of the valley of Deir el-Bahari, immediately in front of the steep cliff face before the Valley of the Kings.

The tombs of officials were cut into the friable rock of the east slope of the mountain. A few of these 'private tombs' were provided with columns to give the impression of a temple; the simpler ones imitate Egyptian houses. The walls and ceilings are painted, and colourful ceiling patterns make the cult chamber look like a tent. An innovation are the wall-paintings, showing the great banquets that were organized in the tomb in honour of the deceased. The worldly character of these feasts inspired the artists to a more detailed representation of feminine beauty and changing fashion, while their more fluid technique

297 The 'gold of honour' is placed around Khaemhet's neck

gave a freer, more expressive rendering of posture and movement. Unity among the figures is achieved through subtle variations in gesture and glance, and in the inclination of the beautiful heads under their heavy wigs (313– 317).

Goldsmiths' Workshops in Tomb Paintings
In the tombs of the New Kingdom it is essentially the gold workshops of the temple of Amun that are represented. In contrast to the Old Kingdom, the scenes no longer follow a strict order, showing successive phases of work from melting, through the beating of foil, to the creation of jewellery. In keeping with the prevailing style of the period, the selection and ordering of activities are more flexible, and scenes are filled with livelier movement. The work processes represented show many innovations. Blow-pipes for increasing and regulating the temperature of the fire have become longer, and the open hearths for melting and soldering are raised on legs so that the goldsmith may sit on a stool (298). To drill several beads at a time, they are set alongside each other in plaster, and craftsmen use drills that are rapidly rotated with a bow string (300).

298 Goldsmith with blow-pipe and pincers sitting at the forge

Scenes of jewellers' work and finished products are represented in the tomb of the 'two jewellers', Nebamun and Ipuki (301). Two men sit facing each other on three-legged stools, and between them is a chest decorated with inlay. One of them holds the lid open so that the contents are visible, probably a pectoral with a kneeling figure between two cartouches of Amenophis III; the other holds two flat inlays in his hands and seems to be matching them together. Above their arms is a stemmed vessel, and a flat dish on which lie materials covered with a cloth, intended for cutting into inlay. At the very top is a double necklace with a pendant representing a lotus flower with lateral buds. Next to this is another pendant in the form of a winged scarab, which holds a *shen*-ring, a sign of protection, between both forelegs and hind legs. The scene immediately to the right of this fell victim to tomb-robbers some time

299 Procession of bearers with funerary equipment

ago. At the top of the lost section was a richly decorated tall-stemmed metal bowl, and under this a seated man with a scribe's palette on his lap, holding on his knee a vessel on to which, with rush pen and ink, he applied the preparatory sketch for the decoration. The inscription above identified him as the painter of Amun, the king's son Paremnefer.

Frit, Glass, Faience and Glazes

Beads and inlays of frit and glass were used for the first time during the 17th Dynasty. To produce these materials, silica-lime sand from the desert was mixed with natural soda from the salt lakes and/or lime and salt-rich plant ash in proportions of between 60:40 and 70:30, together with metal oxides for colour. The salts worked as a flux, the lime as a fixative. The

mixture was presumably heated in earthenware pots; at 930°–1580°F (500°–750°C) the separate particles would stick together superficially but would not fuse. This porous frit could be cut and worked into beads, inlays and other objects. If the frit was further heated to between 1650° and almost 2010°F (900° and 1100°C) – depending on the proportions of the raw materials – it would melt into proper glass. Such glass was relatively opaque, the result of natural impurities, such as air bubbles or of the presence of zinc oxide, an ingredient of the bronze waste used as a colourant.

It seems that for a long time the Egyptians did not manufacture glass, but obtained it from the Near East, where the firewood needed for its fabrication was as plentiful as the raw materials. Imported crude glass was coloured in Egyptian workshops.

300 Drilling beads with several drilling-rods

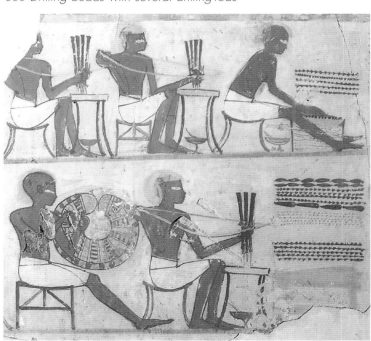

301 Workshop of the jewellers, tomb of Nebamun and Ipuki

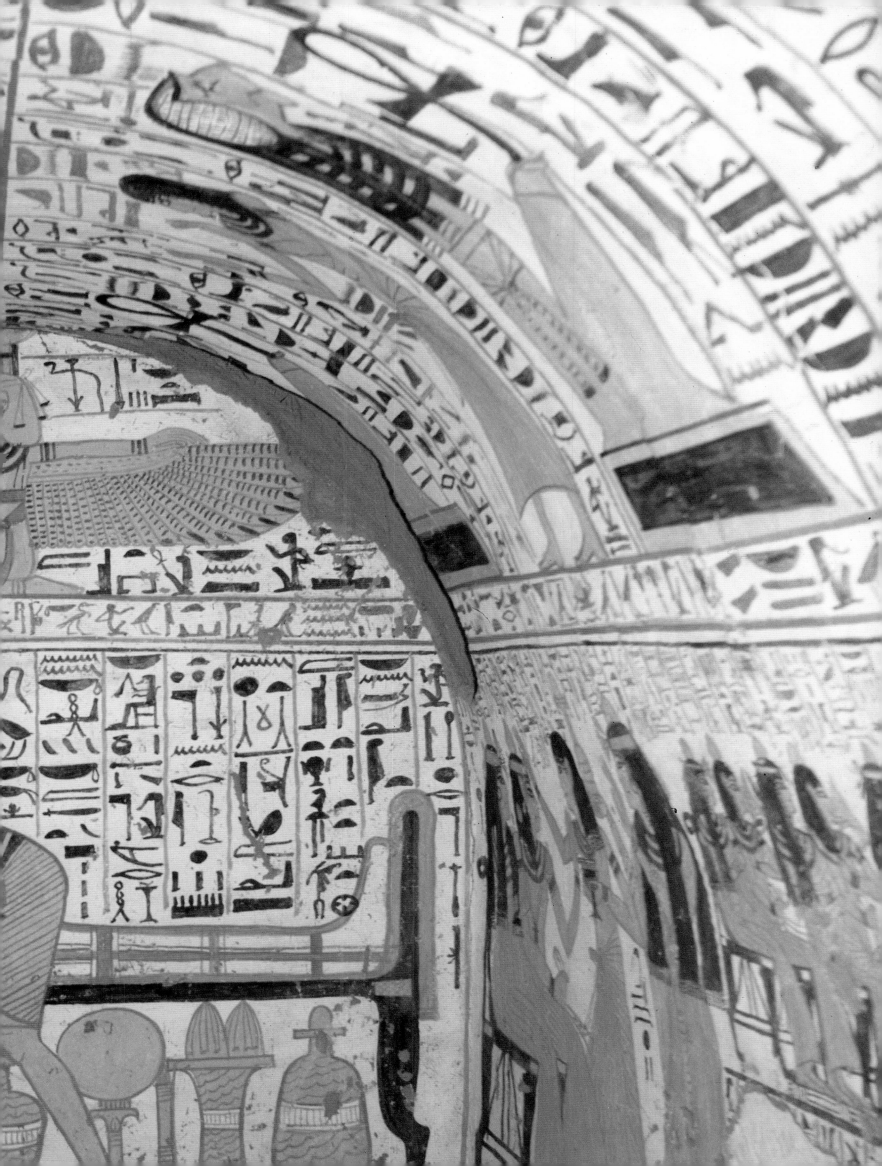

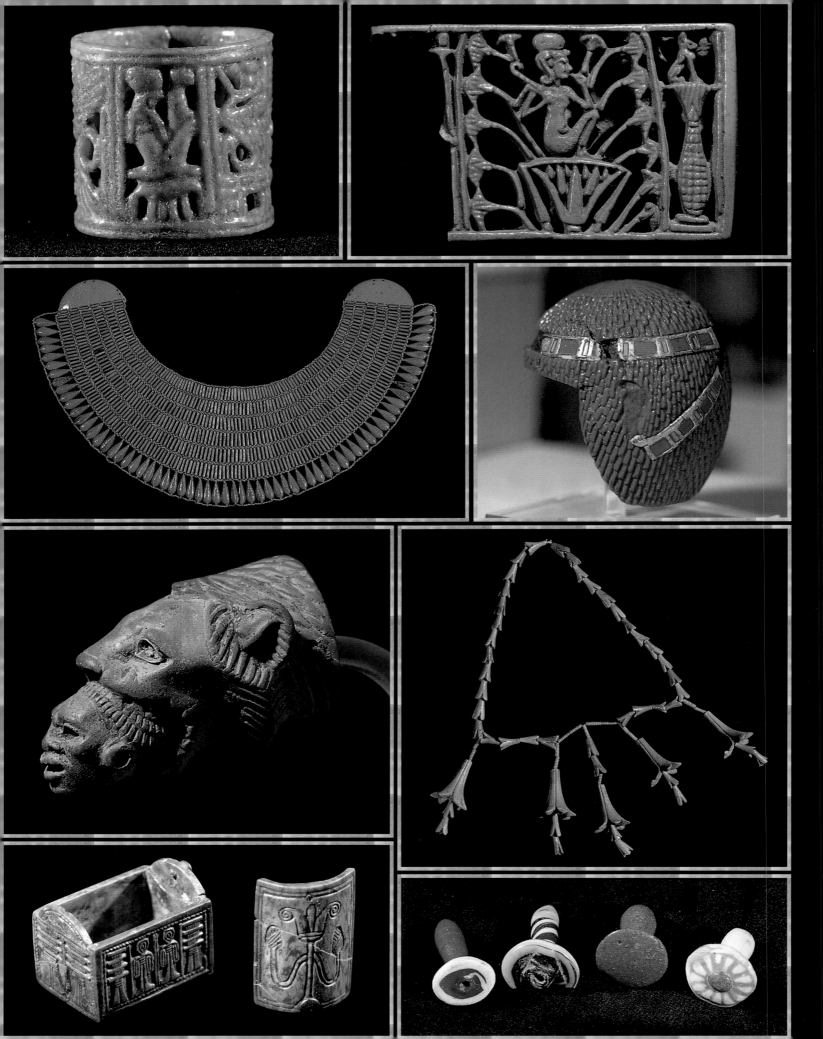

Gold in Abundance

Beads were formed around a wire, from a heated rod of glass, and glass inlay was made in open clay moulds. Masses of viscous molten glass would be pressed into moulds, and very likely glass powder might be melted in a mould placed in the fire. After being cooled down and cut to shape, the inlays were cemented into the prepared cells; the upper surface, which often bore the traces of pressing, would then be placed at the bottom.

the desired hue. Alongside the flat inlays there now appear relief inlays produced in open moulds. Among the best of these are the heads and limbs of the royal couple pictured on the throne of Tutankhamun (405), with their elegant lines and fine relief. Glass and faience inlays can often be distinguished from the coloured stones they mimic only by chemical analysis.

In appearance, 'Egyptian faience' closely resembles glazed ceramics; the interior is, however, porous and

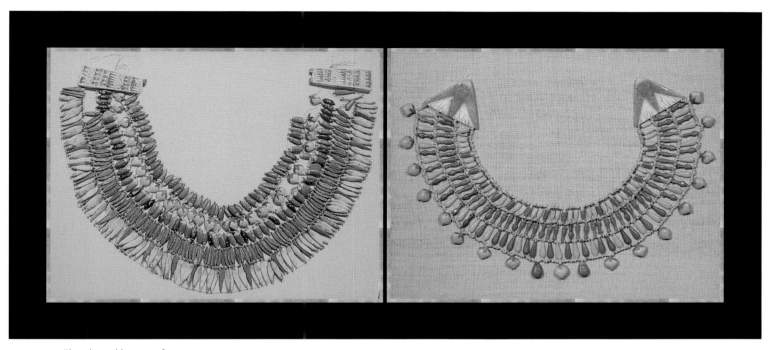

311–312 Floral necklace in faience

Glass, which was used like coloured stone, was called 'molten stone' by the Egyptians. Enamelling, or the melting of glass directly in cloisonné cells, had not yet been mastered in Egypt, the first high-quality examples of this technique being found only in the Ptolemaic period. Apart from gold, no other material was used in such quantity. The reason for this may be that, unlike stones, glass could be exactly coloured to

consists of quartz. The same raw materials were used as for glass, but the ratios and processes differed considerably. The finest possible powdered quartz chippings or sand, with a maximum of 5 per cent impurities in the way of clay, lime and sodium salts, were kneaded with water, together with metal oxides, and then shaped, dried, and fired at 1470° to 1768°F (800° to 1000°C) to form a partly-glazed sinter.

Glazing was achieved by various processes, with countless intermediate stages. One required the unfired piece to be dipped in a slip of pulverized frit and water, or painted with coloured slips, and then fired. As simple as this process might seem, it nevertheless required highly developed skills and long practice.

A second, simpler method was the self-glazing process. Quartz powder, alkaline salts and metal oxide colourants were kneaded into a mass; during drying, the water would evaporate and take some of the salts and metal oxides with it to the surface. Fired at about

1650°F–1768°F (900°–1000°C), a glaze would be formed, usually a rich blue, from copper. In the presence of clay, which always contains iron and/or aluminium oxides, the glaze would take on a markedly green cast, though many green tones only appear only when the glaze decays.

The last of the three most common processes worked in the opposite way. The unfired piece was coated with calcite paste, or powder mixed with soda or vegetable ash, fine quartz powder and metal oxides for colouring. During firing, the surface of the faience reacted with the coating, and a regular, all-round glaze was produced, the surplus coating being removed after cooling. This process was employed to good effect by Egyptian craftsmen and is still used in Iran.

Dynasty. Women's simple white robes, fastened over the shoulder, acquired a refined elegance; pleated and translucent, they now clung to the body. Luxuriant wigs were worn with long curled tresses, and on the top of the head were cones of fragrant unguent. Instead of gold diadems there would be garlands of fresh lotus flowers, or their imitations in faience; a single lotus flower would hang daintily over the forehead. In jewellery, fashionable shapes began increasingly to appear.

Earrings

Earrings had already been known for centuries in Mesopotamia and Troy. They were probably brought to the Egyptian royal court by Near Eastern princesses

313 High-ranking women attending a feast, from a wall-painting from the tomb of Nakht at Thebes

The Egyptians called their faience 'the lustrous', on account of its luminous glaze. It was handled like clay. The difficult process of drilling was avoided by moulding the bead around a reed, which would burn away during firing. Open clay moulds for inlays and amulets in relief have been found in thousands. The reverse was smoothed before firing, generally by hand.

Innovations in Dress and Jewellery

Statues and, above all, wall-paintings in the tombs show how dress changed in the course of the 18th

and were soon worn by both men and women. Records on cuneiform tablets show that the daughter of the Mitanni prince Tushratta, who married Thutmosis IV, took with her over thirty pairs of earrings as part of her dowry. A great diversity of forms developed – rings, studs (310), discs and pendants – executed in a great variety of materials. The thick, hollow-worked gold earrings (360–361) pinched the earlobe in the gap between it and the side of the face; modern trials have demonstrated that the springy rings hold in place very well.

314 Woman with collar and lotus flowers in her hair

315 A bead collar is put round Nebamun's neck

Disc-shaped earrings decorated with spiral patterns or rosettes were very popular with women and are often represented, the small bust of Queen Ti (363) being unique of its kind. On the rosette of her disc-shaped earring, which has been partly uncovered, are alternating segments of gold and lapis lazuli, and in the centre are two royal *uraei* in gold. Computer tomography has shown that under the wig is a white royal hair net in silver. The gold *uraei* that hung down over the ears and the base of the two *uraei* over the brow have been preserved.

With time, pendant earrings became much more splendid and also much heavier – some weighing more than 3½oz (100gm). The Egyptians liked to use plant motifs for pendants, with stylized flowers, fruit or seed-capsules hanging from fine chains (416).

Collars and Necklaces

In the New Kingdom, collars and necklaces continued to be among the most popular jewellery for both sexes. The broad bead collar of the earlier period was still worn, though with slight changes. In place of the gold falcons' heads there now appear lotus-flower terminals in faience (312). Floral collars in faience were a novelty, but only a few have survived (311). We also know of faience collars with stylized lotus flowers from wall-paintings in the tombs (314).

The fine gold wire for braided chains was produced by drawing narrow strips of strong gold foil through successively smaller holes in stone plates until the desired thickness was obtained, and would be artfully braided and soldered (262, 274). Simpler necklaces – whose arrangement often remains uncertain – have

316 A woman with festive jewellery and sistrum

317 A woman putting on her jewellery

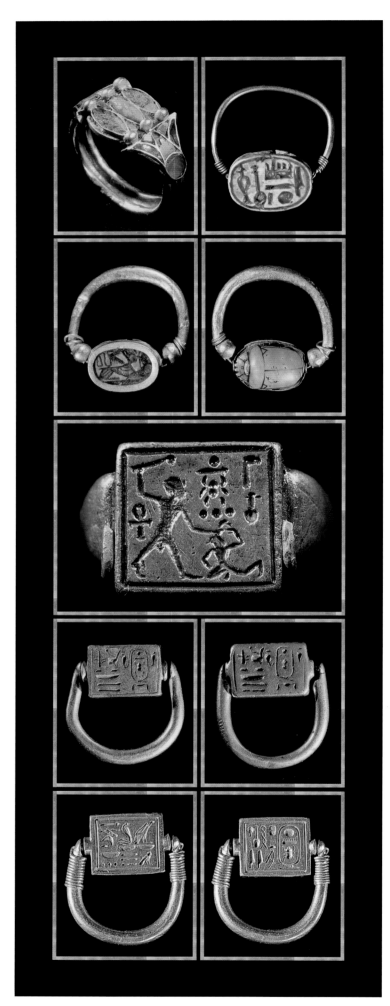

flower motifs, hieroglyphic signs and divine emblems as amulet pendants. One necklace, in blue faience, has pomegranate flowers (308), another cornflowers cast in solid gold (332). The cornflower was a guarantor of reincarnation and participation in the eternal cycle as, like the lotus, it opens in the morning and closes at night.

From a string of beads (333–334) hangs a panther's head, a powerful amulet. It is of beaten gold foil, and the eyes, nose and line of the cheek are cut out.

Another string of beads, in glass, has a jackal and the hieroglyph for 'beauty' in gold (336). Reference has already been made to fly and lion amulets (286–288) as military decorations.

Scarab Rings and Signet Rings

The scarab ring in its early form developed in the Middle Kingdom from the scarab seal with its engraving on the smooth, oval underside. Scarabs, often engraved with the name of the king or of a high official, or with good wishes, lucky symbols or other decoration, continued to be worn until the Late Dynastic Period, and were adopted as amulets by neighbouring peoples.

The scarab, usually made of faience or carved from steatite, and glazed in green, was drilled along its length and bound to the finger with a length of cord or fine gold wire. Later, to avoid the discomfort of a knot on the inside of the hand, gold wire was passed through the hole and the ends attached to the extremities of a U-shaped stirrup, as can be seen in a ring whose scarab bears the inscription: 'Amun-Re with perfect favour' (319).

Over time, the stirrup became more substantial and the fastening more artful. Gold caps at the scarab's drill holes were to protect it from damage; mounting the base in a soldered band of gold foil served the same purpose, as is visible in rings from the funerary treasure of the 'Three Princesses' (352) and in another of the same period (320–321). On the underside of this scarab a sphinx with crown and *uraeus* is engraved, and above is a winged scarab and the throne name of Thutmosis III, Men-kheper-Re,

318 Ring with cloisonné ornament

319–321 Scarab rings, gold and glazed steatite

322–324 Signet rings of Amenophis II

325–326 Signet rings of Thutmosis III

which cryptographically contains the name of the god Amun and so affords a double protection.

It was a simple, logical step to move from the scarab ring, whose complicated assembly could easily be damaged, to produce the seal and stirrup in a more solid form, with a fixed or removable seal. In early days, the solid-cast signet ring was a borrowing from Crete, where it has been found as early as 1700 BC, several centuries earlier than in the Nile Valley. The Cretan signet ring, however, displays considerable differences in form and manufacture. Its oval seal is always placed across the line of stirrup, while the seals of Egyptian signet rings are set in the same direction, and take the form of a rectangle or cartouche (322).

Egyptian signet rings were made by the lost-wax

327 Presentation of the seal

technique. The whole ring, or in the case of a removable seal the seal alone, was modelled in every detail in hard wax, together with ducts and vents. Very fine-grained clay was then pressed around the wax model and allowed to dry. When this was fired, the wax would melt away. Molten metal was then poured through the duct into the hollow space thus created, the air escaping through the vents. When cool, the clay was smashed to release the ring, and the excess metal that had occupied the duct and vents was filed away. The ring was finally polished; remaining traces on Egyptian signet rings show that this was done with a piece of slate and charcoal.

The signet ring was a sign of office presented to officials on their appointment. The presentation of a signet ring to the viceroy of Kush (Nubia) is shown in a wall-painting from the tomb of Huy (327), who held this office under Tutankhamun. Besides the simple scarab and signet rings, there exist others that are more richly decorated. The fifteen rings from Tutankhamun's funerary treasure (393–394), and others such as a ring with cloisonné ornament (318), in which the plate with three faience beads is mounted between two lotus flowers, demonstrate the magnificence and variety of ring design in the 18th Dynasty.

328 Woman with menat *and lotus flowers in her hair*

The *Menat*

Menat was the name given to an item of jewellery of religious and ritual significance that consisted of a sheaf of fine strands of blue beads and a bronze counterweight. The *menat* was known in the Old Kingdom in connection with the cult of Hathor, and was used as a rattle-type instrument to accompany

329 Bronze menat *with gold and silver inlay*
330 Woman with menat *in her hand*

songs and dances by women musicians. In painted representations of the 18th Dynasty it is worn as an amulet or held in the hand as a cult instrument (328, 330). Imbued with the healing powers of the goddess Hathor, it was thought to bring life and protection, joy and love, and to lay it upon someone or to hold it out towards them was believed to have a favourable influence on reincarnation.

Sometimes the bronze *menat* is inlaid with gold and silver or with stones and glass. The inlaid metal decoration on a *menat* from Amarna (329) refers to Hathor. In the circle at the bottom, the goddess, in the form of a cow with the solar disc between her horns, is shown passing in a boat through a thicket of papyrus. Above this she is shown in human form. The

wives and princesses. In one hand she holds a sistrum and in the other the *menat*, both attributes of the goddess Hathor, the protector of the harem.

In front of Sit-Amun stands a Nubian woman who hands her a gold collar. On the inner side of the armrests (365), four ladies of the harem each carry gold that has been cast into rings. On the outer side (364) are Thoeris and dancing Bes-figures, who protect the child.

The Treasure of the 'Three Princesses'
In the early days of his rule, during his joint reign with his sister Hatshepsut, Thutmosis III took three secondary wives into his harem, whose names indicate their Near Eastern origin. They probably all died at

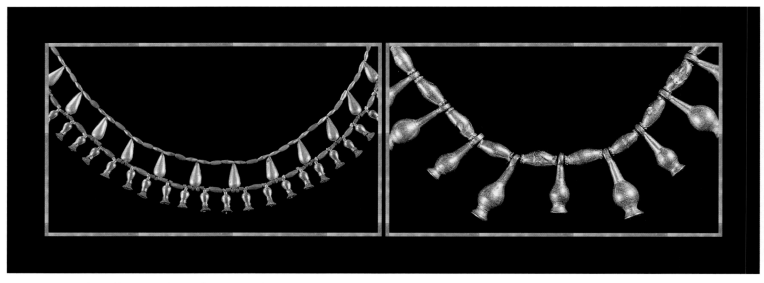

331–332 Bead necklaces with cornflower pendants

upper part terminates in the head of a woman with a vulture headdress.

Gold Jewellery of Princess Sit-Amun
Sit-Amun was the eldest daughter of Amenophis III by Queen Ti (363) and sister to Akhenaten. Her small child's chair was placed in the tomb of her grandparents Yuya and Tuya. The backrest and two armrests have gilded relief decoration, the scene depicted on the inside being explained by a hieroglyphic inscription: 'The arrival of the gold from the foreign lands of the south, Sit-Amun, his greatly beloved royal daughter'.

On the backrest (366) is a symmetrically mirrored scene: the enthroned princess wears a diadem of lotus flowers and buds, with a gazelle's head on her forehead, the recognized jewellery of royal secondary

the same time – perhaps from a plague, or as the victims of a harem revolt – and were buried together. The entrance to their tomb in the mountains west of Thebes lies high above the Nile Valley, hidden in an inaccessible rock crevice.

In 1916 the local villagers made a curious discovery: after a heavy rainstorm, the water that streamed down the cliffs suddenly disappeared into the rock, reappearing far below. They investigated the point at which the water disappeared, letting themselves down into the dark opening by a rope,

333–334 Necklace with panther's-head pendant
335 Bead necklace with gold ducks (top right)
336 Necklace with jackal and Nefer pendants (right)
337 Pectoral with the god Shed
338 Rings of Nefertiti and Akhenaten

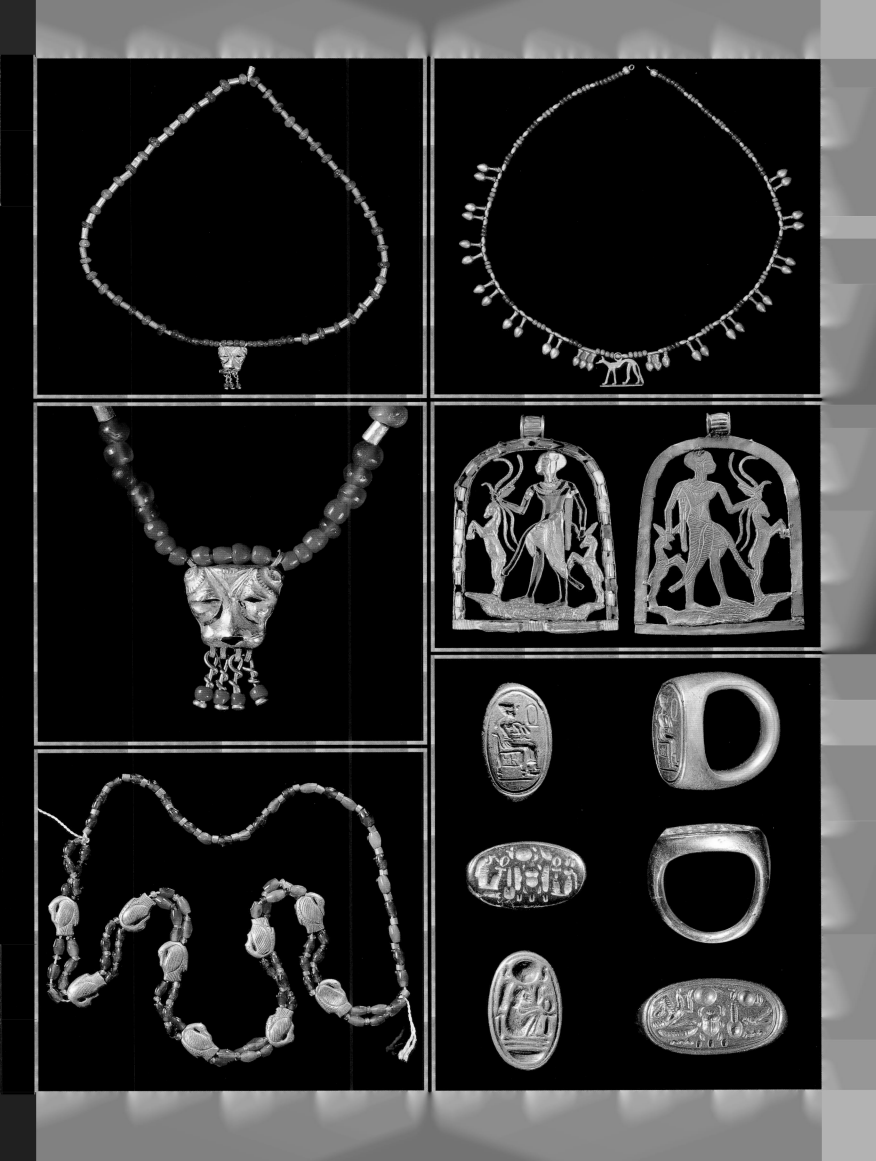

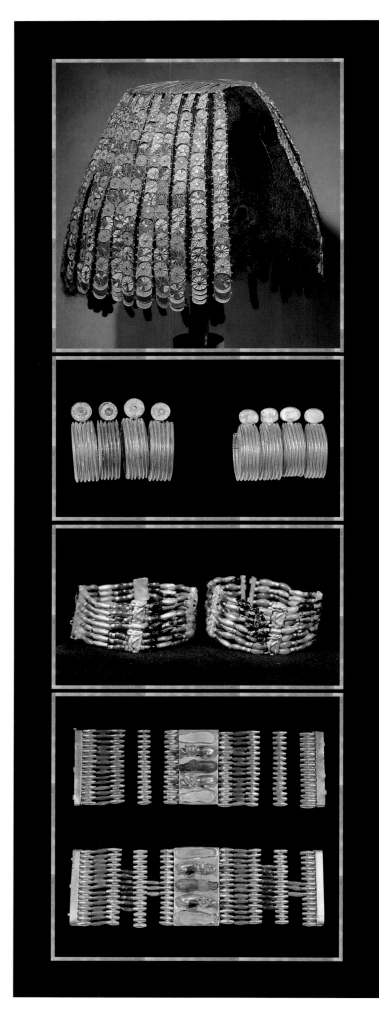

and found the entrance to a rock chamber, the hidden burial place of the 'Three Princesses'.

Like almost everything else that was not made of stone or precious metal, the coffins and mummies had been destroyed by periodic flooding of the tomb, and the glass and frit inlays of the surviving jewellery were mostly corroded. In all secrecy and haste, the villagers emptied out the burial chamber, seizing what they could and packing it into baskets in order to sell their precious discoveries as quickly as possible to dealers in Luxor. Whatever might still have provided some information about the buried women, their funerary equipment or the arrangement of the jewellery, was destroyed by the robbers.

The largest part of the discovery was bought by the Metropolitan Museum of Art in New York. When the dealer had reassembled the jewellery he had skilfully replaced some missing pieces; a few years ago, after careful examination, all these additions were removed, and now only the original parts that had been found are on display.

The three princesses had probably all been provided with funerary equipment with almost identical jewellery, and the most important pieces are presented in the following section. Parts are missing in many cases, and the arrangement remains uncertain, particularly in the case of bead collars and bracelets.

Jewellery for Headdresses

The diadem with two gazelles' heads over the forehead (343–344) is cut in a T-shape from strong gold foil, and a panther's head of beaten gold foil is soldered on each of the three rounded ends. In the mouth of each is a ring by means of which the ends were tied together at the back of the head. The two gazelles' heads in the middle are modelled in full relief, beaten from thick gold foil and set on two tapering tubes of gold. Below them, at the edge of the circlet, there are several small soldered rings that once held an ornament for the forehead, which has not survived. Above the two gazelles' heads and on either side, two daisy-like flowers have been soldered, their petals inlaid in carnelian and green and blue glass.

339 Headdress of a secondary wife of Thutmosis III

340 Golden earrings with rosettes

341 A pair of bead bracelets

342 A pair of bracelets for the upper arms with cats in relief

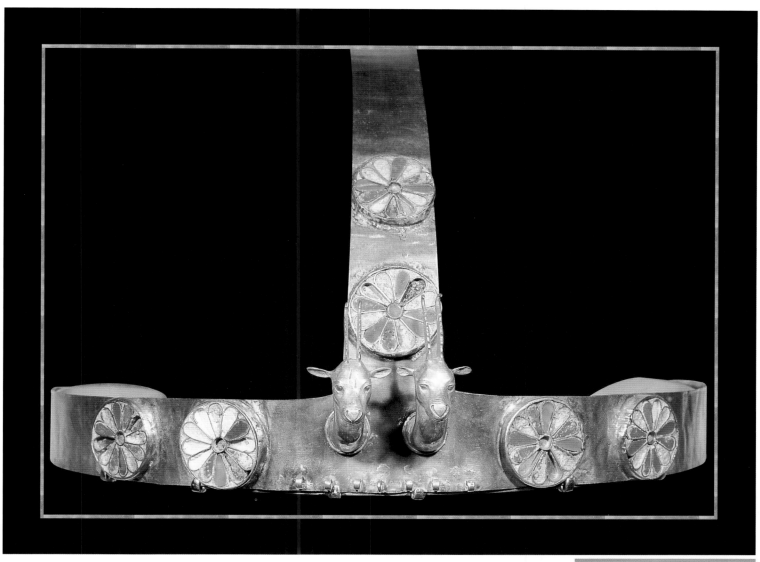

343–344 Diadem with two gazelles' heads

The gazelles may have been introduced as ornament for such circlets when princesses from the Near East joined the pharaoh's harem. This motif appears in visual representations until the Ramesside period, and symbolizes the gazelle-like grace of the ladies of the harem who, as secondary wives, were not entitled to wear a vulture or *uraeus*.

The headdress (339), in the form of a flexible wig made of hundreds of golden rosettes in cloisonné work, is a unique and heavy ornament for the head. The vertical strands are fastened to an oval gold plate that lies on the top of the head. This plate is engraved with a palm emblem, once inlaid with coloured glass.

The rosettes, cut into semicircles at the bottom, are suspended from each other by thread that passes through overlapping eyelets on each side. Each of the strands starts at the top with a rhomboid element that is rigidly attached to the first rosette, and ends at the bottom with a rosette with three crescent-shaped cells.

The rosettes increase in size from the top of the head downwards towards the shoulders. Except for the carnelian, their coloured inlays in the form of flowers have mostly fallen out. As the rosettes vary in their size and execution, they must have been the work of several goldsmiths. Signs of repair lead to the supposition that at least one of the princesses wore the headdress during her lifetime.

Gold rosettes with cloisonné inlay were also used for a series of earrings (340), each one consisting of six gold foil tubes soldered together. The two tubes in the middle are longer and were passed through the pierced earlobe.

The New Kingdom

Collars

One of the collars from the funerary treasure of the 'Three Princesses' has gold falcon's-head clasps (347). The brows over the obsidian eyes are inlaid in carnelian, the curve of the cheek and the head plumage with faience, which has now lost its colour. These details are chased on the reverse of the falcons' heads, as are royal cartouches with the name and titles of Thutmosis III. Seven rows of vertically arranged

delicate appearance. The coloured glass inlay of the gold hieroglyphs has mostly decayed. At the bottom are gold palms, a motif from the Aegean coast of the Near East.

Bracelets

The rigid gold bracelet (349–350) and its pendant bear signs of wear, and must have been worn in life. The two halves are connected by hinges, one of which

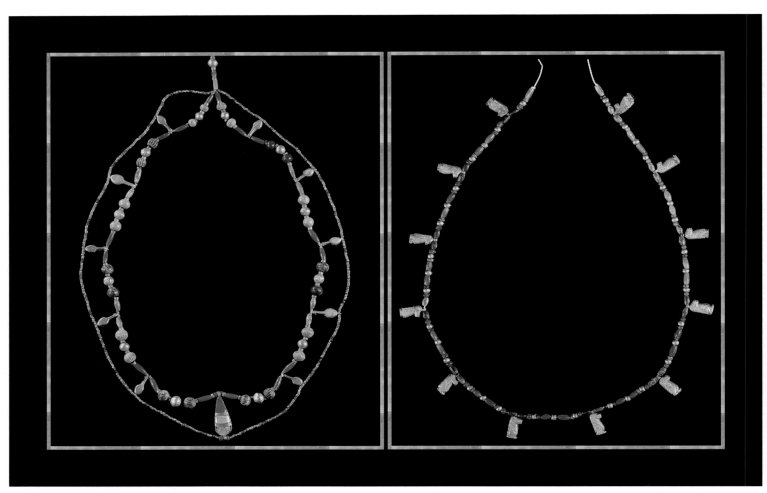

345–346 Two necklaces, with nefer *('beauty') pendants and with Thoeris pendants*

tubular beads of carnelian and blue-green frit alternate with rows of small gold beads, and at the lower margin is a row of drop-shaped inlaid pendants finished with a similar row of gold beads.

The same arrangement is shared by a bead collar with semicircular terminals. These are decorated in masterly cloisonné work, with the name and titles of Thutmosis III between lotus flowers. A counterweight in the form of a lotus flower hangs down from the back of the neck.

The collar with the hieroglyph 'beauty' (*nefer*) repeated through five rows (348) is of light and

can be opened and closed with a long gold pin. 'Windows' have been cut into the gold foil of the outside, in which ribbed plates of turquoise, carnelian and blue frit have been set, mimicking rows of cylindrical beads. The smooth inner surface bears the name of Queen Hatshepsut and the inscription: 'Beloved of Amun, who rules the harem'.

As it is unclear how many pairs of bracelets there originally were in the tomb, the reconstruction from

347 Large falcons'-head collar
348 Gold collar with nefer *signs*

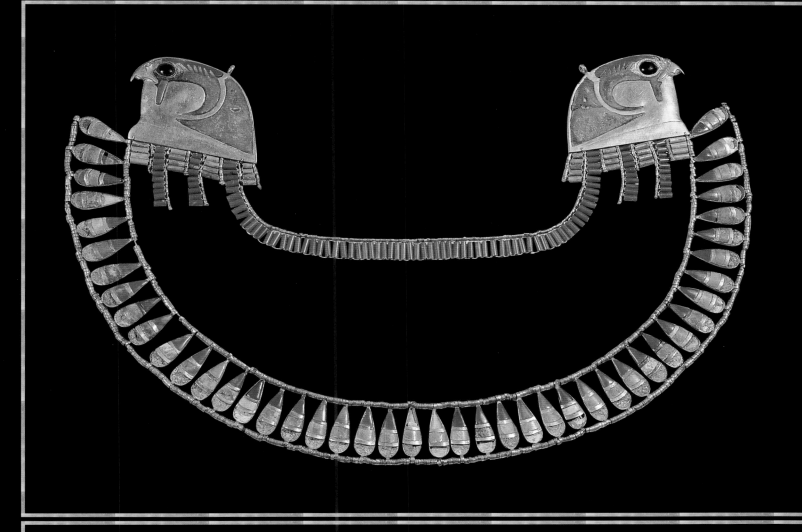
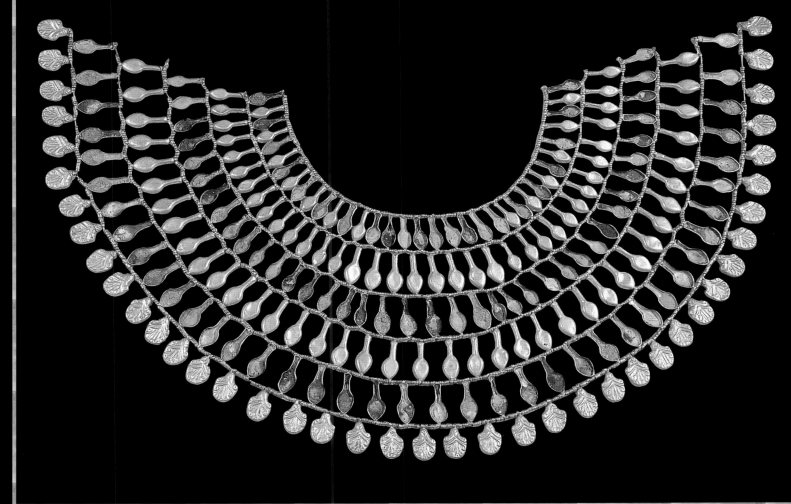

surviving parts of two bracelets for the upper arms (342) remains uncertain. Each is made up of fifteen rows of buoy-shaped beads in gold, carnelian, green feldspar and blue frit. The gold beads are soldered together into bands.

On a rectangular gold plate in the middle of the bracelet are five cats represented in relief with sideways-turned heads and crossed paws. The two outer cats, made of frit, have crumbled away because of the damp; like the middle cat, they were set in a gold mount. The two gold cats were soldered directly on to the plate.

Another pair of bracelets (19, 341) consists each of seven strands of gold, blue, light red and dark red beads of different sizes and shapes. Four evenly spaced hollow gold stiffeners hold the rows together, each being decorated by two figures of the goddess Thoeris in repoussé, one above the other.

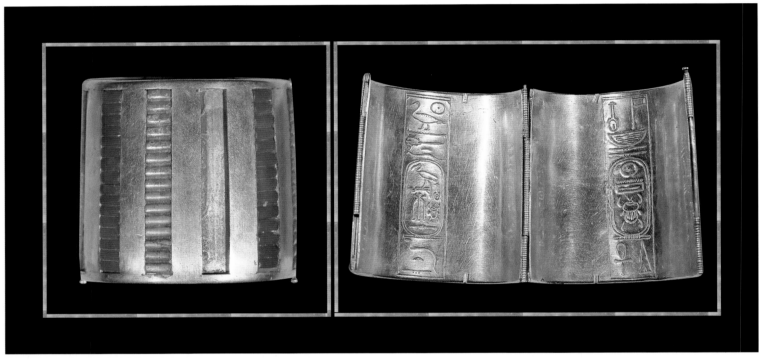

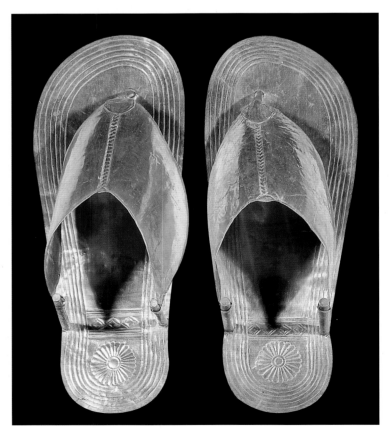

349–350 Rigid bracelet of a secondary wife of Thutmosis III
351 A pair of gold funerary sandals

Thoeris 'the Great' is represented as a pregnant hippopotamus with the back and tail of a crocodile; she walks on lions' legs and her front paws – or sometimes human hands – rest on the sign for 'protection'. Amulets of this popular fertility goddess, the protector of birth and of mother and child in the weeks that follow, appear in costly women's jewellery from the early 18th Dynasty (346).

Other Jewellery

The wealth of jewels with which the 'Three Princesses' were provided was completed by necklaces (346), rings (351), belts and anklets. A girdle with twenty-two gold Nile perch (*Tilapia nilotica*) deserves notice (353–354). The fish were made by pressing two halves in moulds that were then soldered together at the edges. There are holes at both ends to receive the thread with the gold beads. The triple strings of beads are shorter than the fish with which they are alternated. Fish amulets are frequently found from the Middle Kingdom onwards (194). On the girdle of a young princess, worn immediately next to the body, there are Nile perch with acacia seeds and cowrie shells as fertility-amulets.

The three pairs of gold sandals (351), which come from the same location, may be assumed to have been intended for the mummies of Thutmosis' princesses.

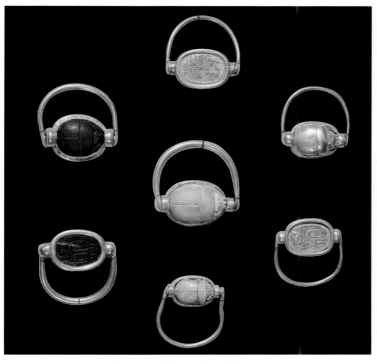

352 Scarab rings of a secondary wife of Thutmosis III

The soles and uppers are cut from thick gold foil. The two halves of the upper are riveted together in the middle and bent into shape, the ends being fastened to pegs fixed to the soles. Like leather sandals, these have lines stamped round the edges and a daisy flower at the heel. On her golden shoes the deceased was supposed to start on the road to the hereafter and to reach the 'house of eternity'. Gold served to protect the body and maintain it intact, safeguarding the functions of its members. Fingers and toes were then fitted with gold caps.

The Funerary Treasure of Tutankhamun

Tutankhaten (later called Tutankhamun) was the last legitimate ruler of the 18th Dynasty; he lived his short life at a time of internal and external political threat. He had grown up in Akhetaten (now Tell el-Amarna),

353–358 Girdles of a secondary wife of Thutmosis III

at the court of Akhenaten, and on the death of Akhenaten he was about ten years old. To ensure the continuation of the dynastic line he was married to Ankhesenpaaten, third daughter of Akhenaten and Nofretetes, and was made a pharaoh. He seems to have continued to reside at Akhetaten for a short period, but opposition to the monotheistic cult of the sun imposed by the 'heretic king' Akhenaten soon prevailed; Tutankhaten changed his name to Tutankhamun and moved his residence to the old capital of Memphis. There he issued the edict of restoration that re-established the traditional gods and

their priests. He reigned a further nine years before dying, research on his mummy suggests, at the age of about nineteen.

The Discovery of the Tomb
It was through the discovery of his tomb, the only Egyptian royal tomb to have survived through millennia almost untouched since it was sealed, that Tutankhamun became the best known of all the pharaohs. The tomb lies amongst the burial sites of the pharaohs of the 18th, 19th and 20th dynasties in the Valley of the Kings. In comparison to the tombs, furnished with halls and long corridors, that other pharaohs had carved into the rock to provide their final resting place, Tutankhamun's tomb is disappointingly modest. The entrance to the small underground chambers had been hidden by rubble that had been heaped over it during the building of the later royal tomb of Ramesses VI close by; workers at the necropolis had then built themselves basic huts upon this debris. In this way, any memory of the royal burial was erased: the tomb remained safe from ancient robbers and modern plunderers alike, and hidden from the archaeologists who systematically explored the Valley of the Kings.

In 1907 some jars containing embalming materials used for Tutankhamun were discovered in a shallow pit in the Valley of the Kings. Encouraged by this find, which bore the name of a pharaoh whose tomb was still missing from the series of royal tombs from the New Kingdom that had already been discovered, the British archaeologist Howard Carter and his patron Lord Carnarvon took up the search.

There followed years of failure and disappointment, during which hundreds of tons of sand and rubble were moved without result. In November 1922, Howard Carter and Lord Carnarvon made a final attempt, ordering the ancient workers' huts below the tomb of Ramesses VI to be removed. Carter is supposed to have been given a hint about this location from a local man, Mohammed Hassan Abd el-Rassul, a member of the famous family of tomb-robbers. His son Hussein recalls: 'Carter worked here for twenty years and didn't find anything. My father showed

359 Penannular rings of jasper
360–362 Gold earrings
363 Head of Queen Ti with disc earrings

The New Kingdom

Carter the grave, and then Carter opened it and took out all the gold; at the end, he hung a necklace around my neck and took my photograph wearing it.'

As soon as the huts had been removed and the underlying rubble cleared away, Howard Carter came upon stairs cut into the natural rock. A few steps lower down was a sealed door covered in mortar, upon which Carter found not a king's seal but that of the

when Lord Carnarvon, unable to stand the suspense any longer, inquired anxiously, 'Can you see anything?', it was all I could do to get out the words, 'Yes, wonderful things'.

The discovery of Tutankhamun's tomb was the most sensational archaeological find the world had ever seen, and Tutankhamun became the very embodiment of pharaonic splendour. Years of work were required to catalogue and remove the coffin and shrines of gold

364–365 Armrests from the chair of the princess Sit-Amun, outer and inner sides, with the god Bes dancing on either side of Thoeris

necropolis guards. He realized that here was a tomb that had been opened by robbers and that the administration of the city of the dead had resealed it.

When the door at the foot of the steps was totally uncovered, however, the seals with Tutankhamun's name also came to light. As soon as it had been opened and the corridor behind it cleared of rubble, Carter came upon another door with the seal of Tutankhamun alongside that of the guardians of the necropolis. He carefully pulled out a few stones from the wall and held a candle through the opening:

> At first I could see nothing, the hot air escaping from the chamber, causing the candle flame to flicker, but presently, as my eyes became accustomed to the light, details of the room within emerged slowly from the mist, strange animals, statues and gold: everywhere the glint of gold. For a moment – an eternity it must have seemed to those standing by – I was struck dumb with amazement, and

and gilt, the gold jewellery of every kind on the mummy of the pharaoh, and the thrones, chests, chariots, weapons and other goods that were piled up in the neighbouring rooms. The treasures have since then become world famous and the principal attraction of the Egyptian Museum in Cairo.

In the narrow burial chamber (368), with its painted walls, there remains only the stone sarcophagus and a gilt wooden coffin within which lies the mummy of Tutankhamun; here, in accordance with Howard Carter's wishes, it is to rest for eternity.

Jewellery and Amulets from the Mummy

The ancient Egyptians believed that the complete preservation of the body was a precondition for the continuation of life after death. To help ensure the deceased person's successful passage to eternal life, amulets were placed close together over the neck,

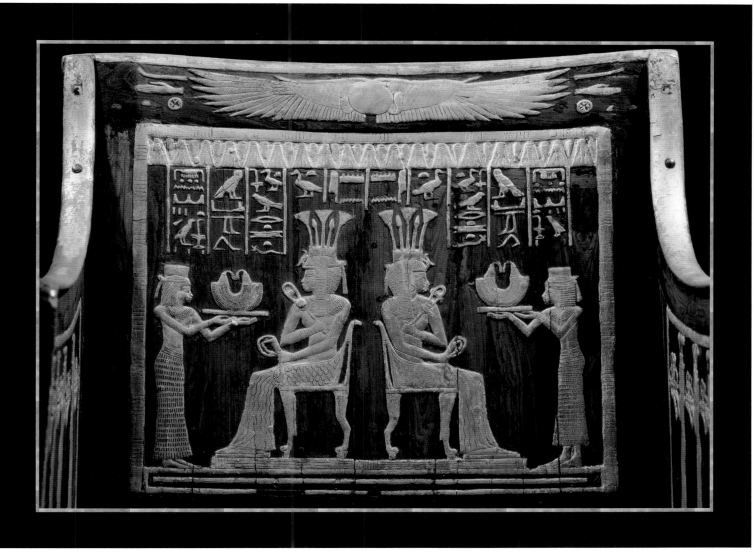

366 Back rest from the chair of the princess Sit-Amun (364–365)
367 Another chair of the princess Sit-Amun

breast and heart of the mummy; in Tutankhamun's case, 143 items were found inserted between the linen bandages. These amulets gave tangible meaning to the spells from the Book of the Dead that were recited during the embalming and the burial, and reinforced their magical potency.

The undamaged adornments of Tutankhamun's mummy provide a unique illustration of the religious beliefs and funerary customs that were supposed to secure the king's rule in the afterlife. There was a great variety of ways in which gold and precious stones were used to ensure the immortality of the pharaoh and his favourable reception before the gods; nowhere is this more impressively shown than in the treasure of Tutankhamun, with its thousands of objects.

Four wooden shrines covered in gold, a sarcophagus of yellow quartzite, two wooden coffins overlaid with gold leaf and a coffin of solid gold with coloured inlay

The Valley of the Kings

The discovery of the tomb of Tutankhamun – an Egyptian royal tomb with its contents almost completely intact – was the most sensational archaeological find that the world had ever seen. The fabulously rich funerary treasure made this young king, who lived his short life at the end of the 18th Dynasty, during a period of great political problems, the most famous of all the pharaohs.

The discovery was not merely a matter of luck, when in November 1922, beneath rubble and some rough huts, Howard Carter uncovered the first of the steps leading to Tutankhamun's 'house of eternity'.

Above: The tomb of Tutankhamun in front of the tomb of Ramesses VI

For six years he had been almost obsessed by the search for this particular tomb in the Valley of the Kings, which the American Egyptologist Theodore Davis believed he had already found in 1907, in the form of an almost totally empty chamber. But Carter always doubted that this chamber was the tomb still missing from among those resting places of the pharaohs of the New Kingdom that had already been discovered.

After five years of searching, Carter's patron Lord Carnarvon was disheartened. Given the difficult economic situation in the post-war years, he felt unable to continue financing the quest. Carter, however, was not ready to give up; his tenacity impressed Lord Carnarvon and persuaded him to allow Carter a last chance. Only four days after the

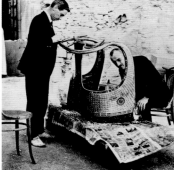

Above: The King's mummy had thirteen bracelets on its arms

Left: The treasure of the tomb of Tutankhamun and its recovery

beginning of what was to be positively the last season of excavations, Carter was able to send Lord Carnarvon a telegram: 'At last have made a wonderful discovery in the valley; a magnificent tomb with seals intact.'.

(369) surrounded the mummy. This inner coffin, weighing approximately 240lb (110kg), is the largest and heaviest gold object ever found in Egypt. It has the shape of a mummified Osiris, the god who rose from the dead, and whose fate the deceased king would hope to emulate. He wears the striped royal head-cloth with the *uraeus* (a cobra) and vulture's head over the forehead, has his god's beard, and in his crossed hands he carries sceptre and flail. A double chain of gold and faience beads lies over the wide collar, which is decorated with inlays of lapis lazuli, carnelian and turquoise. On the breast, shoulders and arms, the protective divinities, represented as a vulture and cobra worked in cloisonné enamel with coloured stone and glass inlays, stretch out their wings. The lower part of the body is protected by the winged

figures of Isis and Nephthys, sisters of Osiris, and protective inscriptions encircle the coffin.

The mask that covered the head and shoulders of Tutankhamun's mummy (371–373) was beaten out from heavy gold foil, and it is a masterpiece of the Egyptian goldsmith's craft. It is an idealized portrait of the young Tutankhamun. The striped royal headcloth (*nemes*) and the woven god-beard are inlaid with blue glass. The vulture and cobra on the headband are cast in solid gold. The vulture's beak is made from glass, the cobra's head from dark blue faience. The cobra's eyes are set in gold and inlaid with red-pigmented quartz discs, and its chest is inlaid with lapis lazuli, quartz, carnelian and turquoise glass.

The eyes of the mask are made of glass, with pupils of obsidian. The rims of the eyelids, cosmetic line and

The Funerary Treasure of Tutankhamun

eyebrows are of glass inlay. A wide necklace with end-pieces in the form of falcons' heads completed the royal attire. The rows of cylindrical beads of lapis lazuli, quartz and green feldspar are edged at the bottom by a row of droplet beads in cloisonné enamel.

On the reverse of the gold mask and on the parts of the gold coffin in contact with the mask is inscribed verse 151 of the Book of the Dead:

Your right eye is the barge of night, your left eye is the barge of day, and your eyebrows are the divine novelty. Your parting is Anubis [god of the dead], the back of your head is Horus [son of Osiris], your fingers are Thoth [god of wisdom], your lock of hair is Ptah-Sokar [god of the necropolis].

On the mummy's head, beneath the gold mask, was the slim diadem (6), that Tutankhamun probably also wore in life. This is suggested by the fact that the frontal goddesses, the vulture and the cobra are removable, and so they could also be attached to the pharaoh's other diadems. They were actually found within the mummy's bandages on the right and left upper thighs. The circlet on the mummy is a further development of the simple head-band tied at the back of the head that was worn during the Old Kingdom. It is covered with carnelian discs set in gold and held in place by nails with golden heads, the background being formed of bands of light and dark blue glass. The golden vulture's head is skilfully modelled and the

368 Burial chamber with sarcophagus and coffin of Tutankhamun

bird's expression, conveyed by its obsidian eyes, is captivating. The cobra rises up over the pharaoh's forehead. Its head and chest are inlaid with lapis lazuli, carnelian, faience and glass. From the knotted fastening at the back hang two long ribbon ends each with an erect cobra modelled in gold foil.

Verse 85 of the Book of the Dead contains the phrase 'to take on the shape of living Ba', and verse 89 the words 'so that Ba may enter his body again'. By the word Ba, the Egyptians designated the soul, which during life dwelt in the body and was liberated by death. The purpose of the transfiguration rites in the Book of the Dead was to ensure that the deceased can leave his tomb on the outspread wings of a falcon, that he can move freely everywhere and return to the mummy again. Such a 'soul bird' (*ba*), a convincingly fine likeness of Tutankhamun as a child, lay on the royal mummy between the linen bandages (370). The head, depicted in profile, wears a diadem, the cobra insignia and the royal beard. A wide bead necklace

covers its attachment to the bird's body. In its claws the bird holds solar discs of carnelian, enclosed by the ring of eternity.

Placed within the bandages, no fewer than seven large collars covered the breast and shoulders of the mummy. They are all of the same kind: winged creatures, whose outspread wings almost form a circle. In this way the falcon, the vulture and the cobra were supposed to envelop the king, to take him 'under their wing' and provide him with magical protection. Four of the collars are fragile burial jewellery cut from thin gold foil and chased (374, 375). The other three are in cloisonné enamel and consist of several sections linked together with gold wire threaded through eyelets soldered on to the metal (376, 377).

Tutankhamun was also buried with pectorals of the most varied type and function. On the breast of the mummy lay a pectoral with the *wedjat*-eye, or eye of Horus (378). The *wedjat*-eye symbolizes the indestructibility of the body and offers help in rebirth.

369 Gold coffin of Tutankhamun

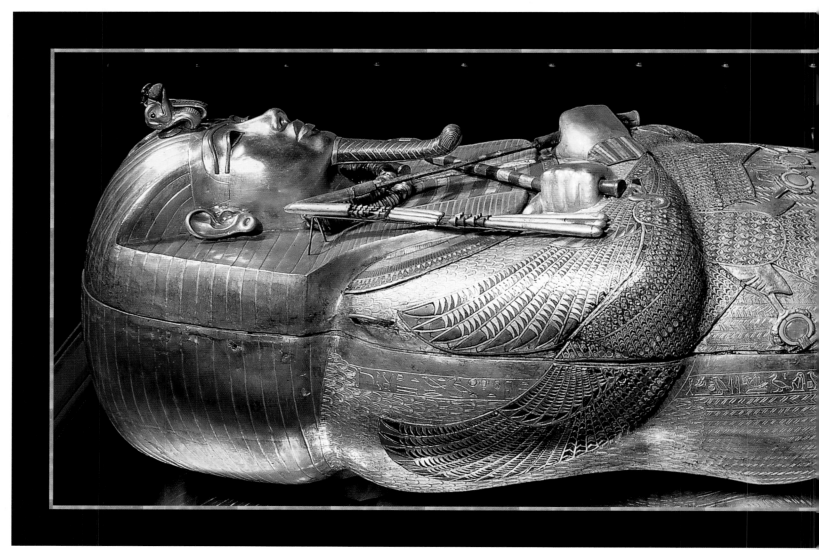

The Funerary Treasure of Tutankhamun

Combining elements of human and falcons' eyes, it is the eye of Horus, god of the heavens, in both his human and animal embodiments. According to Egyptian mythology, Horus lost his eye during a fight with his uncle, the evil god Seth, to avenge the death of his father Osiris and to regain the throne of kingship from the usurping fratricide. Seth tore the eye of Horus to pieces; but Thoth, god of wisdom and magic, found the pieces, put them together and made the eye whole again by spitting on it. Horus then gave it to the dead Osiris to eat so that he could come back to life.

When placed in burials, the *wedjat*-eye is an amulet with the power to reawaken the dead, in the same way as Osiris was returned to life. There are right and left *wedjat*-eyes. The right eye of the god of the heavens is the sun, and the left is the moon. As the symbolic embodiment of the life-giving sun, the right *wedjat*-eye had greater magical powers and was more common. It also appears on this pectoral, and is protected by the cobra with the crown of Lower Egypt and the vulture with the *atef*-crown, symbol of lordship over the whole of Egypt. The borderless pectoral in cloisonné enamel hangs on a triple chain of gold and coloured beads. The counterpoise at the back of the neck is made of hieroglyphs that stand for 'rebirth' and 'permanence'.

The pectoral with the 'sun on the eastern horizon' (379) is also without a frame. On a strip of lapis

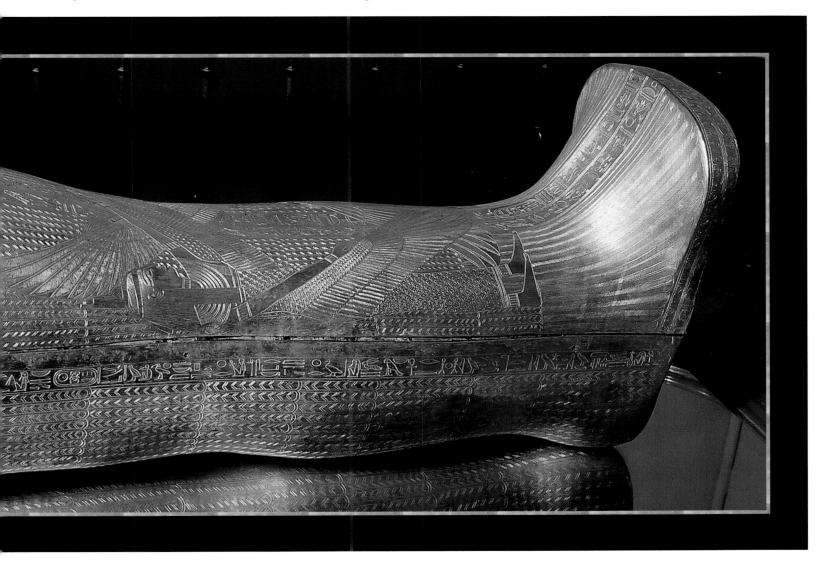

370 Ba-bird of Tutankhamun

lazuli, symbolizing the waters of the underworld, sails the barge of the sun-god in the form of a scarab pushing the hieroglyph 'horizon' with the rising sun in front of it. The scarab is of lapis lazuli and the solar disc of light red carnelian; during its voyage through the heavens it is protected by the cobra, daughter of the sun-god. The scarab is flanked by cobras, with solar discs on their heads and at their tails the hieroglyphs 'perfection', 'life' and 'stability'.

The two bands that taper slightly towards the top winged scarab, the young sun-god, the king wishes to rise every morning rejuvenated, reborn from the underworld in the depths of the earth, to traverse the daytime sky as a falcon and pass through the underworld at night. Thus the cartouche with his name is placed significantly between the scarab and the falcon-winged sun. Isis and Nephthys ward off the dangers that attend rebirth. The beaded robes of the goddesses, inlaid with fine cloisonné enamel, represent the star-spangled night sky. The reverse of the pectoral

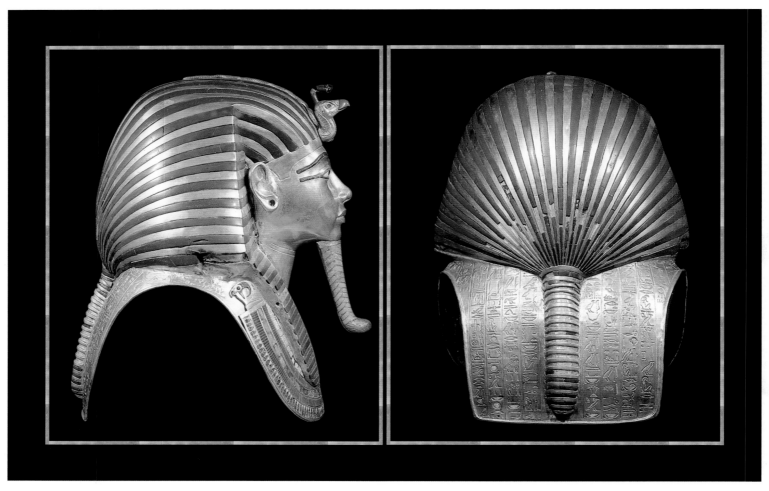

371–373 Gold mask of Tutankhamun

show similar motifs: two lapis lazuli scarabs with gold solar discs, each followed by a pair of cobras, crowned with carnelian suns with the hieroglyph 'life' between them; above this are the hieroglyphs 'celebration' and 'stability' under a carnelian disc. Vultures with outstretched wings are bent into shoulder-pieces. The clasps are formed of two upright cobras on chains.

The metamorphosis of the sun on his cyclical journey is represented in another pectoral with a large scarab (15). The plane of the earth, the celestial pillars at the side and a winged sun floating in the heavens are to be read as a depiction of the world. Like the

alludes to the subterranean kingdom of their brother Osiris. On the flat underside of the scarab is engraved the chapter from the Book of the Dead that beseeches the heart not to bear witness against the deceased at the tribunal of the dead. Only the righteous can enter the cycle of rebirth. It is Aten, the sun-god of the Amarna period, to whom appeal is made, so the pectoral must have been produced at the beginning of Tutankhamun's reign.

The piece known as the rebus pectoral (383) displays complex motifs of transformation. The composite creature, part-scarab, part-falcon, both

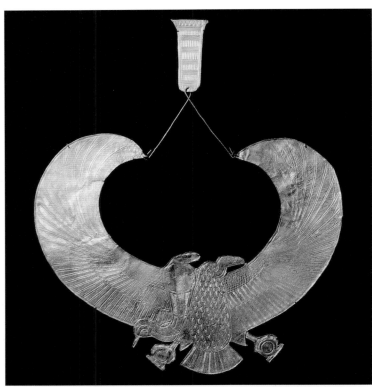

incarnations of the sun-god, is a figurative representation of the line from the Pyramid Texts: 'He flies as a bird and lands as a scarab'. The front legs and wing tips carry the celestial barge with the left *wedjat*-eye – the one identified with the moon – protected by two cobras. Above it hang the full and crescent moons, representing phases of the transformation. The relief on the lunar disc represents the pharaoh's ascent to the heavens. There he is, greeted by the falcon-headed sun-god Re-Horakhte and the ibis-headed god Thoth, the former with the solar disc, the latter with the lunar crescent and disc, with which the king is also crowned.

The sun-god, Khepri in the form of a beetle, has a composite body incorporating vulture wings and legs, and holds *shen*-rings in each of his talons, together with a lily and lotuses. The lower edge of the pectoral

374–375 Collar ornament with two guardian-goddesses

The Funerary Treasure of Tutankhamun

is made up of flowers inlaid in bright colours, alternating with stylized daisies.

A large cloisonné enamel pendant (23, 24) bears hieroglyphic elements of Tutankhamun's throne-name, Nebkheperure ('The Lord of Transformation is Re'). Over the basket character ('lord') the scarab ('transformation') rises and pushes the rising sun ('Re') with its front legs. The scarab is cut from dark blue lapis lazuli, the solar disc is of luminous carnelian, and the falcon's wings are inlaid with strips of turquoise, green feldspar, lapis lazuli, calcite and red carnelian. The motifs on the pendant front are repeated on the back, engraved on the gold surface.

The vulture pectoral (388, 389) from the room known as the Treasury in the tomb of Tutankhamun probably stored part of the pharaoh's personal jewellery that would have been worn by him during

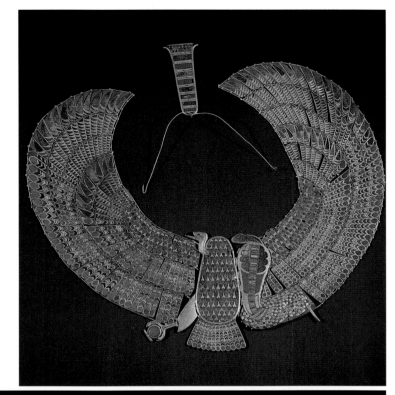

376–377 Collar ornament with two guardian-goddesses

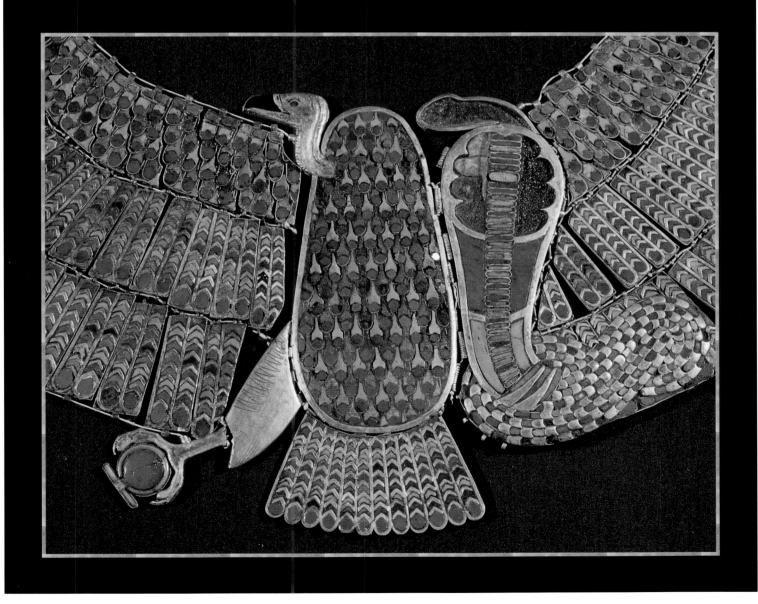

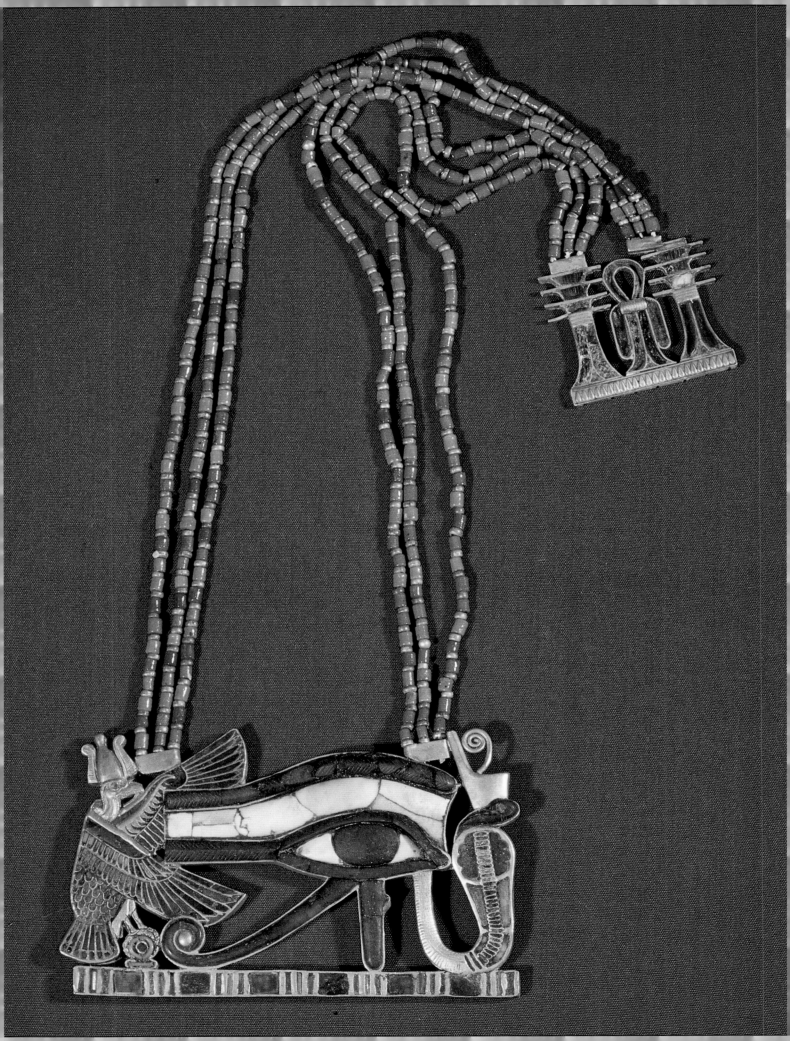

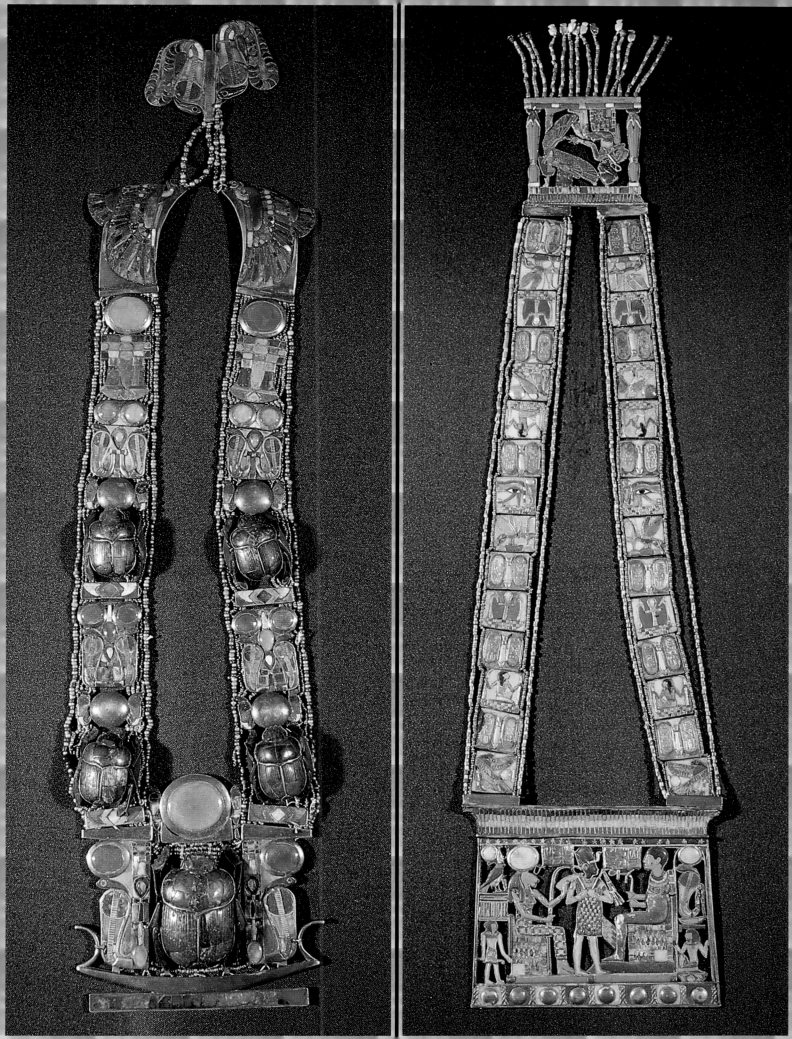

The New Kingdom

Page 178: 378 Pectoral with wedjat-eye
Page 179: 379–380 Pectoral with the 'sun on the eastern horizon'
and coronation pectoral of Tutankhamun

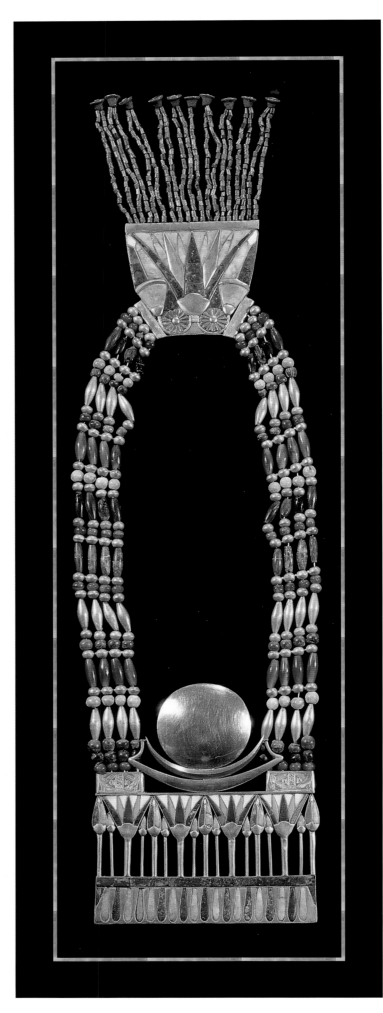

his lifetime. The vulture spreads its wings protectively, and in each extended claw it holds a ring of eternity with a solar disc. The cloisonné enamel of the feathers is inlaid with lapis lazuli and carnelian. The vulture's head, modelled in full relief on the flat body, is unusual. It is turned towards the wearer's face and wears the high *Atef*-crown, symbol of lordship over all Egypt.

The figurine cast in solid gold (5), representing a seated pharaoh with pleated loin-cloth and the so-called Blue Crown, crook and flail, with multicoloured bead necklace, has an eyelet at the back of the neck, through which, at the time of its discovery, a long gold chain was drawn. It lay wrapped in a cloth in a gilt box, which also contained two miniature coffins, one inside the other; the inner carried the name of Queen Ti and contained a lock of her hair. Howard Carter saw a likeness of Ti's husband Amenophis III in the gold statuette, as he thought that the statuette and the lock of hair were heirlooms placed in the tomb with the last direct descendant of the Theban royal house. However, images with the same costume and attitude and bearing Tutankhamun's name are to be found on several objects that formed part of the pharaoh's funerary treasures. The posture of the child-king who

281 Pectoral with moon barque
382 Scarab bracelet
383 Rebus pectoral of Tutankhamun

crouches on the floor in full regalia is a child-like squat that recalls the young god Nefertum on the lotus flower, the 'sun-child' at the moment of his rebirth each morning. The image may thus symbolize daily resurrection, and was perhaps used as an amulet.

In a chest in the form of the royal cartouche was found the pectoral that Tutankhamun probably wore

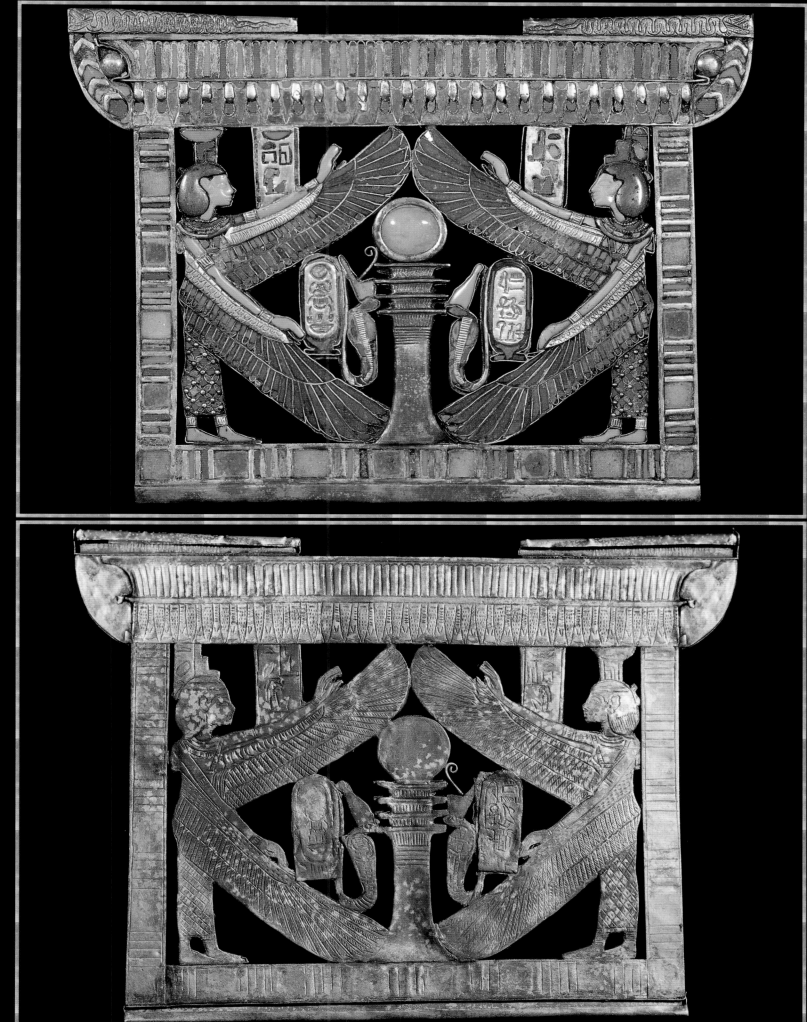

The New Kingdom

Page 182: 384–385 Pectoral
with Nut, goddess of the
heavens, her wings protectively
outspread
Page 183: 386–387 Djed-pillar
pectoral with Isis and Nephthys

at his coronation (380), together with armbands and earrings. The pectoral takes the form of a shrine; the base is formed by eight groups of eternity-hieroglyphs, while the upper end is made up of a strip of sky with golden stars and hollow moulding. In the centre is the king with the Blue Crown and knee-length coronation robe, a sceptre and flail in his hands. He stands between two enthroned divinities from Memphis: on the right the god Ptah, who gives him 'life, power and well-being', and on the left the god's wife, the goddess Sekhmet, with a palm-frond in her hand, who offers him 'years of eternity'.

Behind Sekhmet is the king's *ka*, a small standing figure of Tutankhamun, crowned by the palace façade on which sits the Horus falcon with its double crown and solar disc. Behind the god Ptah kneels Heh, the god of endless time, holding two notched palm ribs, the sign for 'million years'.

388–389 Vulture pectoral of Tutankhamun

The Funerary Treasure of Tutankhamun

The broad chain is edged on both sides with gold and blue beads; it has the king's cartouches and elements of the royal titulary as well as wishes for a long reign, happiness and well-being. Like the pectoral itself, the counterweight has the form of a shrine, the moulding at the top being supported by green papyrus columns. In the shrine sits the king, enthroned before Ma'at, the goddess of justice with protective wings outspread, and he receives from her the sign 'Life'. The lower edge is hung with strands of beads; the eight in the middle with gold fish pendants – Nile perch, symbols of fertility.

The corslet worn by Tutankhamun at his coronation (391) is a particularly lavish piece of jewellery work. This type of corslet appears in numerous representations as part of the royal robes or of the sumptuous dress of the gods. Tutankhamun's, with its representation of the coronation ritual, is the only example actually to have survived. Its chest and back pieces were made separately, and fastened together at the sides and shoulders with hinges.

The corslet itself is made in two rectangular parts with a feather pattern, the usual decoration for such dress. Scale-shaped pieces of light and dark blue glass, inlaid with little chevrons of gold and triangles of red glass, are fitted together like a mosaic and then strung together with thread that passes once through the little scale plate and then again through its 'stem'. Half-length scales were used for the top row, set in gold cells and provided with eyelets so that they could be attached by thread to matching eyelets on the upper border. The last row on the bottom is made up of gold half-scales with eyelets. The two borders consist of elongated cells inlaid with gold and coloured glass, alternating with small square plates and groups of vertical bars. Beads have been inserted

390 Falcon pectoral of Tutankhamun

between the eyelets, so that the borders look as if they are edged with strings of beads. The straps of the corslet, attached to the upper border, are made in the same manner; their inlays have lines of interlocking chevrons on both sides.

Between the straps on the front and back is a broad collar, made up of five rows of square cells inlaid with light blue, dark blue and red glass. The ribbed glass inlays look like cylindrical beads and the caps on their ends like rows of gold beads.

391 Corslet worn by Tutankhamun at his coronation

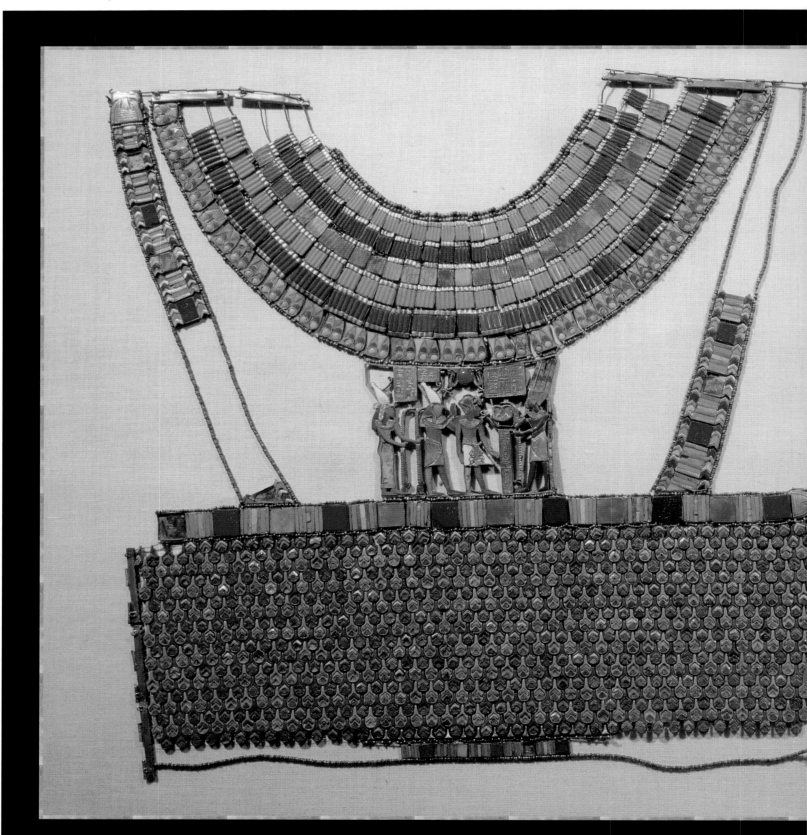

The collar is edged at the top by two rows of coloured beads, and at the bottom by drop-shaped pendants in cloisonné. On the chest, between the collar and the bodice, hangs a pectoral in cloisonné open-work inlaid with glass, ivory and beaten and engraved gold. Beneath the red solar disc protected by two *uraei* with life signs, Tutankhamun stands in the centre wearing the Blue Crown, a broad gold collar and a richly decorated apron. With one hand, Amun-Re of Thebes holds the sign of life to the king's nose,

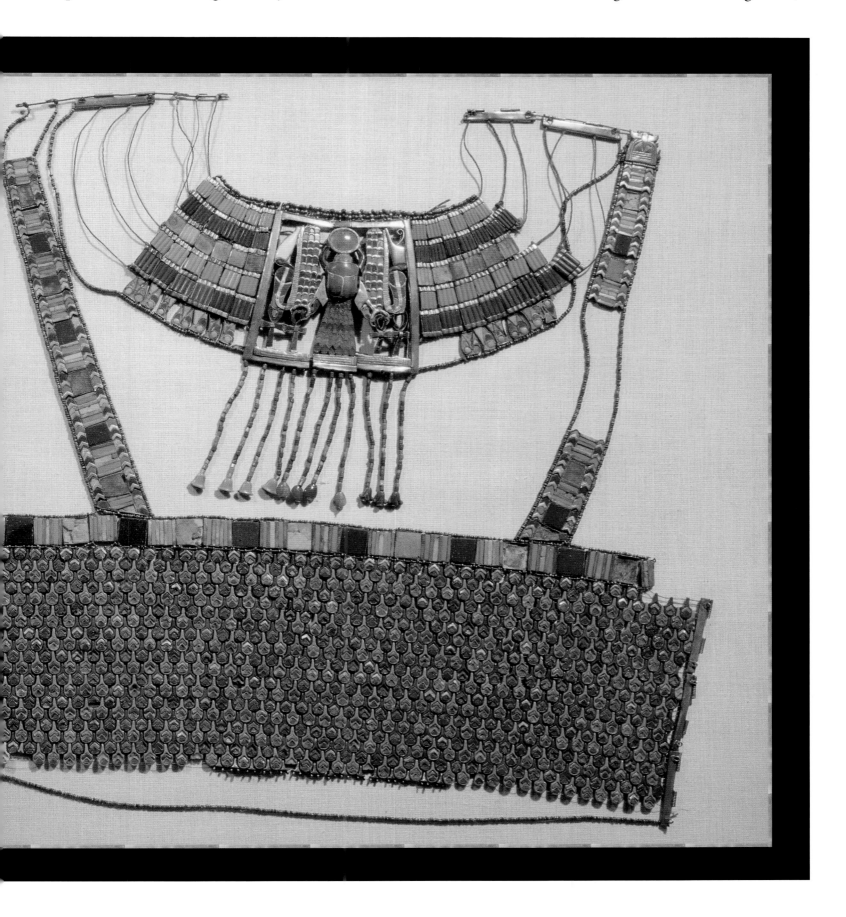

and in the other one he carries a branch with the sign for the coronation feast. The creator god Atum of Heliopolis, with falcon's head and Double Crown, and his goddess companion Jusaas, with the vulture headdress and Double Crown and holding two branches, bring the king before Amun. The branches in the hands of the deities bear the tadpole, the sign for 'one million', meaning that the coronation should be ever renewed.

Tutankhamun, here crowned as son of the sun-god, is identified in the composition on the back of the collar with the sun-god himself. Elements of his throne name, like the beetle and the sun, are fused with the divine forms of the scarab and falcon. From the bottom edge of the trapeze-shaped frame hang

'button' endings passed through the ear and fitted together. An ornamental connector holds the earring and its pendant. In one example (398), the bell-shaped connector is granulated and the ring is made of beads – hollow spherical beads of red gold with light granulation alternating with smooth resin beads of the same size, separated by discs of dark blue faience. Below the central gold bead a band with a granulated spiral pattern is soldered. Seven short strands of gold, carnelian and blue glass beads hang from this, the strands ending alternately with pomegranate and drop-shaped beads.

In another earring (397) a falcon with outspread wings serves as connector between fastener and ring. The gold ring, decorated on the outside with notched

392–394 Amulet with the serpent-goddess Weret-heqau suckling the king, richly ornamented ring, and double ring

strands of beads that end in pendants in the form of papyrus umbels and lilies, the heraldic plants of Upper and Lower Egypt.

Why Tutankhamun's mummy should have been laid to rest without earrings is unknown. The pierced ears of the mummy and signs of wear on the earrings found in the chests show that the young king did wear them – a custom that had become fashionable at the Egyptian court early in the 18th Dynasty. The examples illustrated (396–398) are all constructed in essentially the same manner. Two grooved tubes with

gold thread, encircles the tiny figure of the young ruler with gold sceptre and *uraeus*, carved from carnelian, which stands on the sign for 'jubilee celebration' between two *uraei* crowned with solar discs. Around the ring is a string of gold and coloured disc-shaped beads. The pendant part is made of strands of coloured beads with interspersed discs of granulated gold, with heart-shaped pendants.

395 Scarab pectoral of Tutankhamun
396–398 Earrings of Tutankhamun

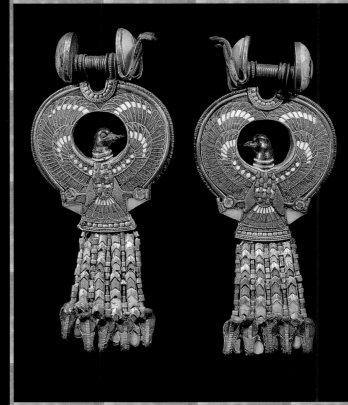

The New Kingdom

The dead king wore seven bracelets on the right forearm and six on the left; more were found wrapped within the mummy's bandages or elsewhere in the tomb. A noticeably large number of pieces have the scarab as a motif, for example a bracelet (12) with hieroglyphic elements of Tutankhamun's name. The large scarab (*kheper*) of lapis lazuli inlaid in gold cells stands on a basket (*neb*) inlaid with light blue glass, holding the royal cartouche with the throne name Neb-kheperu-Re between its forelegs. The bead bracelet is attached by hinge fastenings on either side of the beetle. Elongated beads of gold, electrum, lapis lazuli and alabaster, round beads of glass and carnelian, and smooth and granulated gold rings are symmetrically patterned between narrow bands of gold and framed by strands of gold beads.

Apparently surprised by the necropolis guards, the thieves who penetrated Tutankhamun's tomb fled, dropping a number of heavy gold rings, simple signet rings and also double rings, wrapped in a piece of cloth. The cartouches on one of these double rings (394) show, in gold on a dark blue ground, two manifestations of the god Thoth facing each other: on the left as a baboon squatting on a plinth, on the right in human form with an ibis-head and with a sceptre in the right hand. Both are crowned with a lunar disc and sickle. Below the cartouches, on the shoulder, a baboon is engraved in an attitude of adoration. Some of the fifteen rings from Tutankhamun's tomb have three-dimensional motifs on the bezel. A particularly fine example is a triple ring (393) on which the lapis lazuli scarab in full relief wears the *atef*-crown flanked by two *uraei* and pushes the moon barque before it. Behind it the ascending Horus falcon unfolds its wings protectively. Cloisonné lotus flowers and poppy buds are soldered on to

399 Dagger with an iron blade

the gold base; their stems form the basis of the ring's shoulder. Engraved on the inner side is the throne name of Tutankhamun, described as 'beloved of Thoth'.

Tutankhamun's mummy was buried with two daggers, one with an iron blade (399), the other with a blade of tempered gold. The sheath of the gold dagger (400) is decorated on the front with a feather pattern in cloisonné technique, and on the back (401) with relief ornament beaten and chased in gold foil. The top rim has a line of inscription praising the king as 'the great god, strong arm, bestowed with life'. Below a band of spiral decoration are hunting scenes: a leaping ibex is attacked by a lion; a dog has jumped on a bull calf and bites its tail; a leopard and a lion both fall on an ibex; a dog sinks its teeth into a bull, while a calf runs away with a backward-turned head. Stylised plants fill the gaps and the tip of the sheath. The motifs and techniques

400–401 Sheath for gold-bladed dagger
402 Vulture pectoral of Tutankhamun
403 Scarab pectoral with Isis and Nephthys

of this masterpiece of goldsmith's work suggest a Near-Eastern or Aegean origin, or the work of foreign goldsmiths in the pharaoh's service.

Distinctive Features of Tutankhamun's Jewellery
Individual pieces from Tutankhamun's treasure are still marked by the characteristic style of the Amarna period, with the grace, expressive power and colour of the art of the time of Akhenaten and Nefertiti. The gold relief panels of the statue shrine (407), their intimate scenes, so full of lustre and sensuous charm

name, it appears in ever-new variations to symbolise and guarantee the rebirth of the dead king, who wishes to ascend to the heavens from the underworld, reborn like the sun.

Apart from the abundant use of scarabs, there is also another innovation in the design of the jewellery. Many of the pectorals no longer hang from chains but from luxurious and ornate broad bands, with counterweights of the most diverse forms. Several pieces (379, 383, 397–398) are made of red gold, an invention of the Amarna period. Copper, which

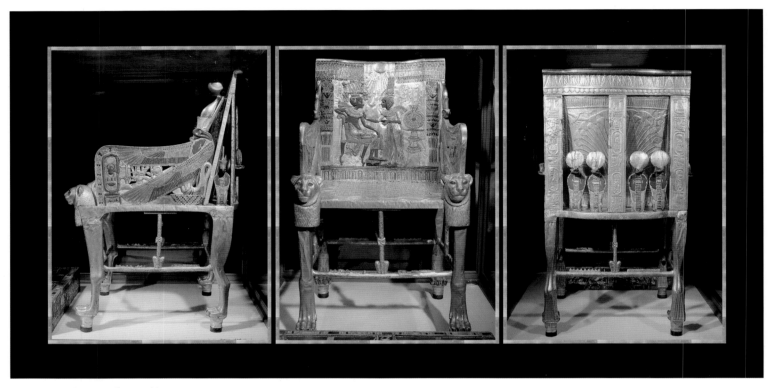

404–406 Throne of Tutankhamun

but nonetheless retaining a symbolic significance that contributes to the regeneration ritual, fall completely within this tradition. In a related scene on the backrest of the throne (405) the *Aten* sun-disc appears over the royal couple, bestowing life and well-being with its rays; the inscriptions on the back still use the old names of Tutankhaten and Ankhes-en-pa-Aten. Unless such pieces came from the king's childhood or the early years of his reign, they came from workshops that continued to work in the style of the Amarna period. On the whole, however, Tutankhamun's jewellery was made after the restoration of the cult of the old gods, by goldsmiths who had adopted the traditional formality of the restoration period.

The scarab makes a noticeably frequent appearance in Tutankhamun's jewellery. As part of his throne

oxidises and therefore turns the gold a darker shade, is added to the molten metal.

With a few exceptions, Tutankhamun's jewellery seems over-ornate. The subtlety and balance of form and colour of the masterpieces of the 12th Dynasty are almost never achieved, and the real significance of the find is the fact that it has provided us with an almost complete inventory of a royal tomb from a significant period in Egyptian history.

The Ramesside Period
At the end of the Amarna period the pharaonic kingdom was in severe crisis. This led to a military take-over by General Haremhab, who after his accession to the throne designated as his successor an officer named Paramessu. Under the name of

The Ramesside Period

Ramesses I the latter founded the 19th Dynasty, whose greatest days are associated with the names of Sethos I and Ramesses II.

While the practical task was to rebuild the kingdom of Thutmosis III, psychologically and spiritually it was a matter of appeasing the gods angered by Akhenaten's coup, and this required a colossal temple-building programme. Impressive as the constructional achievements of the period are, evidence of goldsmith's work from the 19th and 20th Dynasties is very rare, as the content of the tombs was plundered by robbers.

Discoveries of Treasure at Zagazig

During the building of a railway line in the Eastern Delta in 1906, silver and gold vessels were discovered at Tell Basta near Zagazig, the former Bubastis. A few of the objects from this find found their way through the antiquities market to the museums of Berlin and New York; the larger pieces, however, were saved for

407 Tutankhamun and Ankhes-en-pa-Amun in a papyrus thicket

the Egyptian Museum in Cairo. In the same year, not far from the first site, workers came upon a second hoard which, thanks to the vigilance of the Antiquities Service, was taken to Cairo in its entirety. These treasures presumably came from the temple of Bubastis, and may have been hidden during the turmoil at the end of the Ramesside period.

From the first find comes a group of three vessels of gold and silver with the inscription 'Atumemto-neb, royal cellar-master, pure of hands', among them a silver vase (408–409) with a gold handle in the form of a he-goat standing upright. The animal was cast in two halves and soldered together, with horns, ears and nose ring added. While the body of the vessel is decorated with rows of embossed chevrons, the shoulder and tall cylindrical neck are covered with engraved and punched decoration. The upper part has groups of fighting animals and a winged griffin, separated by palm trees, motifs which, like the

handle, betray foreign influence; below these are depicted scenes from the marshes of the Delta.

The finest item from the second Zagazig find is a pair of bracelets of Ramesses II (411), possibly a gift from the king to adorn a cult statue. The two bracelets of solid gold each consist of two halves, connected by a hinge and a rod fastener. On the bowed upper side a curved piece of lapis lazuli represents the body of a duck, which is provided with two backward-turned heads and a fanned-out tail in gold. The gold setting of the stone and the border of the bracelet are sumptuously decorated with granulation and plain, braided, and beaded wire. Between the birds' heads and the hinge is the royal cartouche with the name of Ramesses II, embossed in the gold foil.

Finds of Jewellery in the Serapeum of Saqqara

For roughly 1,400 years, from the days of Amenophis III, the Serapeum was the final resting-place of the holy Apis bulls. They were mummified there and buried in sarcophagi, and new galleries had constantly to be added. In 1851 Auguste Mariette began to investigate the subterranean crypts hewn in the rock. He found galleries several hundred yards long whose floors and ceilings were once covered with fine limestone. In chambers on either side stood twenty-four huge sarcophagi of polished red and black granite dating from the 7th to the 1st century BC, every one of which had been looted (108).

During his second expedition in 1852, beneath a piece of rock from the collapsed ceiling of one of the older galleries, Mariette came upon a wooden coffin with the intact mummy of Prince Khaemwese, a son of Ramesses II who was high priest of Ptah at Memphis. The face was covered with a gold mask, and around the neck lay two gold chains with amulets

408–409 Silver vessel with goat handle of gold and engraved decoration

of green feldspar and red jasper. A gold falcon with outspread wings in cloisonné protected the breast. Khaemwese had had the gallery constructed for the burial of twenty-eight Apis bulls and had himself buried nearby. In the intact tomb of two Apis bulls, one could still see in the sand on the floor the footprints of the priests who 3,000 years before had laid the sacred bull to rest. The reliefs on the walls show Ramesses II and Khaemwese making a funerary sacrifice before the holy Apis-Osiris.

Two black painted wooden coffins contained funerary offerings. In the first were found amulets of carnelian and serpentine, and also numerous small gold plates; in the second, together with other offerings, was a pectoral with the cartouche of Ramesses II (414). The rectangular silver frame, with

410 Signet ring of Ramesses II

the throne name of Ramesses II stands out against a gold background. Between the cartouche and the heads of the guardian goddesses a falcon with a ram's head spreads out its wings. Falcon and vulture hold rings of eternity (*shen*) in their talons. The front of the pectoral is rather sombre in effect, as most of the inlay has either decayed or fallen out. On the silver reverse the motifs of the front have engraved detail: instead of the ram's head, the falcon here has a human head with a short beard.

From the same Apis tomb comes a finely worked falcon pectoral with ram's head and horizontally outspread wings, and eternity rings in the extended talons (413). The ram's head, which faces upward, is soldered onto the falcon body. The feathers in cloisonné were inlaid with lapis lazuli, turquoise and

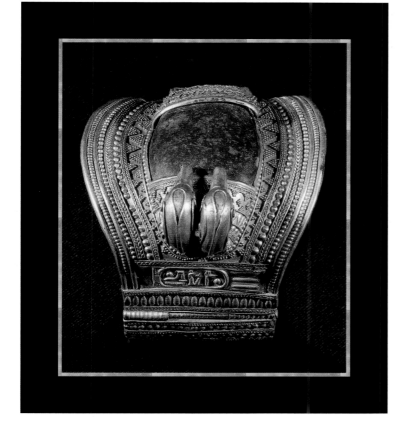

411 Bracelet of Ramesses II with a central motif in the form of a double-headed duck and rich granulation

412 Ramesses II as the young sun-god seated on a lotus flower

its customary cavetto cornice at the top, is inlaid with glass of various colours and blue faience, and the space within is tightly packed with motifs: two Djed pillars flank the guardian goddesses, the cobra of Lower Egypt with its coiled tail, and the vulture of Upper Egypt, the tips of whose wings enclose the horizontal royal cartouche. Framed in silver and blue,

carnelian, only traces of which arev still visible today. The gold reverse has chased detail.

A gold pendant of unknown origin has the portrait of Ramesses II as the young sun-god rising from an opened lotus flower (412). The squatting figure with hands on knees is highly stylised, and only the head has any detail. It was beaten from gold foil in two parts, which were filled and soldered together. The *uraeus* on the forehead and the solar disc on the head were worked separately and soldered on. A depression running from the top of the head to the neck held the customary child's side-lock. The lotus flower and the collar with its counterweight at the back are in cloisonné, inlaid with coloured glass, most of which is now missing, and soldered to the body.

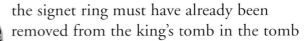

On the oval bezel of a solid cast ring of electrum (410) are hieroglyphs in deep negative relief with much finely-executed detail, which read: 'beloved of Amun-Re, Ramessu'. Apart from a small scratch on the upper edge of the bezel, which was caused by the removal of material for analysis, the ring is perfectly preserved and shows no signs of use. This suggests that it belonged among the funerary equipment of the king.

The tomb of Ramesses II in the Valley of the Kings was plundered soon after his burial. Around 1000 BC, the high priest Pinodjem ordered the king's mummy to be wrapped in new bandages and transferred to the hiding-place provided for the royal mummies near Deir el-Bahari. When it was examined after its discovery in 1881, no jewellery was found on it, so the signet ring must have already been removed from the king's tomb in the tomb robberies of the 20th Dynasty.

In several representations in her tomb in the Valley of the Queens, Nefertari, the favourite wife of Ramesses II, is shown wearing the vulture crown, the jewelled headdress of a 'great royal wife' or goddess (415). Actual examples of such crowns have not been preserved; they must, however, have consisted of plain or inlaid gold elements assembled in such a way as to produce a flexible head-covering. Enveloping the wig, the vulture crown is surmounted by a circlet, which itself normally supported a solar disc and two tall gold feathers.

413 Falcon pectoral with ram's head

The Jewellery of Sethos II and Queen Ta-usret

After the death of Sethos II, his wife Ta-usret acted as regent for the young heir to the throne, and after his early death she reigned in her own name for about another two years, until General Sethnakht, the founder of the 20th Dynasty, ascended the throne. Like Hatshepsut, Ta-usret adopted a royal titulary and as a reigning pharaoh had a rock-cut tomb prepared for her in the Valley of the Kings.

In 1908, Edward Ayrton, who was working for the American Theodore M. Davis on a dig in the Valley of the Kings, discovered a small shaft tomb; it was filled with hardened mud, presumably washed down into the shaft after robbers had opened the tomb in ancient times. Near a decayed miniature coffin a number of pieces of jewellery were found, among them some inscribed with the names of Sethos II and his wife Ta-usret. What remained unanswered was whether this was a cache of plunder from the tomb of Queen Ta-usret herself, or perhaps the burial of a daughter of the royal couple who had died in infancy and for whom the parents had provided the jewellery.

414 Pectoral with the name of Ramesses II

415 Nefertari with gold vulture crown

The New Kingdom

The floral diadem (417) has the names of the royal couple chased on the inner side of the petals. The sixteen gold flowers were pressed in a mould and very simply attached to a narrow strip of gold foil, two pieces of wire being soldered onto each of the hemispherical pistils, threaded through two holes drilled through the flower and the circlet, and then bent outward on the inside.

A pair of gold pendant earrings (416) has a fastening like those on Tutankhamun's earrings (396 – 398), made up of two grooved tubes that pass through the pierced ear, the one sliding into the other. At the end of each is soldered a domed disc, the one plain, the other beaten into the form of a flower, every other petal being inscribed with the name of Sethos II. From the tubes hangs a trapeze-shaped element, again with the name of Sethos II. Beneath this hang ribbed seed-capsules from stalks fitted with eyelets, three large alternating with four small. The proportions of these pendant earrings are inharmonious, and the work itself is quite rough: the soldering of the hemispherical parts of the seed-capsules are clearly visible.

While clearing the tomb, Ayrton found numerous beads and pendants, which have now been strung as two necklaces; one is at the Metropolitan Museum in New York, the other at the Egyptian Museum in Cairo (418). The beads alternate with pendants in the form of cornflowers. Both are made of artfully braided and soldered rings of wire – this delicate necklace is the earliest example of filigree work.

Jewellery of the 20th Dynasty

The son of Sethnakht, the founder of the dynasty, Ramesses III modelled himself so closely on the example of Ramesses II that he copied his throne name and mortuary temple. This last significant ruler of the New Kingdom fought successfully to defend Egypt against the double threat from the Libyans and the 'Sea Peoples'.

In the following period he and his successors, who all took the birth name Ramesses, had to contend more and more with internal political difficulties. Officials acted increasingly independently, and

416 Pendant earrings of Sethos II

417 Floral diadem with the names of Sethos II and Queen Ta-usret

418 Filigree chain with cornflower pendants

incompetence and corruption endangered the provisioning of the population. The consequences were famine, strikes, rebellion and the breakdown of law and order. Tomb robbers were able to plunder the Theban necropolis undisturbed, and when legal inquiries were finally organised, corruption proved to have penetrated to the very highest levels of the administration itself.

Ramesses XI, the last of the Ramessides, was in the end the ruler of Egypt in name only. In the northern part of the kingdom, real power was in the hands of the vizier Smendes, high priest of Amun at Tanis; in Thebes in Upper Egypt, Herihor was able to accumulate the offices of viceroy of Kush, generalissimo, vizier and high priest of Amun, and then even to lay claim to kingly status and introduce a new calendar.

With the economic and political decline of the late Ramesside period came an artistic deterioration clearly visible in the wall paintings of the rock-cut tombs in the Valley of the Kings. Nor are the few surviving pieces of jewellery of a particularly high standard. One outstanding example that runs against this trend is a sumptuous pair of pendant earrings with the name of Ramesses XI (419); these were found by Mariette on the decayed mummy of a woman of the royal household who was buried in a sarcophagus beneath the inner sanctum of the temple of Osiris at Abydos.

The Hildesheim Museum has a bracelet with Herihor's name (420), which continues the tradition of the rigid hinged bracelets of the early 18th Dynasty. Examples of this type of bracelet with a central motif appeared for the first time among Tutankhamun's jewels, and later in the find of jewellery from the temple of Bubastis (411). The bracelet proper is made from three bands of gold, linked by five vertical strips. Small half-cylinders of gold foil are soldered on the outside at close intervals, pre-shaped pieces of glazed faience being set between to produce a geometric pattern. The centre motif is framed by the same decoration. A turquoise, left in its irregular natural shape, is fixed to the gold plate with gold nails, the unoccupied surface being filled with motifs in gold cloisonné with coloured inlay. Still recognisable is a coiled *uraeus* with the remains of dark blue frit on the flared breast and red carnelian in the coils, while the crushed gold setting on the other

side can no longer clearly be made out. In the uneven gold on the back are roughly inscribed hieroglyphs: 'First prophet of Amun-Re, king of the gods, Herihor, the blessed [the departed]'. This designation, together with the somewhat fragile construction of the bracelet, suggests that it was perhaps an item of funerary jewellery.

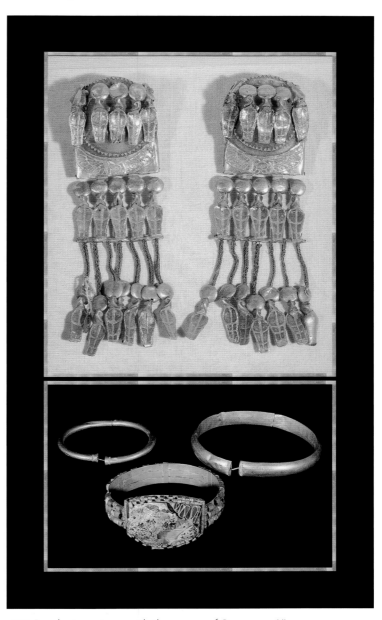

419 Pendant earrings with the name of Ramesses XI

420 Bracelet with name of Herihor

The Late Dynastic Period

With the end of the Ramesside period around 1100 BC came the disruption of political unity and the loss of the Nubian and Near-Eastern territories – typical features of the so-called Intermediate Periods – that signal the end of the New Kingdom. Like the two earlier Intermediate Periods, which followed the fall of the Old and Middle Kingdoms and brought with them poverty and cultural decline, this Third Intermediate Period was a consequence of internal processes of dissolution. At the same time, however, it was part of a more wide-ranging pattern of collapse that affected all the Mediterranean and Near-Eastern states during the transition from the Bronze Age to the Iron Age. After the death of Ramesses XI, Smendes ascended the throne and founded the 21st Dynasty. The new royal house took pains to maintain the traditions of the Ramesside period even if it no longer ruled from the 'city of Ramesses' but from Tanis, the Zoan of the Bible, thirteen miles further north. In the south, the Theban rulers had won autonomy and established the 'theocracy of Amun', in which the all-powerful divine ruler directed every activity by his oracular pronouncements. Formally, the unity of the state was preserved.

421 Pendant
422 Snake-headed bracelet

The Late Dynastic Period

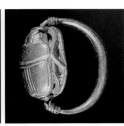

423–425 Scarab ring of Mendes, with two gods

In Upper Egypt dates were still defined by the regnal years of those who ruled over the north, after Herihor himself had given up the new dating system of his 'era of rebirth'. When the high priests of Amun on occasion adopted the title of king, they seem to have done this with the approval of the rightful pharaoh. The houses that ruled in Tanis and Thebes were linked by blood, and there were close and amicable relations between the two centres. This time, unlike the earlier Intermediate Periods, internal order in the land of Egypt was preserved.

While there is little to show for the building activity of the period, the goldsmith's art underwent an astonishing revival. The funerary equipment commissioned by the kings at Tanis and the high priests at Thebes leaves one in no doubt that their workshops not only continued the best of the old traditions but were also capable of creating new types of jewellery in masterly designs. The uncluttered forms of the cloisonné work in cool blues and greens are enchanting. One now rarely finds rings and earrings, but rather heavy collars of several rows of disc-shaped gold beads, and pectorals and bracelets from which hang cascades of fine chains terminating in finely executed blossoms. Hinge fastenings are much in evidence, now also being used for the attachment of pendants. The art of metal casting reaches its high point.

The Jewellery of the High Priests of Thebes
Pinodjem I became high priest at Thebes at about the same time as Smendes came to the throne. He was given Smendes' daughter Henuttaui in marriage and took the title of king. When he died, he was laid to rest in a coffin of Thutmosis I. Among the offerings were a pectoral (426), which has his throne name, Kheper-kha-Re, flanked by two bees, the heraldic emblem of Upper Egypt, over the sign for gold. Bees and hieroglyphs are partly in embossed and finely chased gold foil and partly in cloisonné with lapis

lazuli inlays, as is the rectangular pattern of the frame. The triple-stranded chain is made up of tiny grooved rings and has embossed pendants in the form of hexagonal calyces. From the lower edge of the pectoral hang nine chains with the same blossoms soldered at their ends.

Pinodjem II ordered that the royal mummies that had been moved several times already as a consequence of the plundering of their tombs should be brought to Thebes, together with the remains of their equipment, and placed in a rock tomb in the cliffs south of Deir el-Bahari. He also had himself buried in the same place, where his mummy remained undisturbed until local villagers found its hiding place in 1871. Precious items stolen from the tomb were offered around in Luxor for years, but Maspero eventually identified the robbers and was able to rescue almost all this enormous hoard for the Cairo Museum.

On the mummy of Pinodjem II was found an identical pair of bracelets of the rigid type (427). They are almost circular in cross-section, each being made up of two half-circles with symmetrical decoration. A piece of wire hidden by a bead of lapis lazuli serves as a hinge; one end is soldered, the other passed through an opening. The fastening opposite consists of a hook that engages in a slot and is held by a pin pushed through it. Near the clasp two small rings hold a further ring on which two types of chain are hung, three of cylindrical beads of gold, lapis lazuli and carnelian, the other two of grooved gold rings. The strands of beads end in hexagonal gold calyces with stone inlay, the gold chains in similar blossoms of lapis lazuli. The flower pattern decoration is repeated all round the bracelet between soldered bands of gold, and is inlaid in lapis lazuli and carnelian to lively and colourful effect. The construction of the bracelet is reminiscent of Tutankhamun's bracelets, while the fastening is similar to that on Herihor's (420). The flower pendants, however, are typical of the 21st Dynasty and were fashionable in Tanis as well as Thebes.

The Royal Necropolis of Tanis
One result of the high incidence of tomb robbery in the Valley of the Kings in the late Ramesside period was that the new rulers in Tanis chose a better protected location for their tombs, in the temple

complex of their capital. In the temple of the 'Northern Thebes' the same triad of gods was revered as in the south: Amun, his wife Mut and the child-god Khons-Neferhotep. The layout of the shrine also follows the great example of Karnak. It was within the protection of its massive surrounding wall that the kings of the 21st and 22nd Dynasties built their 'houses of eternity'. The limited space on the hill where the town was built did not, however, allow the building of extended funerary complexes. The constructions above ground have not survived. The chambers sunk into the ground, built of limestone blocks, were covered with stone slabs and decorated with wall reliefs; the building materials were taken from the nearby 'City of Ramesses,' which now served as a quarry. Even the coffins of some of the earlier kings were usurped.

Given the modest extent and the inferior construction of these royal tombs, the wealth of gold and silver grave-goods is surprising. The high humidity in the Nile Delta allowed the use only of permanent materials for funeral equipment. Furniture, chests, wooden statues, war-chariots and textiles, even the wooden shrines around the sarcophagi – all subject to decay – had to be forgone, but there was an abundance of vessels in precious metal, found in the burials at Tanis in quantities that are unmatched elsewhere in Egypt.

A French expedition under Pierre Montet began digging in Tanis in 1929. Montet had earlier uncovered in Byblos, among other significant discoveries, a group of royal tombs from the period around 1800 BC, and a few of the finds proved to be presents from pharaohs of the Middle Kingdom to the rulers of this Phoenician city. In order to learn more about the relationship between Egypt and the Near East, he turned to a site in the north-east of the Nile Valley, the 998-acre (400-hectare) hill-settlement of Tanis, which rose 115ft (35m) above the flat Delta.

Years passed with no striking discoveries, while in the barren desert, in very taxing conditions, the remains of the great temple were cleared of sand and rubble. Perseverance was finally rewarded when, during Montet's eleventh season in 1939, beneath brick ruins, the diggers came upon the blocks of a

426 Pectoral of the priest-king Pinodjem I
427 Bracelet of Pinodjem II

The Discoveries at Tanis

The huge settlement on the hill of San el-Hagar in the Eastern Delta had for a long time been thought to be the location of the 'city of Ramesses', because of the many inscriptions of Ramesses II on obelisks and architectural elements found there. In the meantime, Pi-Ramessu had been located near Qantu, from where the kings of the 21st and 22nd Dynasties had taken building materials and monuments for their capital of Tanis.

In 1929 a French expedition under Pierre Montet started to dig at Tanis. Year after year they toiled in the difficult conditions of the barren desert, clearing sand and rubble from around the buildings.

Their perseverance was to be rewarded when on 25 February 1939, during the eleventh season of the dig, they came across the roof of a burial chamber under brick ruins inside the outer walls of the temple

The gold mask of Amenemope, damaged by grave robbers

The entrance to the tomb of Osorkon II is uncovered by the Montet expedition

dozen precious metal vessels are among the treasures found at Tanis.

Many of the precious finds were removed to the Cairo Museum, but the imminent outbreak of the Second World War meant that many lesser items were left on site in sealed magazines. These were broken into early in 1943 and the objects they contained, such as *ushabti* figurines, were dispersed in the antiquities market.

The gold mask under the silver coffin of Sheshonq II

Collar and pectoral of the mummy of Sheshonq II

The French Egyptologist Pierre Montet in front of the silver coffin of Psusennes I

Right and below right: Ruins of Tanis: the temple of Amun and the royal necropolis

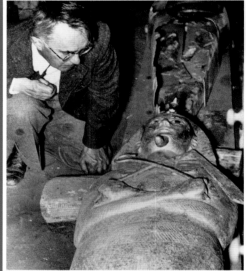

of Amun. The burial place of the Tanite kings had been found. Within the tombs were found the burials of six kings and high dignitaries of the 21st and 22nd Dynasties, three of them remaining untouched since the burial. But even the plundered tombs of those whose mummies had been transferred in ancient times contained valuable jewellery. Four gold masks, two silver coffins and two

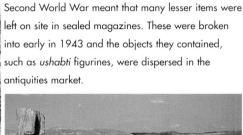

tomb covering. One stone was missing, and through this hole made by the grave robbers one of the archaeologists lowered himself into the small chamber. In the half-darkness he deciphered the inscriptions on the wall reliefs. This was the funeral complex of Osorkon II, who ruled in Tanis as the fourth king of the 22nd Dynasty.

Openings in the wall led from the chamber into a little labyrinth of subterranean rooms, containing plundered sarcophagi and a few objects scattered in the muddy deposits.

The archaeologists' disappointment over the robbery of the new-found tomb evaporated when a second tomb of similar type was discovered very close by, its 66ft-square (20-square) covering still intact. A block was removed, and Montet himself went down

into the chamber to read the name Psusennes I, a king of the 21st Dynasty, on the wall.

The floor was covered with canopic jars, *ushabti* figures and equipment, but Montet's attention was caught by a silver coffin with a falcon's head, whose lid had been slightly moved. Gold shimmered through the gap. When the coffin was opened, in the presence of King Farouk, it became clear that it was not Psusennes' mummy inside but instead that of Sheshonq II, a ruler of the 22nd Dynasty, who had been laid to rest a century later in the antechamber of his predecessor Psusennes.

The Intact Burial Chamber of Psusennes I
The wall of Psusennes' burial chamber was still completely covered by a painted layer of stucco, the

entrance being barred by a huge granite block – part of a broken obelisk, which the excavators were able to remove using the bronze rollers that had been used to put it in place. It was so humid in the small, deep burial chamber that water dripped from the walls. The front part was filled with funerary equipment, a bronze offering table, vessels, implements, canopic jars, and hundreds of *ushabti* funerary statuettes. But what caught the eye was the gleaming gold of the king's cult vessels and tableware.

In the back part of the chamber stood a large sarcophagus of pink granite, its seal intact. The lid was raised to reveal a black granite sarcophagus, and in the space between the sarcophagi were weapons and sceptres, among them a bronze sword of which only the gold-foil-covered hilt survived, finely chased with a falcon's head on the pommel (431). The inner of the two sarcophagi, both of which came from earlier burials, contained a silver coffin (428).

Unlike the re-used granite sarcophagi, the mummy-shaped silver coffin was made for Psusennes himself. The facial features are stylised and reminiscent of royal portraits of the Ramesside period. The god-beard and folded arms holding the crook and scourge crossed over the breast represent the divine figure of the king as transformed into Osiris. Around the forehead is a band of thinly beaten gold foil, above which rises a gold *uraeus*. The eyebrows and eyes are inlaid in glass. The beard of beaten silver was worked separately, like the silver royal insignia held in the hands, and attached to the chin with rivets.

The lid and base of the coffin were beaten out and riveted together. The stripes of the royal *nemes* head-cloth, the broad floral collar, the bracelets, the hieroglyphic inscriptions and the protective deities that envelop the body with their wings, are all chased. On the interior base of the coffin, the goddess Nut envelops the dead king with winged arms outspread. An inscription on the lid reads: 'Oh my mother Nut, spread your wings over me. Grant that I should be like the eternal and tireless circumpolar stars.'

Montet's team had discovered the entrance to the tomb of Psusennes I on 15 February 1940, and two weeks later the lid of the silver coffin was raised.

The mortal remains of the pharaoh were covered by

428 Silver coffin of King Psusennes I

Pages 206–207: 429–430 Gold mask of Psusennes I

a gold mask and a sheet of gold foil over 3ft (1m) in length, chased with protective formulae and representations of gods. Of the mummy there remained only a few bones, covered in jewellery: necklaces of gold and lapis lazuli, three gold collars 'of honour', which had fallen apart into hundreds of disc-shaped beads, six inlaid pectorals, twelve bracelets on the left arm, ten on the right, four more elsewhere, thirty amulets; also a gold incision plate covering the embalming cut, finger caps, toe caps and sandals of gold that had once protected and adorned the royal mummy. Such a find could not be kept secret, and it was protected by teams of guards day and night, to thwart any attempt at robbery. Within a few weeks the treasures were recovered and on 3 May they were transferred to the Cairo Museum.

The gold mask of Psusennes I (429–430), with its dignified and remote expression, is the most perfect of the four masks discovered at Tanis. It is the only one made in two parts, the face-mask framed by the royal *nemes* head-cloth and the floral collar, and then the continuation of the head-cloth over the back of the head. At the join, the parts are lapped and riveted together. Beaten from extremely thin gold foil, finely chased but not polished, so that light is reflected in a gentle glow on the surface, this mask is a masterpiece of the Tanite goldsmith's art. This mastery of craft skills can be seen too in the *uraeus* which, like the god-beard, is worked separately, assembled from three parts and fastened with rivets, and in the inlays of glass and lapis lazuli.

'Greetings, fair of face, lord of vision… fair of face among the gods!' This is how in the Book of the Dead (Chapter 151) 'the embalmer' Anubis addresses the deceased prepared for the journey to the afterlife. The mask surrounded the head and breast of the mummy as a protective covering and an everlasting portrait, its gentle modelling preserving the king's

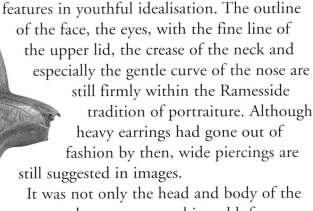

431 Sword-hilt

features in youthful idealisation. The outline of the face, the eyes, with the fine line of the upper lid, the crease of the neck and especially the gentle curve of the nose are still firmly within the Ramesside tradition of portraiture. Although heavy earrings had gone out of fashion by then, wide piercings are still suggested in images.

It was not only the head and body of the mummy that were covered in gold, for even the fingers and toes needed an everlasting protective envelope. Artfully bound, they were covered with gold caps that were chased with the outline of the nails. The feet were shod in gold sandals for the long journey to the hereafter. Before the body was embalmed, the priests removed the brain through the nasal cavity. The viscera were removed through a long incision on the left of the lower abdomen and replaced with a filling. The incision was closed with thread and covered with a layer of wax, faience and a gold plate. Psusennes' mummy had such a covering made of gold foil with embossed and chased motifs and inscriptions, perforated at all four corners and stitched onto the bandages above the abdominal incision. The central motif is a *wedjat*-eye, the eye of Horus, injured in a fight with Seth and restored by Thoth, which became the quintessential symbol of protection from bodily harm. Like the eye of Horus, the pharaoh's body was supposed to be healed of its wound. On left and right stand the four tutelary deities of the viscera, who will protect the deceased against hunger and thirst. The silver coffin and gold mask of Psusennes both have broad collars in fine chasing which, though so common in the New Kingdom, was however missing from the opulent jewellery of the mummy. There were instead three multi-stranded gold collars 'of honour'. Images of the presentation of 'gold of honour' to deserving officials are frequent, and a relief at Tanis shows Psusennes at just such a ceremony. The

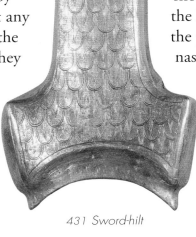

432 Ba-bird

decorations shown are astonishingly similar to those found in his tomb. These were the first to be found, and show the worth of such jewellery, which since the Ramesside period had increasingly also been used to adorn the images and boats of the gods.

Around the mummy's neck lay a collar of over five thousand gold discs, weighing over 18lb (8kg) (433–434). It still has five strands, although the outer strand no longer exists. The clasps that fasten the rows of beads are hidden by a flat box-like closure with narrow rounded ends. The long sides, with six holes each, have been lost since its discovery.

The front of this closure has a winged scarab and beneath this, framed by friezes of *uraei*, the throne and birth names of Psusennes inlaid in lapis lazuli. On the reverse is the same design in delicate engraving. A thin rod passes through eyelets at the bottom of the closure to support the interlocking eyelets from which hangs a cascade of finely-woven gold wire, the chains branching out successively to end in flower pendants of beaten gold foil.

The winged scarab, in ancient Egypt a symbol of the rising sun and of rebirth, accompanies the king on the journey to resurrection. Psusennes took no fewer than four scarab pendants with him to his grave. Almost identical in form, they are distinguished only by their inlays, the decoration of the wings and the inscriptions engraved on the underside. The sayings chosen were intended to guarantee the king's continued life by identifying him with the sun-god and enabling him to move at will in the afterlife as he had done on earth. 'My heart is Re's, Re's heart is my heart', declares the inscription on the scarab of carved granite (435). Mounted in a gold setting, it spreads out its narrow wings. Their vertical striped decoration is of coloured stone inlaid between soldered strips of gold. Rather than the customary solar disc, the scarab pushes a gold cartouche with the king's name 'Psusennes, beloved of Amun' in coloured inlay on the front. At the other end of the beetle is a *shen* ring, the symbol of eternity, which encloses a solar disc in the shape of a domed carnelian.

The scarab motif had appeared in jewellery since the time of Amenophis III, and achieved greater significance in the funerary treasure of Tutankhamun. In Tanis, reduced to its essentials, it is heightened in

433–434 'Gold of honour' of Psusennes I, back and front

artistic effect. While the jewellery of Tutankhamun's time often seems over-ornate, the clarity of line and the harmony of colours here are impressive.

In the two pectorals with their shrine-like frames, too, the course of the sun symbolises the ever-recurring theme of rebirth and life after death. Like an open gateway, the frame affords a view of the scene within. In one of the pectorals (436–437), the kneeling Isis and Nephthys support the wings of a scarab that pushes the royal cartouche and the winged sun up towards the hieroglyph for the heavens (*pt*)

conjured up the underworld of Osiris by setting Chapter 100 of the Book of the Dead in a vignette:

> Saying, to perfect the deceased and to allow him to descend to Re's boat with those who are in his entourage. I have ferried the phoenix (Benu) to the east, and Osiris to Busiris.

On the right of the composition, designated by his throne and birth names, the king rows the phoenix to the east, towards the rising sun; on the left he rows Osiris to Busiris, the god's home in the Delta.

Winged deities envelop the deceased pharaoh and

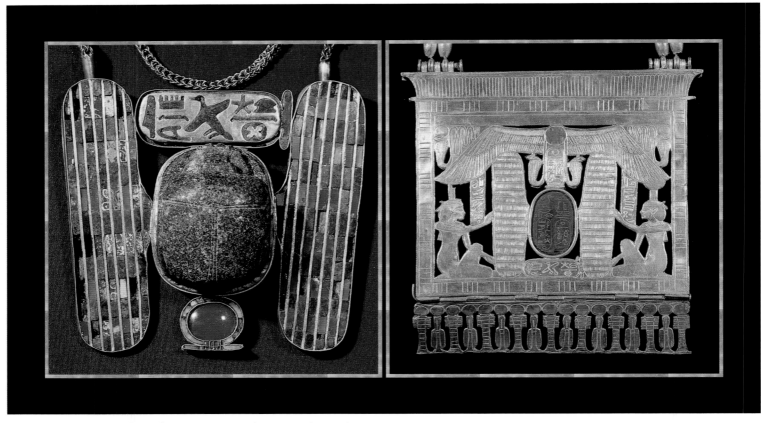

435–436 Scarab pendant of Psusennes I, and reverse of scarab pectoral with Isis and Nephthys

beneath the cavetto cornice.

The second pectoral is a variation on the same theme: assisted by *uraei* and *wedjat*-eyes, Osiris' sisters protect the rising sun with outspread wings. Above a row of Djed pillars, a symbol of Osiris, it rises from the underworld in the form of a scarab to fly up to the hieroglyph for the heavens (*pt*). The king's cartouches with his throne and birth names serve as wings – sun-god and king have become one – and *shen*-rings guarantee the eternal cycle.

The strict composition of this cloisonné openwork derives its charm from a basal strip attached with hinges. In this very restricted space the artist has

protect him on his journey to rebirth. Finely chased, they cover the coffin with their wings or lie over breast and shoulders as pendants or collars. In the funeral equipment of Psusennes I, small amulets in the form of shoulder collars replaced the actual jewellery. Made of embossed and chased gold foil, they represent Horus-Behedeti, the god of the heavens, in the form of a falcon, the goddess of Upper Egypt in the form of a vulture, and the guardian goddesses in the double form of vulture and snake. The human-headed falcon with a *uraeus* on his

437 Scarab pectoral with Isis and Nephthys

The Late Dynastic Period

forehead (432) embodies the soul-bird (*ba*), which can move unhindered between the body in the sealed burial chamber and the outside world. All these winged creatures carry rings of eternity in their claws, and like the broad collars, they have counterweights between their wing tips. They were fixed in their ordained positions on the mummy's bindings by eyelets soldered on to their backs.

Psusennes' funerary treasure includes twenty-six bracelets. One of the matching pairs, of the

of gold in a lapis lazuli inlay that goes round the outside of the bracelet:

> Long live the king of Upper and Lower Egypt, lord of both lands, Aa-kheper-Re, favoured by Amun, bestowed with life eternally. The son of Re, lord of manifestations, Psusennes-beloved-of-Amun, bestowed with life like Re eternally.

Two simple bracelets of a type not found elsewhere in royal jewellery bear dedicatory inscriptions by the royal wife. The bracelets are made in two halves,

438 Solid gold bracelet of Psusennes I

439–440 Rebus bracelet of Psusennes I

same type as the bracelets of the high priest Pinodjem (427), has 'East' and 'West' inscribed on either, meaning 'left' and 'right', but they were on the wrong arms. Each consists of two unequal parts, whose ends are pushed into each other. Made of thin gold foil, these hollow bracelets are very light. Decoration hides the soldered seams. Two bands of interlocking gold spirals on a blue background frame an inscription also

each consisting of seven hollow half-rings soldered together, smooth and ribbed alternately. On the inside of the third and fifth rings the following inscriptions are engraved:

> 'King, Lord of the Two Lands, first prophet of Amun-Re-king-of-the-gods, son of Re, Psusennes-beloved-of-Amun. Made [by the] first great royal wife of his majesty, mistress of both lands, Mut-nedj-met.

The Royal Necropolis of Tanis

On the left arm of the mummy was a solid gold bracelet (438) weighing almost 4lb (1.8kg); this is clearly too heavy to have been worn by Psusennes during his life. Inside the bracelet is the very finely engraved inscription:

> Speech of Amun-Re, king of the Gods: 'I grant you strength and courage, that you may strike the heads of your enemies'. The king of Upper and Lower Egypt, Aa-kheper-Re, the chosen of Amun, son of Re, lord of manifestations, first prophet of Amun-Re, king of the gods, Psusennes-beloved-of-Amun.

King of Upper and Lower Egypt, lord of both lands, lord of strength, first prophet of Amun-Re-king-of-the-gods, Psusennes-beloved-of-Amun, bestowed with life.

The hieroglyphs have inlays of coloured stone, some in mosaic-like arrangements of different colours, some in fine relief. The central motif is a distinctive *wedjat*-eye, making (together with a baboon) a rebus for 'king' in the epithet of Amun-Re 'king-of-kings'.

On the plain inner side, written in the opposite direction, are two finely chased royal titularies with the same beginning:

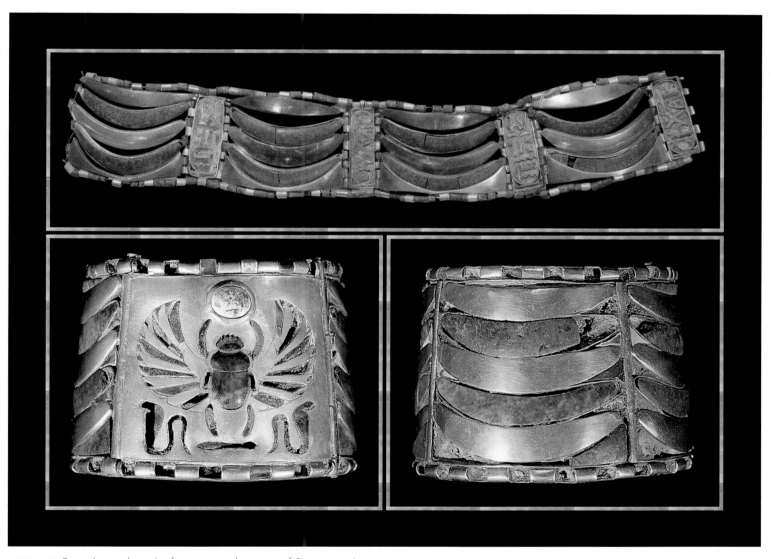

441–443 Bracelet and armlet from a matching set of Psusennes I

Its smaller counterpart on the right arm has the same blessing, but pronounced by Amun's wife, Mut.

One of the cylindrical bracelets was not made in two parts but beaten from a single piece of gold foil (439–440). On the outside of the bracelet, between two grooves inlaid with feldspar and without any other ornament, is an inscription in large and impressive hieroglyphs:

Long live the perfect god, with terrible arm, with courageous heart like Montu [the god of war] at his hour, the king of Upper and Lower Egypt Aa-kheper-Re, chosen by Amun, bestowed with life like Re eternally. Long live the perfect god, ruler of all joy, the lord of whom one can be proud, son of Re, Psusennes-beloved-of-Amun, who lives eternally.

A pair of armlets and a pair of bracelets make up an

The Late Dynastic Period

unusual matching set (441–443). The two identical armlets are more or less cylindrical, widening a little towards the bottom, and are made of two unequal parts, the smaller, a more or less square plate of gold, being incised with the throne name of King Aa-kheper-Re, inlaid with lapis lazuli and carnelian and chased. It is attached by hinges to the larger part, which is divided into three fields, each with the same decoration of alternating crescents of gold and lapis lazuli on a gold base, the first soldered to it and the second inlaid in gold cells.

The edges of the bracelet are of tubular beads, gold and lapis lazuli.

The plate that bears the name is both an amulet and an unusual piece of jewellery. The winged scarab with a solar disc fuses elements of the royal name with the symbol of the young sun-god, king and god becoming one. The scarab's wide-spread wings stand out from the gold ground, the

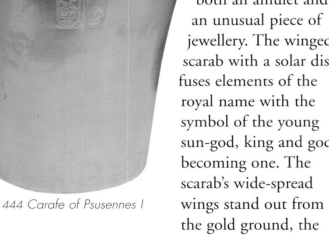

444 Carafe of Psusennes I

sun-drenched air, with geometrical rigour. The curved blue and gold elements of the wings link the lucid design of this plate to the choppy blue and gold crescents of the bracelet proper, heightening the effect of both parts through the contrast of rigour and mobility. On the back is engraved the inscription: 'Made by the first prophet of Amun, Smendes, son of Men-kheper-Re', showing that this piece was given by the high priest of Amun of Thebes.

Separated into their constituent parts, two identical bracelets were found near the knees of the mummy.

Each has four rectangular gold plates with cartouches of blue lapis lazuli; two of them with the name 'Psusennes-beloved-of-Amun', the other two with the title 'King of Upper and Lower Egypt, first prophet of Amun'. The backs are also inscribed: 'King, first prophet of Amun, Psusennes, son of Nes-ba-neb-djed [Smendes]'. Between each pair of these are four loosely hanging crescent elements, alternately of gold and of lapis lazuli in a gold setting, attached to the plates by eyelets. The bracelets are edged with tubular beads of gold and lapis lazuli. This beaded edge, the colours, and especially the crescent motif, unknown elsewhere, link the armlets to the bracelets to make a single ensemble.

Over the mummy's gold finger caps were no fewer than thirty-six rings, many more than have been found on any other pharaoh. Most of these are simple bands of gold; other rings have revolving ornamental plates, scarabs or *wedjat*-eyes. The right thumb was adorned by a ring like a miniature bracelet, beaten from gold foil and decorated in cloisonné technique. As in a full-size bracelet, the decoration is arranged in vertical fields. Four have rhomboids and squares inlaid with lapis lazuli and carnelian, two the cartouche of Psusennes I, the hieroglyphs being cut into the lapis lazuli.

The wide variety of Egyptian cult vessels is known from representations in temples and tombs, and in Theban tomb paintings the guests at the banquets feast from precious tableware and are served from expensive utensils. Only a pale shadow of this wealth survives. Vessels of precious metal were far too attractive to robbers, being so easily melted down for other purposes. About seventy silver vessels and twelve of gold or electrum are all that have been found in archaeological excavations from the two millennia of the kingdom of the pharaohs. In this context, the ten pieces in gold and electrum and the dozen silver vessels found in the royal tombs of the 21st Dynasty were a spectacular discovery, still unsurpassed by later finds at el-Kurru and Nuri. With one exception, all the gold vessels from Tanis had been the possessions of Psusennes I. Six of them, together with other funerary offerings, were laid in front of his sarcophagus, the others, equally worthy of a pharaoh, being contributed by the king to the funerary equipment of his follower Wen-djebau-en-djed. These vessels are enchanting in their clear lines and simplicity of form and decoration, typical features of Tanite art. The artists used the most precious metals to create works of timeless beauty. They had mastered to perfection the skills of embossing and chasing, of riveting and soldering, and they understood how to combine metals of different colours to the best effect.

They achieved great effects on the matt polished surface with accents such as floral decoration on handles and rims, and economy in inscriptions and inlays.

A particularly beautiful example of this is a carafe of thinly beaten gold foil (444). The narrow neck broadens out into a many-leaved papyrus umbel, with a plain band winding around it several times at the bottom. The tips of the petals are rolled into a rim to maintain the shape. The body of the vessel rises from a flat base, its sides gently concave. Carefully chased on the shoulder are the throne and birth names

445 Goblet

of Psusennes I. This slight concavity of the sides, the flat base and the chased royal names are found again in a basin. Attached to the rim by three rivets is handle of sweeping lines, in the form of a bunch of lotus flower and buds. The stalks, bent sharply inward, end in a palmette, whose end is riveted down for firmness. As papyrus and lotus are the complementary heraldic plants of Lower and Upper Egypt, the carafe and bowl form a unity, and they stood next to each other on the floor of the burial chamber. Such vessels are often depicted in tomb paintings and were probably used for washing, the water being poured over the hands from the ewer to the basin – a custom known in the Old Kingdom and

446 Beaked vessel

still practised in the Orient today.

The hemispherical vessel with a beak-shaped spout (446) was used in the funerary ritual. The handle ends in a duck's head with an elegantly bent neck and it carries the meticulously chased dedication: 'Made by the great royal wife, mistress of both lands, Mut-nedj-met'; the epithets, title, and throne and birth names of Psusennes I follow. The goblet (445) is of a type frequently found in pottery. The slim bowl, in the form of a stylised, half-open lotus flower, and the trumpet-shaped foot were beaten from gold foil and soldered together. The bowl is finely chased all around with the pointed leaves of the blue lotus. Just as precisely rendered is the columnar inscription on bowl and stem: 'High priest of Amun-Re-king-of-kings, Pinodjem, justified, son of Piankhi, justified. King's daughter, mistress of the harem of Amun, lord of both lands, Henut-taui. This drinking vessel had therefore been made for the Theban high priest

Pinodjem before he took the title of king and wrote his name in a cartouche. He was married to a daughter of Smendes, the founder of the Tanite dynasty, and probably offered the goblet to a successor of his father-in-law, who took the magnificent vessel to his grave, as a gift of profound symbolic significance: lotus flowers open with the rays of the rising sun, so the unfolding lotus flower is a symbol of sunrise, rebirth and resurrection.

The Tomb of General Wen-Djebau-en-Djed

The Second World War halted excavations at Tanis for five years, a worrying time for the archaeologists as they were certain that there were still treasures waiting to be uncovered. On 15 April 1945 they were finally able to resume work. The expedition's architect, Albert Lézine, suspected that there was another tomb hidden behind a last, unexplored, exceptionally thick section of wall in the south-eastern part of Psusennes' complex, near the smaller, completely looted burial chamber of one of the king's generals, and he found it before a year was out. With a surveyor's rod he poked through a crack in the wall to find emptiness behind. A covering slab was removed and the paintings and

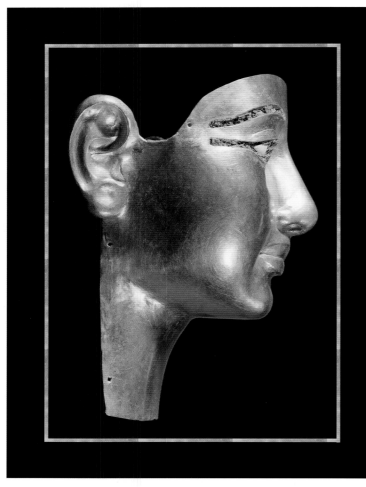

447–448 Gold mask of Wen-djebau-en-djed

inscriptions of a burial chamber were revealed: the intact burial of a companion in arms and favourite of Psusennes I, who had been laid to rest in the tomb complex of his lord.

The stone coffin, a 20th-Dynasty granite example taken from Thebes, contained only a few remains of the gilded wooden coffin; even the silver coffin containing the mummy had decayed in the humid chamber. What survived, in amazingly good condition, were the gold mask, the jewellery, and vessels of precious metal of high quality, gifts made in the royal workshops. But there were also objects from

the time of the New Kingdom, among them a heart scarab of feldspar in a gold setting, which had originally been intended for a Ramesside king; it probably came from a plundered royal mummy, and is the only surviving royal heart scarab from the Ramesside period.

Among the remains of the decayed coffins and the mummy the golden mask of Wen-djebau-en-djed shone out unscathed, an expressive face with straight nose, full lips and large protruding ears (447–448). The face and neck of the mask were beaten from gold foil which had been nailed to wood at the edges. The gentle sheen of the unpolished surface, the dark coloured inlays of the brows and eyes, the fine engraved lines around eyelids and nostrils, the firmly delineated mouth and the suggested piercing of the ears – all these details indicate that the mask came from the same workshop as the king's. This, too, is an idealised portrait suspended in time, with Ramesside overtones, but it seems more lively than Psusennes' mask, which is more conventional and closer to the style of the New Kingdom. Given the small number of royal masks to have escaped the grave robbers – Tutankhamun's and the three Tanite examples from the tombs of Psusennes I, Amenemope and Sheshonq II – and the few surviving masks of high dignitaries in precious metal, this mask, outstanding in its expressive power and execution, is a significant find.

All four gold masks from Tanis, and also the mummiform coffins, have the suggestion of piercings for earrings – like other iconographic details, a relic of times past. Heavy pendant earrings were no longer in fashion, and among the rich jewellery from the royal necropolis at Tanis there is only one example: the spiral earrings from the burial of Wen-djebau-en-djed.

This general, covered with decorations from his king, had three pectorals, and there were five costly rings over his gold finger caps. One of these had been the personal property of his master, a gold ring with an elongated revolving ornamental bezel of green stone, whose concave upper side has a *wedjat*-eye in high relief. The tiny inscription on the flat reverse bears the name of 'the king of Upper and Lower Egypt, Psusennes'. A ring of the same kind, with an almost square bezel of lapis lazuli and a *wedjat*-eye in delicate high relief, has the birth name of Ramesses IX, 'Neferkare-chosen-by-Amun', engraved in the same place.

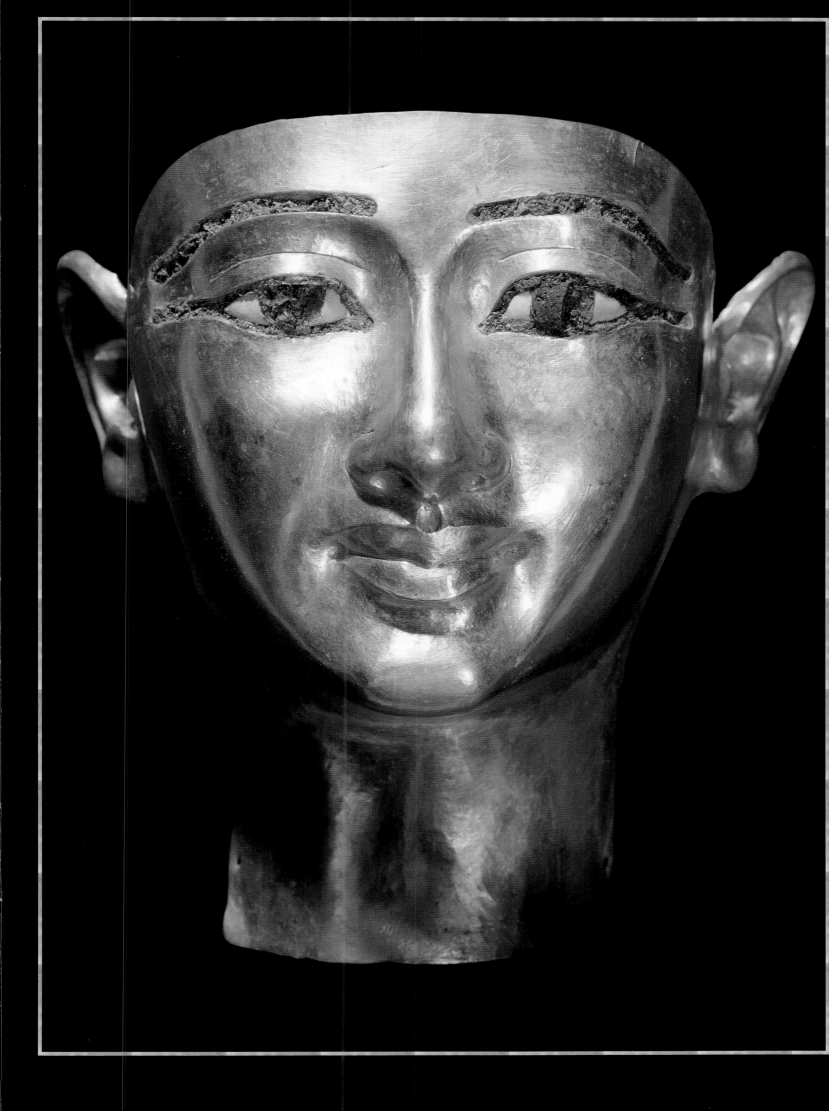

Another gift from Psusennes I is a ring of solid gold. Around the outside of the ring runs a meticulously chased inscription:

> An offering, which the king Khons-the-great-Neferhotep gives, to bring life, well-being and health, to Khons's major-domo, the general and commander Wen-djebau-en-djed.

The mummy was protected by numerous amulets. In addition to the usual types in faience and stone, there were small figures of divinities in gold and gilt, as well as little figurines of lapis lazuli these were apparently older heirlooms that could be worn around the neck as a talisman, set in gold and mounted in a miniature shrine.

In this exceptional goldsmith's work, Psusennes' general had a treasure such as no Tanite king could call his own, because the other amulets found in Tanis are more poorly worked examples of purely funerary jewellery. Yet the finely modelled solid gold figurines of the goddesses Isis and Bastet – perhaps gifts of honour from the king – and the lapis lazuli figurine of the god Ptah-Tatenen, and another of a ram, an embodiment of the god Amun, with its precious setting, give the impression that they had already been used by the deceased during life.

The vessels of precious metal, particularly valuable presents from the king to his loyal general, had been placed on the gilded wooden coffin. Among them, as in the funerary treasure of Psusennes I, there is a ribbed gold dish that suggests an open daisy. Twenty-three petals radiate from a rosette decorated with plant motives in cloisonné. The rosette, which was made separately, is surrounded by a heavy ring of gold and fixed to the cylindrical base of the dish by a rivet at its centre. This makes it more robust, as does the rolled rim. On the outside is a handle of thick, tightly curved, drawn gold, hanging from two eyelets on a plate riveted to the dish in four places. The ends of the eyelets have chased palmettes, and between the eyelets of the handle smooth and notched rings are soldered on alternately. Opposite the handle on the outside is engraved the inscription: 'The administrator of Khons, the prophet of Khons, Wen-djebau-en-djed, the justified'. Ribbed bowls of this type occur throughout the Eastern Mediterranean, and handles decorated with palmettes have been found in Syria and Cyprus: they make their first appearance in Egypt in the 19th Dynasty.

The king of Upper and Lower Egypt, Aa-kheper-Re-chosen-by-Amun, son of Re, Psusennes-beloved-of-Amun: gift as royal decoration for the administrator of Khons-in-Thebes-Neferhotep, servant of god of Khons, general, commander of the pharaoh's archers, high priest of all gods, Wen-djebau-en-djed, justified in the house of Osiris, lord of Mendes.

With these words, finely engraved and running round more than half the inner margin of the dish, Psusennes I dedicated an exceptional piece of metalwork (449) to his loyal follower.

On the bottom of this flat silver dish a cloisonné rosette edged by a beaded border is surrounded by gold foil with embossed decoration, at whose centre it is anchored to the bottom of the dish with a rivet. The artist has used the embossed gold to depict life and activity in the water: finely embossed and with lively chased detail, four naked girls swim among fish and aquatic plants, trying to catch ducks. Three of the swimmers wear shoulder-length wigs, the fourth a short wig. Their jewellery consists of earrings, bracelets and anklets, broad bead collars, girdles and strings of cowrie shells. The circular dance of these graceful figures through the watery element symbolises the cycle of life and the eternal renewal of a world that has its origin in the primeval ocean.

With a sure feeling for form and colour, the goldsmith has created a masterpiece. The plain, dark surface of the silver dish makes an effective contrast with the brighter, livelier gold, further accentuated by the way the inscription avoids the area around the handle, creating a space for the four round gold rivets. The technique used for the handle is the same as for the ribbed bowl from the Zagazig treasure. The motifs of the embossed decoration can be found on the tiled walls of the palace at Qantir. Wen-djebau-en-djed's stemmed bowl, presumably a drinking vessel, is of unusual form. The bowl resembles the stylised open flower of the white lotus, while the stem has the form of an upturned cup. Elegant and simple as this appears to the eye, it is a technically complex work. The petals are of beaten gold and electrum alternately and are soldered together. The foot is worked in a similar way, but provided with staggered fields of decoration. On one of the gold petals are inscribed the names of the royal couple and a wish: 'The King of Upper and Lower Egypt, lord of the Two Lands, Aa-kheper-Re, son of Re, lord of the crowns,

449 Dish from the tomb of Wen-djebau-en-djed

Psusennes-beloved-of-Amun. Royal wife, mistress of the two lands, Mut-nedjmet. Life, well-being and health'.

The Second Burial of King Amenemope
Another walled-up door was discovered behind intact painted plaster, just south of the burial chamber of Psusennes I. It was the end of the season, but King Farouk insisted that it be opened to avoid the danger of the newly discovered tomb being robbed. He had a tented encampment for himself and his entourage set up near the site, and the sarcophagus was to be opened in the King's presence. There was great expectation, and tension ran high. The lower register

of the painting on the plaster showed King Amenemope before the gods Isis and Osiris, and a burial chamber destined for this king had been discovered in the immediate vicinity, with an empty sarcophagus. The hopes of the assembled audience were not to be disappointed.

Detailed investigation showed that it was originally Queen Mut-nedj-met, the wife of Psusennes I, who had been buried in the newly discovered chamber, but that she and all her funeral equipment had been

450 Water vessel (hes vase) of King Amenemope

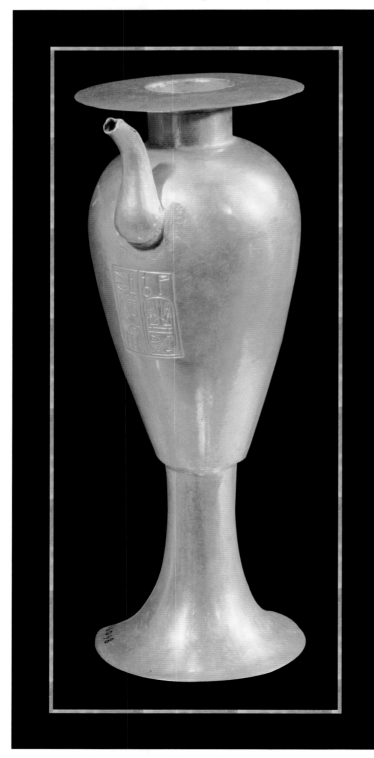

moved after tomb robbers had struck at the neighbouring tomb of Amenemope. The desecration of the king's tomb had apparently been noticed in time, and a more secure place was sought. Mut-nedj-met's name was chiselled from the sarcophagus and the walls of her burial chamber, to be replaced by the cartouches of Amenemope. In its gilded wooden coffin, the king's mummy was transferred to Queen Mut-nedj-met's sarcophagus, and his remaining funerary equipment spread on the floor of the

451 Pectoral of King Amenemope

chamber. The cult and household vessels of metal and pottery and the numerous *ushabti* figures had obviously been set down in a hurry in front of the sarcophagus before the burial chamber was sealed, to remain untouched for almost three thousand years.

When the heavy lid of the granite sarcophagus was lifted once again, in front of King Farouk, the wooden coffin had decayed and its gold foil crumpled. Beneath this, on the remains of the decayed mummy, appeared the king's mask, its thin gold foil creased and dented. This had obviously suffered a great deal at the hands of the tomb-robbers, and was only a pale shadow of the gold mask of Psusennes I.

Amid the remains of the mummy were two pectorals, scarabs, heart amulets, a great gold falcon with inlaid wings outspread, and bracelets, rings and batons. In workmanship, these finds compare very unfavourably with the offerings of King Psusennes I and his general Wen-djebau-en-djed.

The pictorial composition of one of the two pectorals is unique to Tanis (451) and alludes to the ritual for the celebration of the royal jubilee: the king in festive robes, with royal headcloth, royal kilt, animal tail hanging down behind, brings a burnt offering to the god Osiris, who sits enthroned in mummy form with a bead shawl, holding a crook and fly whisk and wearing the *Atef*-crown. The inscription identifies him as Osiris, lord of eternity, and the pharaoh as Osiris, king, User-Ma'at-Re-chosen-of-Re, Amenemope-beloved-of-Amun. The column in the centre refers to his action 'bringing his father Osiris a burnt offering and an offering of drink'. Above the scene hovers a winged solar disc. The basal strip is decorated with alternating eternity symbols of Osiris and knots of Isis.

The pectoral consists of two pieces of beaten gold foil joined together over a core. On the front are the frame, figures and blocks of inscription in raised relief; detail, hieroglyphs and symbols are chased. On the reverse the composition is repeated in mirror image, in generally rather cursory engraving.

The second pectoral, also framed, is in open-work cloisonné. It exploits a common motif: Isis and Nephthys on either side of a scarab that pushes the solar disc before it.

One slender gold jug (450) stands out among Amenemope's funerary equipment, otherwise carelessly designed. This is made of five separate elements in very fine beaten gold, soldered together. The body and neck are created as one unit. The broad rim is bent at the inside margin and set into the neck, the curved spout is attached at the shoulder, and the trumpet-shaped base is closed off by a gold plate. Beneath the spout is the only decoration, a rectangle with the owner's name: 'The perfect god, Amenemope-beloved-of-Amun, beloved of Osiris, the lord of Abydos'.

From vessels of this kind (known as *hes* vases) consecrated water was poured for rituals of purification and revival. An almost identical vessel, though much smaller, with the name of King Ahmose, ended up in the tomb of Psusennes I, a curious instance of a 500-year-old heirloom.

The Burial of Sheshonq II

On 18 March 1939, in the antechamber of the tomb of Psusennes I, Montet came upon the first intact burial to be found at the royal necropolis of Tanis. A silver coffin with falcon's head lay on a plinth of stone blocks, without the usual stone sarcophagus, and beside it two decayed royal mummies.

The owner, identified from the engraved throne name 'Heqa-kheper-Re setep-en-Re', was Sheshonq II, a ruler of the 22nd Dynasty appointed by his

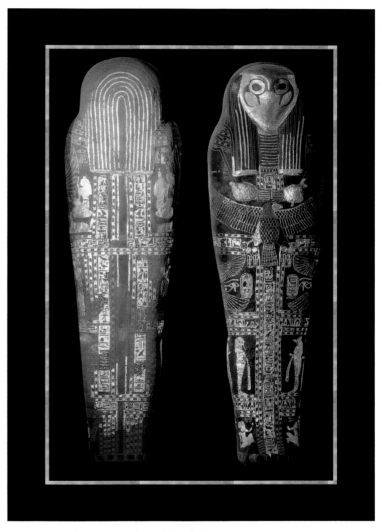

452 Falcon-headed inner coffin of Sheshonq II

father Osorkon I as co-regent and high priest at Thebes, who is not generally included in the traditional king list. After Psusennes II, who died in 945 BC, Egypt was ruled by a house of Libyan tribal chieftains. Long established in the delta cities of Bubastis and Herakleopolis, they had seized power as the leaders of mercenaries in the service of the Tanite kings. The founder of the Bubastite dynasty was Sheshonq I, the 'Shishak' of the Bible. The First Book of Kings tells of his raid on Jerusalem and of the gold and silver treasures from the temple and the palace of Solomon which fell into his hands.

For the burial of Sheshonq II, the funerary complex of the earlier royal house, now over a century old, was opened up again. This was apparently done in great haste. The heavy silver coffin was placed in the antechamber in such haste that the lid came off and was damaged. Nobody took the time to close it, and the mishap was hidden beneath a linen cloth. The canopic chest with four little silver coffins for the entrails and a chest with *ushabtis*, vessels and other offerings were placed in front of the coffin in no apparent order.

When the lid of the coffin was carefully raised, the king's undamaged gold mask looked out from among the remains. With no royal headcloth or collar, it covered only the face, like the mask of Wen-djebau-en-djed. An inner coffin of dark blue painted cartonnage was almost completely reduced to dust but still recognisable from the falcon's head, hands, decorations and inscriptions that had been applied to it in thin gold foil (452). The mummy, enclosed in a net of tubular beads of gold and faience, had also decayed.

Among its jewellery were gold finger caps and sandals, and the only large collar found in Tanis, in the form of a vulture with outstretched wings, a gold collar 'of honour' whose chain pendant terminated in bell-shaped blossoms. There were also pectorals, bracelets, rings, amulets and a kilt in the form of a gold foil mount filled with beads.

Among the most important funerary offerings of Sheshonq II were heirlooms belonging to the founder of the dynasty, among them a cloisonné pectoral (462) that symbolises the nocturnal course of the sun. Under the starry night sky the sun-boat glides on the waves of the primeval ocean. The gold stars are fixed with pins into the lapis lazuli inlay of the hieroglyph for the heavens, on both ends of which sits a royal falcon in gold with the Double Crown. It is supported on the left by a lotus, and on the right by a papyrus plant, the heraldic plants of Upper and Lower Egypt, which grow out of the water. This is depicted by zigzag bands of gold and lapis lazuli, and beneath it hang lotus flowers and buds, inlaid with

453 Sun-bird

lapis lazuli and turquoise. Tall crescent-shaped posts decorate the stern and prow of the boat on which rests the nocturnal sun, a disc of lapis lazuli in a gold setting.

On its gently curved surface are engraved two divinities with inscriptions: the enthroned god-king Amun-Re-Horakhte, the feather crown on his head, a sceptre and a sign of life in his hand; and in front of him his daughter Ma'at, ruler of the order of the world, who has an ostrich feather, the sign of her name, and a solar disc on her head, raising her hands in praise. Two goddesses, Hathor on the left, Ma'at on the right, protect the sun with winged arms outstretched. In the angle of the wings is the *wedjat*-eye, a sign of healing and salvation, over a basket, the sign for 'everything'. The two lower corners of the pictorial space contain two gold rectangles with engraved text:

> Amun-Re-Horakhte, may you cross the sky every day to protect the great one of Meshwesh, the great of greats, Sheshonq, the justified, son of the great Meshwesh, Nemrot (Lamintu).

This indicates that the pectoral was made for Sheshonq at a time when he was still 'chief of chiefs of the Meshwesh', but, as can be seen from the motifs and the quality of the piece, was already able to have work done for him at the royal workshops. Sheshonq must have worn it during his life, for there are unmistakable signs of wear and some of the flower pendants are missing.

A pectoral with heart scarabs (456–457) bears the name of Sheshonq II. The scarab of carved green jasper, symbol of the rising sun and of rebirth, dominates the pictorial field within the shrine. Rather than the sun, it pushes the king's cartouche before him: sun-god and king have become one.

Here the scarab is also an amulet for the heart of the dead man. On the underside is engraved the text of chapter 30 of the Book of the Dead, which begs the heart not to testify against the deceased in the Hall of Judgement.

The pectoral is carried out in cloisonné and inlaid in blue faience. The tutelary goddesses Isis and

454–455 Snake pectoral of Sheshonq II
456–457 Pectoral with heart scarab

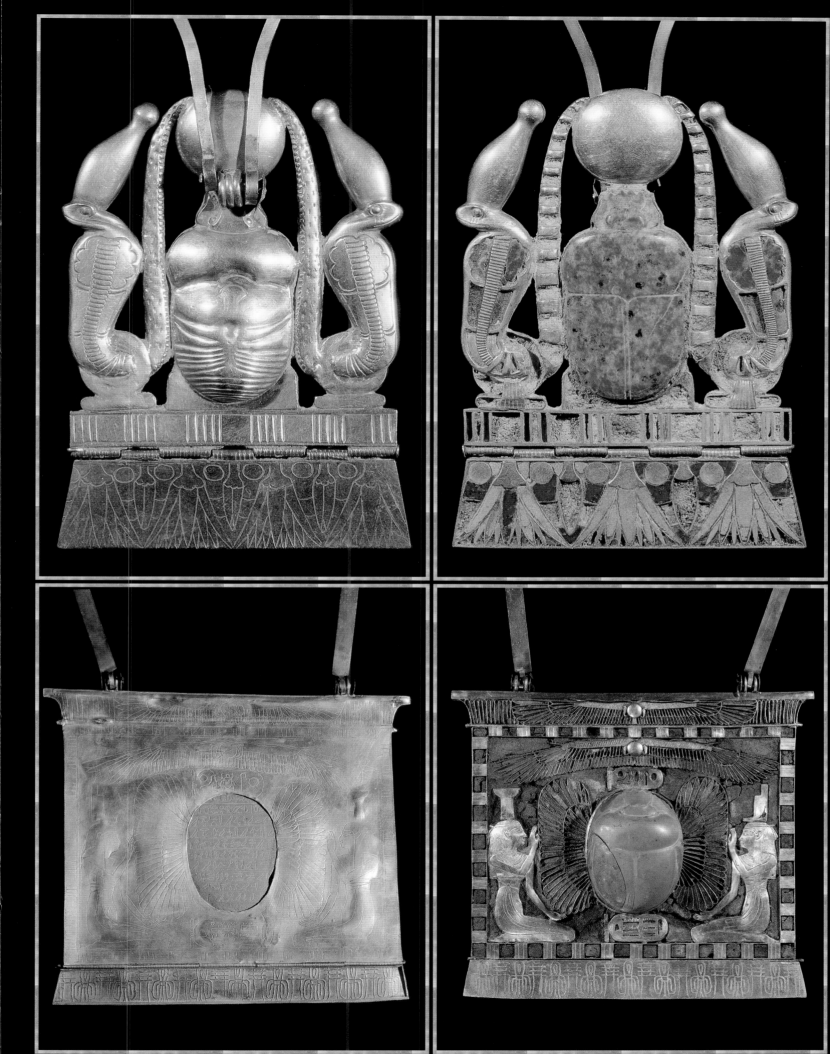

Nephthys, the cartouches, the solar discs and all the flat gold ornament are of embossed and chased gold foil. With its green heart scarab and blue inlay, this pectoral is an example of the Tanite goldsmiths' unique predilection for cool colours. Typical, too, are the hinge fastenings for the necklace and the plinth hanging from a multi-part hinge.

The snake pectoral (454–455), made from separate cloisonné elements soldered together, is as graceful as it is charged with meaning. The two *uraei* wearing the crown of Upper Egypt raise their extended hoods and curl their bodies protectively around the scarab,

which rises from the earth over the horizon sign, pushing the sun up into the sky. This lively composition is in sharp contrast to the geometric forms of the base and the plinth with its two-dimensional lotus frieze, hanging from hinges.

A solar disc and crowns are also rendered in low relief on the reverse of the piece (454), while the segmented underside of the scarab is embossed in gold foil and the detail of the snakes' bodies is chased. Behind the scarab's head are soldered two eyelets, which take the looped ends of the gold band that serves as a necklace.

458–461 Bracelets of Sheshonq I and of his son Prince Nemrot

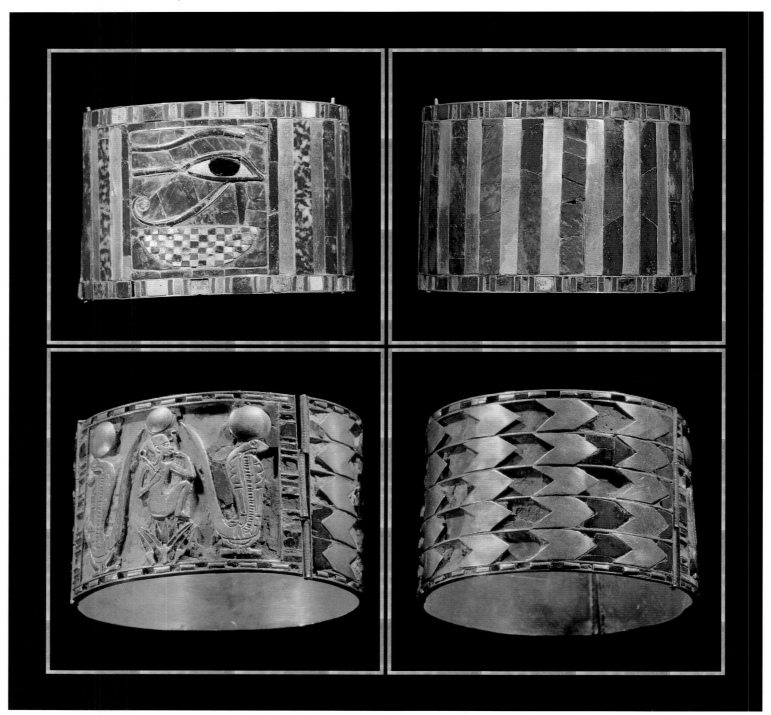

The Royal Necropolis of Tanis

Like one of the pectorals, a pair of bracelets (458–459) is an inheritance from the former belongings of Sheshonq I. The more-or-less cylindrical, slightly tapered bodies of thick gold foil were made in two unequal parts linked by hinges. The outer side is covered in alternating vertical strips of gold and inlaid lapis lazuli. On the smaller part of the bracelet, this pattern is interrupted by a square field of cloisonné work in which a *wedjat*-eye with black pupil and white eyeball appears against a lapis lazuli background, the eye resting on a basket sign in a chequered pattern of gold, red and blue squares.

These colours also appear in the 'ladder' borders on the edges of the bracelet.

On the gold inner side of the bracelet, opposite the *wedjat*-eye, the inscription of ownership is engraved:

> King of Upper and Lower Egypt, lord of both lands Hedj-kheper-Re, chosen by Re, son of Re, lord of the crowns, Sheshonq, beloved of Amun, bestowed with life like Re eternally.

A pair of bracelets that belonged to Prince Nemrot, one of the sons of Sheshonq I, and which presumably comes from Saïs, is constructed in exactly the same way as his father's, although the decoration is less

462 Pectoral of the King Sheshonq II

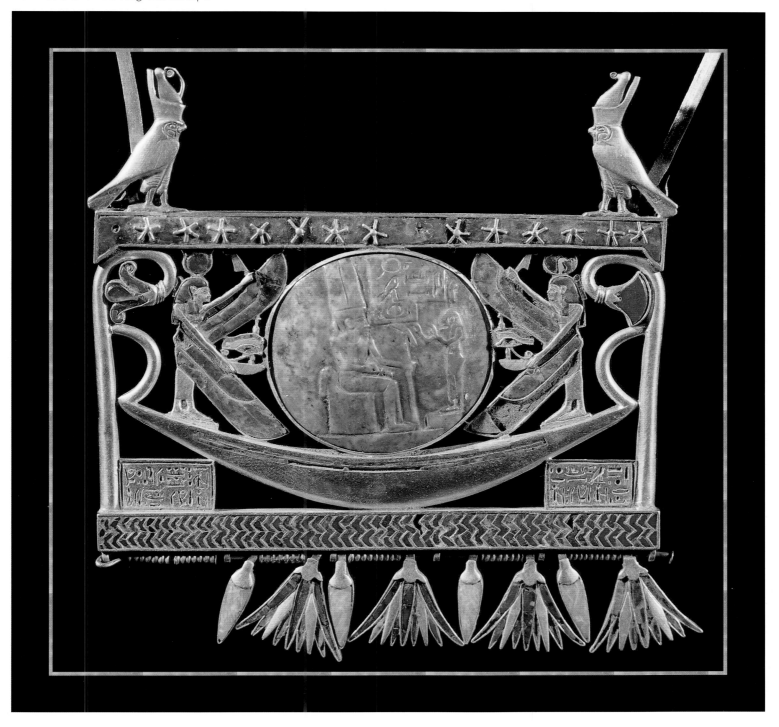

carefully executed. Here, too, the smaller of the two halves has the principal motif, while the larger is covered in a chevron pattern. Above a flowering lotus flanked by two buds sits the naked child-god Horus, with his prince's side-lock, *uraeus* on the forehead and a sceptre in his left hand, crowned with the crescent moon and solar disc. He is protected by two rearing *uraei*. The embossing and chasing of the god and the *uraei* are exceptionally fine, and the solar disc is slightly domed. The lotus, the coloured 'ladder' border to the left and the right of the scene, the background and the decorative pattern on both edges of the bracelet are inlaid with red and blue glass or with faience. Lapis lazuli alternates with gold in the

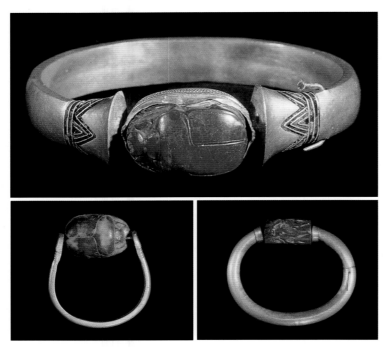

463–465 Bracelet with scarab, scarab ring, bracelet with antique Mesopotamian cylinder seal

decoration of the larger part, complementing the coloured ladders.

A pair of bracelets of Sheshonq II (463) are made of a gold band with a lightly bowed outer side and end in papyrus umbels whose chased geometrical design is filled in with several colours. Between the umbels sits a scarab of lapis lazuli in a setting of beaten gold foil whose rolled edges are decorated with a plaited pattern. Drilled lengthways, it rotates on a rod fixed into the umbels. The remarkably finely carved scarab bears on its base the man's name Djed-Khons-auf-ankh, and its pair has the royal name Men-kheper-Re. The construction of this pair of bracelets resembles that of signet rings with rotating

bezels, and the ensemble is completed by a ring that is a miniature version of the bracelets (464). Here, too, the amulet does not bear the name of Sheshonq; according to its inscription it was made for a priest of the early 22nd Dynasty.

Only one of the seven bracelets of Sheshonq II was not part of a pair (465). It is made of two segments of gold tube of differing length. The ends, which are closed off with gold caps, are joined together by a rod, on which is mounted a rotating amulet: a Mesopotamian cylinder seal of lapis lazuli with an animal-tamer motif, which was about 1,400 years old when it was incorporated into the jewellery of the Bubastite king.

An exceptional find is the sun-bird from the king's regalia (453). This swallow, of beaten gold foil finely chased and provided with an eyelet for hanging, bears on its back a solar disc in a *shen* ring, the symbol of the eternal cycle. As one of a number of different creatures that escort the sun across the sky, the swallow is a guarantors of the cyclical renewal of nature. Shown sitting as a nestling or young bird, it represents the young morning sun. In Tutankhamun's funerary treasure it appears carved in carnelian, the fiery red of the rising sun.

In the representations discovered to date, the sun-bird is always seen on the hem of the beaded hanging that was worn on a belt over the royal kilt, and the example from the coffin of Sheshonq II was the first of its kind to be found.

The Plundered Tomb of Osorkon II

The burial site of Osorkon II, the most significant ruler of the 22nd Dynasty, was the first sensational discovery to be made at Tanis. It meant that Pierre Montet, who excavated it in 1939–40, had found the royal necropolis so long sought for, even if robbers had beaten him to it. In an antechamber stood the stone sarcophagus of Osorkon's successor Takelot II. Beads, fragments of gold jewellery and his electrum coffin, left by the thieves, gave some idea of the riches with which the pharaohs had once been buried there.

As the excavators opened the chamber destined for the owner of the tomb himself, they were full of expectation, for they had discovered the wall still intact; the entrance was covered with a layer of dust

466 Divine triad of Osorkon II: Horus, Osiris and Isis

and blocked by a broken piece of an obelisk. The chamber and sarcophagus within, however, were found to have been plundered, the robbers having forced their way in through a side wall. All that was left were remnants of the mummy, the canopic jars and the gilt bronze ceremonial beard from a wooden anthropoid coffin.

Behind the colossal pink granite sarcophagus of Osorkon II lay a small child's sarcophagus of the same material. According to the inscription, it belonged to Hornakht, the high priest of Amun. The lid was held

amulets cut from gold foil, finely chased and finished with cloisonné enamel.

Nothing found in the tomb of Osorkon II surpasses the famous Triad of Gods (466), which bears Osorkon's name and presumably comes from the robbers' booty. It portrays the family of Osiris, the dead pharaoh being shown in the form of Osiris, wearing the god's *Atef*-crown, beard and garments. His hands on his knees, he squats on a pillar waiting for rebirth like the young sun-god on his lotus-blossom. Beside him stands his sister and wife Isis, her

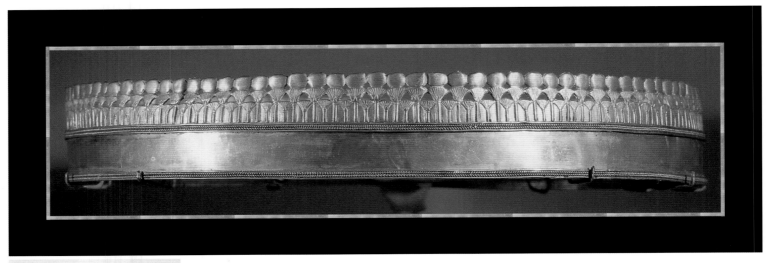

467 Gold circlet with wreath of papyrus umbels
468 King Shabako with crown and ram's-head neck ornament

down by an enormous block of granite, which led the archaeologists to postpone opening it, but in any event the tomb of Psusennes I had now been discovered with all its treasures, and this kept them particularly busy. It was only in the course of the last excavations that they returned and discovered that a boy of between nine and twelve years old, perhaps Osorkon's favourite son who had died in childhood, had been buried in great splendour at his feet.

Through a hole in the side of the sarcophagus, the tomb-robbers had stolen the prince's gold mask and his head and neck jewellery, and also removed parts of the silver coffin itself. Disturbed in their activities, or perhaps distracted by even greater treasures to be found in the burial chamber, they had left behind some forty pieces of jewellery, including a set of

hand raised, crowned with cow's horns and a solar disc, and his son Horus, wearing the Double Crown of Upper and Lower Egypt. The modelling and expressive force of these tiny sculptures compares well with any of the masterpieces of large-scale sculpture of ancient Egypt. The figures are entirely of gold, cast by the lost wax technique and polished, with some engraved detail.

The pillar, of lapis lazuli of a most delicate hue, is crowned by a hollow moulding inlaid with red glass and lapis lazuli. On the front is engraved the inscription:

The King of Upper and Lower Egypt, lord of both lands, User-Ma'at-Re, chosen by Amun, Son of Re, Osorkon, beloved of Amun.

The pillar stands on a flat gold base which, like the feet of Isis and Horus, is soldered onto the common pedestal, the top and bottom of gold foil, which are held together by a gold cloisonné frieze that runs around the outer edge. The lapis lazuli inlay of the frieze, like that on the wigs of Isis and Horus, has in part fallen out. Behind the wigs, soldered loops indicate that the triad, sculpted in the round, was intended not to be freestanding but rather to be suspended, possibly as decoration for a shrine or funerary barque.

Gold from the Pyramids of Kush

From the time of the Middle Kingdom, the lands bordering the Nile to the south of Egypt – Nubia between the First and Second Cataract and the land of Kush, present-day Sudan – were Egyptian colonies and the pharaohs' most important source of gold. In the New Kingdom, they were administered by an Egyptian official, the Viceroy of Kush. With the decline of the Egyptian empire around 1000 BC, these countries – and thus their valuable gold mines – were lost to Egypt, and for two centuries the connection was severed.

In the 8th century BC, a lineage of native chiefs from Napata, on the Fourth Cataract, established a powerful kingdom in Kush. Piy conquered Thebes and in 712 BC his brother Shabako defeated Bakenrenef, King of Lower Egypt, thus becoming the ruler of a vast realm extending from the Nile Delta all the way to Khartoum at the confluence of the White and Blue Niles. As successors to the pharaohs, the Kushites formed the 25th Dynasty, which governed Egypt for barely 100 years. Their capital remained at Napata on Gebel Barkal, the holy mountain. In Egypt they governed through the god's-wife of Amun, a woman of royal descent who passed on her office through adoption. She was responsible not only for the administration of the vast temple properties but also for temporal power.

In order to legitimize their claim to power, the Kushite kings adopted not only the royal robes and titles of the pharaohs but also Egyptian hieroglyphs and the cult of the Egyptian deities, particularly venerating the god Amun and his wife Mut. Important temples were erected to Amun at Napata, where extensive building was carried out by the Kushite kings. Other temples were, however, also erected at Karnak and Luxor. There was a renaissance in art and Egyptian gods and aspects of Egyptian culture now spread far to the south.

When the Kushites were driven out of Egypt by the Assyrians in 656 BC, they withdrew to their original

territories on the Upper Nile. The motifs in their goldsmiths' work reflect the world of the Egyptian gods but show local stylistic variations.

Like the capital, the royal Kushite burial grounds also initially lay in the area around Gebel Barkal. Here, members of the ruling family and their household were buried in small steep-sided pyramids in accordance with Egyptian custom. The oldest burial ground is at el-Kurru, roughly 15 miles (25km) south-west of Napata, while the later necropolis at Nuri, with more than sixty pyramids, lies somewhat to the north-east, on the west bank of the Nile. In the 3rd century BC, the capital and royal burial ground were moved some 185 miles (300km) up the Nile to Meroe.

460 Ram's-head amulet

These royal necropolises, which date from the 8th century BC to the 4th century AD, were explored on behalf of Harvard University and the Museum of Fine Arts in Boston by two leading American Egyptologists: George A. Reisner began excavations in 1907 and, together with his pupil and colleague Dows Dunham, he completed the work between 1916 and 1923. After laborious and extremely exact investigations, the archaeologists discovered, alongside the massive pyramids constructed of stone and rubble, well-secured stairs or shafts cut into the rock and leading to the burial chambers. Very few tombs remained undisturbed, most having been emptied by robbers. The finds were shared between the museums in Khartoum and Boston.

Royal statuettes of the Kushite period (467) show that part of the royal regalia was a very un-Egyptian pectoral: three rams' heads (the ram being the animal representation of the god Amun) are hung on a cord around the neck and shoulder in such a way that the large ram's head with the solar disc stands high in the centre, the two smaller ones without such discs being fastened to the ends of the ribbon, lying on each side of the breast.

An example of such jewellery is to be seen in the ram's head in the Norbert Schimmel Collection (469). Since it has no solar disc, it probably formed one of the side pendants. This skilfully modelled head with its upright cobra is cast in solid gold, the grooves on the powerful horns, the ram's ears, eyes and nostrils and the band on the snake's pectoral being engraved. The snake's tail is shaped into a large loop through which the cord was passed.

A unique piece is a gold circlet now in the Brooklyn Museum (468), of cut and engraved gold foil, decorated with solar discs and the stalks and umbels of papyrus. Along the upper and lower edges of the smooth part lie two rows of intertwined wire. This type of circlet has no counterpart in the Egyptian tradition, but royal images from the Kushite dynasty show similar diadems, and it would therefore seem to be part of the regalia of a Kushite king.

attached to the gold plate at the base by a gold rod that passes through a hole drilled in the sphere.

From the same tomb comes the criosphinx, a ram-headed lion sitting on a column (470). As can be seen where damage has occurred, the figure is formed from a metal core overlaid with electrum leaf. The sphinx turns its head to one side and wears an elaborate wig and broad collar, and the coat on its back is ornately chased. The column is decorated with a cloisonné enamel feather pattern inlaid with red and blue glass. On the capital the remains of an electrum overlay with engraved palm leaves can still be made out.

Gold cylinders have been found in the tombs of Kushite kings, consisting of two parts, the upper part

470–473 Criosphinx, amulet with the head of Hathor and rod attachment

An amulet of rock-crystal with a gold head of Hathor (471) is part of the jewellery of a queen of the second half of the 8th century BC found in a tomb at el-Kurru. The rock-crystal sphere, with its flattened upper and lower surfaces, bears the head of the goddess worked in gold foil and rendered in the round. Her long wig lies over the sphere. On her head she wears the royal cobra, a crown, and her own emblem, the solar disc and cow's horns. A loop is soldered behind the horns. The head of Hathor is

open and the lower closed. Their use is unknown, but they may have had some magical protective function like the cylinder amulets of the Middle Kingdom. An example from the pyramid burial of King Aspelta (477) is made of two strips of gold foil, which after decoration were bent round and soldered together along their lengths. The seam is hidden by partially twisted and notched gold bands. The upper part of the cylinder is divided into three areas: on top, a frieze of cobras with solar discs; in the middle, rams' heads

Gold from the Pyramids of Kush

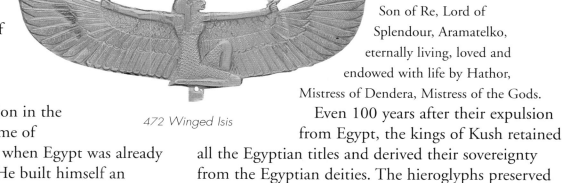

472 Winged Isis

also with solar discs, and at the bottom a row of papyrus umbels. On the lower part is an engraving of the goddess Mut, her wings outspread and the Double Crown on her head.

The hieroglyphic inscription in the royal cartouche gives the name of Aspelta, a king who reigned when Egypt was already lost to the Kushite empire. He built himself an imposing pyramid with three burial chambers and a chapel in the necropolis at Nuri.

Among the accessories found there was an alabaster jar with a gold top (476). On the neck of the narrow vessel are two cartouches with the titles 'Son of Re, Aspelta, King of Upper and Lower Egypt, Meri-ka-Re', and figures of tutelary goddesses with outspread wings are engraved on both sides. The closure is very unusual: the neck of the vessel is surrounded by a cuff of gold foil, decorated with cloisonné enamel inlaid with glass. From the flat projecting cover small drop-

The inscription on the other side (475) reads:

Son of Re, Lord of Splendour, Aramatelko, eternally living, loved and endowed with life by Hathor, Mistress of Dendera, Mistress of the Gods.

Even 100 years after their expulsion from Egypt, the kings of Kush retained all the Egyptian titles and derived their sovereignty from the Egyptian deities. The hieroglyphs preserved their classical form.

A gold amulet from the pyramid burial ground at Nuri (473) portrays Isis. The winged goddess, depicted kneelng, is cut out from thin gold foil with repoussé details. Her hands are outstretched; in the left she holds a sistrum and in the right the *ankh*, symbol of life. Her symbolic attribute, the throne, is shown upon her head. The amulet is perforated in five places, almost certainly so that it could be sewn on to garments, and it was probably intended to adorn the mummy of a queen.

474– 475 Part of a bead collar of King Aramatelko.
476–477 Alabaster vessel and cylinder of King Aspelta

shaped beads of carnelian, turquoise and steatite hang down from little gold chains. Only ten of some thirty of these beads survive.

The middle section of a collar of gold beads belonging to Aramatelko, Aspelta's successor, was discovered under the foundations of a wall in Meroe. On one side (474) is the engraved inscription:

King of Upper and Lower Egypt, lord of both lands,
Wadj-ka-Re, eternally living, loved and endowed with life
by Horakhti, the Great God, Lord of the Sky.

The Late Dynastic Period

The origin of a lion's head cut from amethyst and set in a framework of eight baboons (472) is unknown. The baboons in beaten gold foil are soldered together in such a way as to leave a hollow centre. A gold pin is set through the base and the lion's head to serve as a support. This little artefact perhaps served as the finial of a ceremonial rod.

The Saite and Persian Periods

The radical geopolitical changes into whose turbulence Egypt was inevitably drawn, and the associated alternation between indigenous and foreign dynasties, meant that Egyptian art was now able to develop for only short periods of time at best. The heritage of Egypt's past grandeur remained alive to the very end, however; in terms of art and architecture, it provided authoritative prototypes, and in order to legitimize their claim to power in Egypt foreign rulers adopted not only Egyptian ceremonial but also the style and often the content of Egyptian art.

Goldsmiths produced work of fine quality, although as a result of the plundering of the tombs only very little has survived. The pieces that are still extant show scarcely any sign of foreign influence, adhering to time-honoured forms and remaining thoroughly Egyptian until the end of the 31st Dynasty.

Representative of the funerary jewellery of this period are the tomb furnishings of Hekaemsaef, who held office under Ahmose II, a king of the Saite dynasty. His undisturbed burial was discovered in 1903 by archaeologists from the Egyptian Department of Antiquities, some 57 ft (21m) down one of the sand-filled shaft-tombs to the east of the pyramid of Unas at Saqqara.

Within a limestone sarcophagus, inside a painted wooden coffin, lay the mummy of Hekaemsaef, wearing a gold mask with a net of beads attached to it. The mesh of the net, which like the attached collar is made of lapis lazuli, feldspar and gold beads, represents the starry sky. Beneath the collar with its

478 Isis with the Horus child

gold falcon-head end-pieces kneels Nut, goddess of heaven, with her winged arms protectively outstretched over the body of the dead man. Her wings are decorated in cloisonné enamel, while the inscribed band enclosed in the wrappings beneath the goddess and the Four Sons of Horus who flank her (the gods who protected the viscera) are of chased gold foil. The mummy was adorned with almost seventy gold amulets and other items of jewellery, with gold finger and toe covers, and gold soles beneath the feet for the journey into the hereafter.

The art of Egyptian goldsmiths from the period of the late dynasties can be illustrated by two examples: a wonderfully finely worked *ba* bird (479) and a pendant amulet of Isis enthroned with the Horus child (478). Isis, wife of Osiris and mother of Horus, had become the embodiment of motherhood and marital fidelity. The people turned to her, the goddess so afflicted by the blows of fate, for help and succour in time of need. This painstakingly crafted gold figurine is an outstanding example from among the countless small images of Isis that have been found, mostly popular pieces made of copper or bronze. Under the base is engraved the name Psamtek I, first pharaoh of the 26th Dynasty.

On her head, above a wreath of upright cobras, Isis bears the horns of the 'Mother Cow' with a solar disc, originally an attribute of Hathor. In the full facial features one can still see the formal legacy of the Ethiopian period. The goddess holds her breast with her right hand while with her left she supports the child on her lap. The Horus child, with arms held stiffly to the body and legs together, wears the Double Crown of Upper and Lower Egypt.

Reliably dated representations of the enthroned Isis with the child to whom she offers her breast are otherwise unknown until the 1st century BC. In the Nile Valley during the Coptic period this original motif of the breast-feeding mother of god lived on as the Virgin Mary with the infant Jesus at her breast, entering Western Christian iconography as the 'Maria Lactans', or nursing virgin.

Written sources provide evidence that at end of the Late Period, Egypt was still rich in gold. A tomb relief from the 30th Dynasty (480) bears the inscription, 'The handing over of gold'. The occupant of the tomb is paying weavers for their work, always highly prized in Egypt. Elegantly attired, he sits on his chair looking at the golden collars that lie spread out before him on a mat. A scribe squats on the ground and notes what the man standing behind him is handing out to the five women. Scenes of this sort are already known from the Old Kingdom (141). At the end of Egyptian history the motif was taken up again, and Egyptian jewellery was represented for one last time before Alexander the Great conquered the country and the Egyptian tradition was supplanted by the Greek.

479–480 Ba bird

Jewellery of the Ptolemaic Period

In 332 BC, after his victories at Issus and on the Granicus, Alexander the Great seized the Persian satrapy of Egypt and had himself crowned pharaoh in Memphis, with all due pomp and proper ritual. He then sought out the long-famous oracle at the Oasis of Siwa, to obtain from Amun confirmation of his rank as the son of a god and thus recognition as king of Egypt and ruler of the world.

On his way to Siwa, the Macedonian king founded the port city of Alexandria on the Mediterranean coast. Within a few decades the city had developed into a widely influential centre of Greek culture, a centre that was the cultural focus of the Hellenistic period that now dawned.

After Alexander's early death, Egypt fell to one of his generals, the Macedonian Ptolemy (88), who made Alexandria the capital of his empire. The dynasty that he founded, with its capable and dominant women, ruled over Egypt for almost 300 years. According to ancient accounts, the splendour of the Ptolemaic court was without precedent.

Under the sky of Egypt, and under the eyes of its ancient civilization, there emerged in Alexandria a specific Alexandrine variant of cosmopolitan Hellenistic art. Greek artists borrowed ideas from pharaonic art and portrayed Egyptian motifs in Greek forms. Classic Egyptian elements are rarely found in the gold jewellery of Alexandria (76, 483), which now had to serve the artistic requirements of a prosperous Hellenistic ruling class.

At the end of the 4th century BC, Petosiris, a royal scribe and high priest of Thoth, had his tomb at Tuna el-Gebel decorated with reliefs in a mixed Greco-Egyptian style. The 'goldsmiths' scenes', accompanied by hieroglyphic inscriptions and rendered in the traditional form, show Greek craftsmen working on objects in the Greek style.

New forms of jewellery that spread through the Nile Valley in the Hellenistic period include earrings with antelope-heads (484, 485), a motif of Persian origin, and above all the evidently much-loved snake bracelet (422, 486–492).

According to the Egyptian way of thinking, the *ba* was the soul of the gods, and assumed the form of a snake. Claudius Aelianus tells how vipers were held to be sacred and kept in houses and temples. In Ptolemaic times Serapis and Isis in particular appear in the form of snakes, their portrait busts sometimes

481 Relief showing payment with gold jewellery

Pages 234–235; 482 Outer wall of a sarcophagus

replacing the snake's head in bracelets (490). Alongside the deified Alexander, the snake Agathodaimon was the tutelary deity of Alexandria.

Snake bracelets were popular because they were supposed to ward off evil spirits. They were always worn in pairs, with the serpent's head on the wrist, and remained fashionable as late as the 4th century AD. The cobra does not appear on these bracelets, however; its use even in this Late Period was still restricted to pharaonic jewellery.

The Golden Treasure of Meroe

In the 3rd century BC, the capital of the Kushite empire on the Upper Nile had been moved from Napata to Meroe. The royal tombs in Meroe were built as small steep-sided pyramids, like those at the older capital of Napata.

483 Bracelet with cupids and Gordian knots
484–485 Earrings with antelope heads

As had already been the case under the Kushite kings who in the 8th and 7th centuries BC had extended their dominion over the lower Nile Valley and adopted Egyptian culture, the motifs that appear in the gold jewellery that has survived from this later period are based on Egyptian models. With the centuries-long separation from the empire of the pharaohs, however, local African characteristics also began to make their appearance. Reliefs show how the

rulers are laden with jewellery, and the Negroid features of faces and bodies are accentuated.

A new cultural epoch was beginning, and Hellenistic influences began to make themselves felt. Ergamenes I had received a Greek upbringing in Alexandria and been impressed by the splendour of the early Ptolemies, and objects of Alexandrian manufacture spread Hellenistic forms and motifs through the applied arts of the economically burgeoning empire.

Until the beginning of the 19th century AD, little was known of the remarkable and legendary empire of Meroe, held by ancient Greek writers to be the cradle of culture. It was not until the conquest of the Sudan by the Egyptian Viceroy Mohammed Ali in 1821 that it became accessible to European travellers and adventurers. A French explorer, the mineralogist Frédéric Cailliaud, accompanied these Egyptian campaigns of conquest. He made drawings of the temples and pyramids, the previously completely unknown vestiges of its ancient culture, publishing them in a multi-volume work. The Sudan now began to arouse strong interest worldwide, both among scholars and among adventurers.

Dr Giuseppe Ferlini of Bologna was the most successful of the treasure-seekers. He had served in the Egyptian garrisons at Sennar and Khartoum and, after leaving the army in 1834, inspired by Cailliaud's book, he decided to pursue his archaeological interests and set off for Meroe, where he arrived in August 1834: 'I had decided to return home either penniless or laden down with vast treasure.'

At the royal necropolis, an hour's journey from the Nile, Ferlini selected the best-preserved pyramid as the first target of his treasure-hunt. It stood steep-sided and completely undamaged before him. To the east – as with the older Egyptian pyramids – there stood a small temple with pylons, the gate-towers that marked the entrance to the sanctuary. The pylons and the walls of the sanctuary were decorated with reliefs showing a queen of Meroe, for whom the monument had been constructed.

Ferlini had the pyramid dismantled stone by stone, from the top down. Only a little way beneath the apex – roughly at the height of the niche that can be seen in Cailliaud's diagram – the workers came upon a

486–492 Ptolemaic bracelets

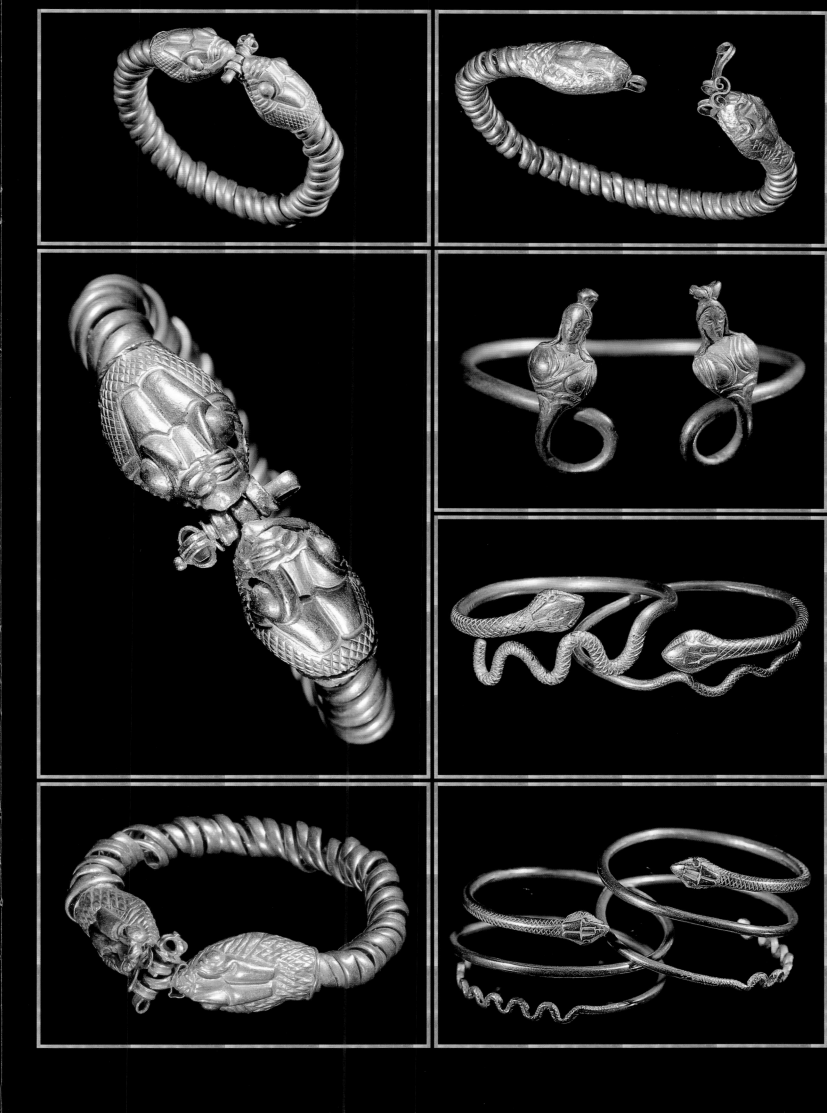

The Ancient City of Meroe

In 1830 Giuseppe Ferlini arrived from Bologna as a military surgeon to the Egyptian garrison in the Sudan. When he left the service four years later, 'keen to make some contribution to history', he asked the military governor for permission to carry out excavations. Like so many other Europeans active in the Nile Valley in the same period, Ferlini of course also hoped to make finds that could be sold profitably in Europe.

Digs in Wadi ban Naqa, Naqa and Musawwarat did not bring the expected results. Excavations in the

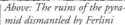
Above: The ruins of the pyramid dismantled by Ferlini

Left: The pyramids of Meroe in 1821, drawn by Frédéric Cailliaud. On the right is the pyramid of Queen Amanishakheto before demolition

Right: Queen Amanishakheto triumphing over her enemies. Relief from a pylon of the mortuary temple

Left: The pyramids at Meroe today.

ruins of the city of Meroe itself and in some of the smaller pyramids of the royal necropolis proved equally fruitless. Ferlini decided to make a last attempt at one of the largest pyramids in the necropolis.

His choice fell on the pyramid of Queen Amanishakheto, according to recent drawings then the best preserved. Ferlini instructed his workers, whom he had recruited from the surrounding villages, to dismantle the pyramid from the top down. Only a little way beneath the apex they came upon a small chamber, and inside it a bronze vessel filled with the

queen's jewellery, carefully wrapped in cloth. Ferlini returned hastily to Alexandria, and then to Rome, with the treasure, fearing that his native workers intended to keep it for themselves. However, he found it unexpectedly difficult to convince European experts of the authenticity of his finds.

small chamber. It contained a bed covered with a white sheet. Under the bed stood a simple bronze vessel filled with the queen's jewellery, carefully wrapped in cloth. Lying on the ground were beads, some loose and others strung into necklaces, and end-pieces for collars and other items.

The dismantling of the pyramid went rapidly ahead. At the halfway stage, the workers came upon another chamber, in which they found two beautiful Greek bronze vessels – but they contained no jewellery. After a little more than a month's further work, the entire pyramid had been razed to the ground, right down to the bedrock.

The valuable finds from the pyramid had excited the greed of the native workers, and Ferlini no longer felt that his life was safe. He hastily boarded his boat

and travelled north to Cairo and Alexandria, and thence to Rome, where he hoped swiftly to convert his gold treasure into hard cash.

In Rome, however, the precious finds so adventurously unearthed did not find a buyer. The Italian scholars to whom Ferlini showed them doubted that they actually came from the famous city of Meroe; others even thought that they were modern fakes. Even his catalogue, published in Italian in 1837 and followed a year later by a French translation, which listed the jewellery with precise descriptions of the pieces and the circumstances of their discovery, did not at first bring the success expected.

This publication must, however, have come into the hands of an important connoisseur of antique art: Martin Wagner, who was responsible for buying art

The Golden Treasure of Meroe

on behalf of King Ludwig I of Bavaria. When the King stopped in Rome on his way home from Sicily in 1839, Wagner visited Ferlini and, trusting in his own artistic judgment, he bought about half the jewellery and the bronze vases of Greek workmanship with relief decoration. These acquisitions were displayed in the Egyptian Room of the royal collection in Munich.

The rest of the gold jewellery was taken to London, although even there it did not at first find a buyer. In the summer of 1842, the German Egyptologist Richard Lepsius took a detailed look at the jewellery before the departure of the Prussian expedition to Egypt and Ethiopia. He recognized its significance at once, and urged Berlin to acquire it for the city's own still quite insignificant Egyptian collection. The authorities, however, dragged their feet.

On 28 January 1844 Lepsius landed with his expedition in Begerawiyeh, the river station near Meroe. In a letter of 12 March 1844, he describes his first visit to the ruins:

> It was only just before dusk that the boat arrived in Begerawiyeh, near where the pyramids are situated.
>
> Although it was already growing dark, I went with Abekon

[an artist on the expedition] to the pyramids which lie just under an hour away inland, on the first slopes of the low mountains which stretch away to the east. The moon provided a meagre light on the level ground, which was covered with stones, low undergrowth and clumps of bushes. After riding furiously, we finally arrived at the foot of a tightly packed row of pyramids which rose up before us in a crescent. Half-reconnoitring and half-groping, I found some sculptures on the outer walls of the small mortuary temples, and could even feel figures and inscriptions on the internal walls. It occurred to me that I had a stump of candle in the donkey's saddle bag. I lit it and now examined several antechambers – Egyptian gods immediately appeared before my eyes with their names written in the well-known hieroglyphics. Our new *kawass*, not wanting to leave us alone in the night, had followed just behind us. He knew the area very well, as he had been with Ferlini and had helped him in his survey of the pyramid. He showed us the location of the pyramid in which Ferlini found the walled-up treasure of gold and silver rings in 1834.

Ferlini was proved right; the origin of the jewellery was confirmed, and in 1844 the remainder of the find was bought for Berlin on Lepsius' recommendation.

493 Broad bracelet with pendants

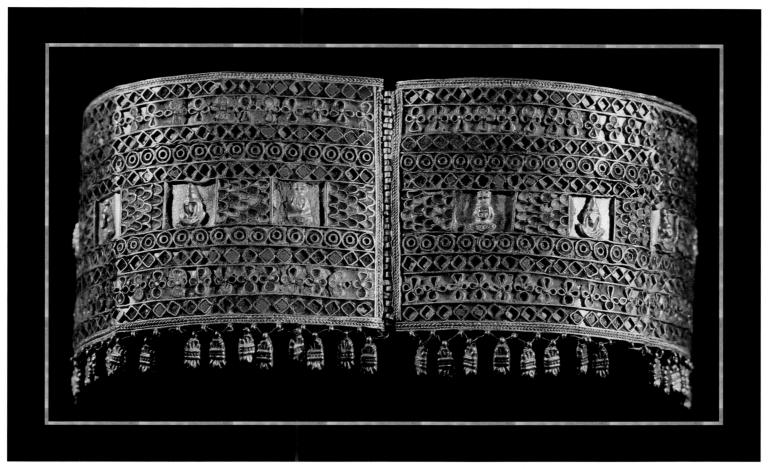

The Late Dynastic Period

A large proportion of the Berlin collection was lost in the Second World War, though the objects in Munich all survived.

Who was the Queen of Meroe?

Since the 2nd century BC the royal throne of Meroe was also occupied by women, who took the title 'Kandake'. The hieroglyphic inscriptions on the reliefs that decorated the small cult temple in front of the queen's pyramid gave her name as Amanishakheto, and she is probably the 'one-eyed Kandake' of Roman military reports of the late 1st century BC. This

The ruler, corpulent and Negroid in features, appears in full regalia. Around her tightly curled hair is a broad diadem, on which, instead of the cobra, we see the ram's head of Amun, together with a high crown of feathers and a bead collar. At the top, a royal falcon – very likely a piece of jewellery in gold foil – stretches out its wings protectively. A narrow band stretches from the nape of the neck to the chin, holding two cobras to the cheek. The queen's neck is adorned by a broad bead collar and necklace. On cords that hang from her shoulders are tassels that reach down to the hem of her garment.

494–495 Bracelet with winged goddess

reference dates her reign to around 25 BC, and this date is confirmed by stylistic features of the numerous signet rings that were found among the treasures in her tomb.

The 'Kandake in the Land of the Moors' mentioned in the New Testament (Acts of the Apostles, 8:26), whose chamberlain, 'a man from the country of the Moors and a powerful man who was set above all her treasure vaults', was converted to Christianity by St Philip, must clearly have been of a later generation.

The relief on the right pylon of the mortuary temple in front of the pyramid of Kandake Amanishakheto shows the queen triumphing over her enemies. In front of her is a group of prisoners, and she herself holds a spear to the back of their necks.

The Queen's Crown Jewels

The gold treasure of Meroe originally consisted of ten armlets of gold cloisonné work with coloured cast glass, to which were soldered figures of gods chased in gold foil; also nine rings with richly decorated interchangeable parts and more than sixty signet rings, some of gold and others of silver. Then there were numerous amulets, earrings, and chain-links, including scarabs, *wedjat*-eyes, Hathor-emblems and *ankhs*. Two collars have been reconstructed from individual beads from the site. The diversity of forms and techniques employed suggests that the individual pieces were manufactured over a lengthy period of time, probably as part of the queen's crown jewels.

The ten rigid bracelets were made in identical pairs and worn in pairs on the forearms and upper arms.

The Golden Treasure of Meroe

All of them were made from two rectangular halves of gold foil, bent into a semicircle and joined by a hinge. The fastening that was common in Egyptian bracelets is absent. Eyelets or small holes at the four outer corners of the bracelets were used to sew them to linen or leather cuffs, as is shown in contemporary Meroitic reliefs. The pair of bracelets with pendants (493) was probably worn on the upper arm without any other jewellery.

The decoration, in rows of repeated circular, square or scale-shaped ornament – and occasional concentric circles – is soldered on in the old technique, in bands

and her husband, the ram-headed Amun of Karnak and Napata. Their cult in far-off Napata and Meroe went back to the days of Egyptian colonisation of the lands of the Upper Nile during the New Kingdom. The bracelet with pendants (493) is covered with symmetrically arranged bands of ornament. As well as the square cells standing on their corners and the concentric circles in the second row from the top and the bottom, there are cruciform constructions that presumably represent the Egyptian sign of life, the *ankh*. They are filled alternately with dark- and light-blue glass. The central band is divided into square

496–497 Bracelet with winged goddesses, outside and inside

between narrow gold foil strips, and filled with coloured molten glass. Since the 4th century BC, even in Egypt, the use of molten glass (which was easier to work with) had replaced the painstaking cutting and fitting into gold cells of semiprecious stone or opaque coloured glass. The molten glass was produced by mixing finely ground glass with a binding agent and pasting it into the hollow cells. On heating this would fuse into a coherent mass which solidified on cooling. Larger surfaces were coated with a thin layer of molten glass, the so-called 'enamel', applied directly to the gold base. Such a coating, however, easily came loose from the setting.

The divinities represented on the bracelets, like those on the flat plates and signet rings, are generally of purely Egyptian origin, primarily the goddess Mut

fields: scale-shaped cells alternate with busts of the gods in beaten gold foil. The outer edges of each half-bracelet are framed with braided wire. From the lower edge, amulet-like pendants hang from wire strung through eyelets. The sheaf forms seem to owe their stylistic origins to Hellenic Alexandria.

Another bracelet (494–495) is constructed of the same elements, but here, over the hinge that links both halves is a figure of the goddess Mut in beaten gold. The winged goddess wears the crowns of Upper and Lower Egypt over the vulture cap; her wings are of cloisonné filled with coloured glass. She

The Late Dynastic Period

stands on a lotus flower that suggests the primeval waters whence she emerged.

The winged goddess Mut appears in the same position on a second pair of bracelets (496–497), standing on a lotus flower and wearing the Egyptian Double Crown on her head. The figure, of beaten gold foil is fastened into the hinge by eyelets. The wings are of beaten and engraved gold, without the customary cells for coloured glass. Corresponding to her four protectively outspread wings, the goddess has four arms, which stretch out diagonally, with *ankhs*

held in the hands. On the two central bands of the bracelet, Mut is faced on either side by two similarly winged goddesses. On their heads they carry the crescent moon and lunar disc. Their wings have gold cells to take coloured glass, which has been lost, though surviving traces show that the background would have been dark blue.

The bracelet is bordered by narrow bands, the upper being a frieze of *uraei* with solar discs on their heads, the lower a row of small squares of gold foil set on their corners; the gaps between were originally filled with coloured glass.

The survival of examples of the Egyptian goldsmith's art at this late period is astonishing. Meroitic gold work, however, shows unmistakably provincial and decadent traits in its handling of the forms and techniques handed down, and in its carefree mixing of Egyptian and Alexandrian divinities and emblems on the same bracelet (493–494). This can also be seen in other pieces of jewellery from Meroe, but more especially in the representations on signet rings.

Escutcheon rings are known only from Meroe; they were not current in Egypt. They consist of a simple ring to which a gold 'escutcheon', or plate, is attached

by a hinge. The escutcheon usually takes the form of an Egyptian collar and symbolises this magical protection worn since time immemorial. At the centre of the semi-circle is a three-dimensional god's head, wearing a crown.

A particularly artfully designed and technically complex example (502) has the ram's head of the god Amun with solar disc before of a shrine facade with *uraeus* frieze. Immediately above the solar disc, whose lower half is decorated with a *uraeus* band, is a round carnelian. From the ram's head hangs a chain of tiny

498–499 Signet rings from the funerary treasure of Meroë: queen or goddess with feather diadem and a crown in her hand, ram-headed Amun enthroned

500 Jewel of jasper with gold band and wedjat-eye

gold spheres; at the bottom this has the tiny figure of a god, probably lion-headed, with solar disc. The chain is flanked by a band of green. The collar has alternating diamond patterns and rows of beads, separated by plain gold wire, and ends at the top with a highly stylised *uraeus* frieze.

An escutcheon ring without a collar (501) has as its central motif a solar disc flanked by *uraei* and inscribed with a *wedjat*-eye, above which is the *hemhem* crown, a complex construction of ram's horns and three conical crowns with solar discs flanked by ostrich feathers and *uraei*. At the base a rectangular plate with a protective sign is held by gold wire passed though eyelets. Less of the coloured glass inlay has separated from the gold foil than in other pieces.

The lower edge of the escutcheon is often hung with a row of cowrie shells (503–504). Cowrie shells had already been popular during the Middle and early New Kingdoms, worn by women on girdles.

The ring part of these escutcheon rings is sometimes decorated with granulation, a row or diamond pattern of tiny gold spheres. The ring was presumably worn on the middle finger and the escutcheon would lie over two to three fingers of the hand. A hinge introduced into very deep escutcheon

The Golden Treasure of Meroe

made it flexible and better adapted to the movement of the fingers.

Among the funerary treasure of Queen Amanishakheto there were also over sixty signet rings, most of them cast from gold, a few from silver. Their round or oval bezels are very skilfully and confidently engraved with representations of divinities and divine emblems (499). Greco-Roman influences can be seen in the depiction of Zeus-Amun. The diversity of motifs makes these signet rings the most important source we have for the religious conceptions in the kingdom of Meroe, which even at this late date were still essentially determined by its powerful Egyptian inheritance.

501–504 Escutcheon rings from the funerary treasure of the Queen of Meroe

Page 245: 505 Statue of Princess Karomama

Chronological Table: The Rulers of Egypt

Up to the First Intermediate Period dates are given in some sources up to 50 years later. The dynastic table is based on Jürgen von Beckerath, 'Chronologie des pharaonischen Ägyptens', MÄS 46, 1997.

Early Dynastic Period

1st Dynasty

Hor-Aha (Menes)	c. 3032–3000
Djer	2999–2952
Djet	2952–2939
Den	2939–2882
Anedjib	2892–2886
Semerkhet	2886–2878
Qa'a	2878–2853

2nd Dynasty

Hetepsekhemwy	2853–2825
Reneb	2825–2810
Nynetjer	2810–2767
Wenegnebti	2767–2760
Sekhemib (Seth-Peribsen)	2760–2749
Neferkare	2749–2744
Neferkasokar	2744–2736
Hudjefa	2736–2734
Khasekhemwy	2734–2707

Old Kingdom

3rd Dynasty

Sanakhte	c. 2707–2690
Djoser	2690–2670
Huni	2663–2639

4th Dynasty

Snefru	2639–2604
Cheops (Khufu)	2604–2581
Djedefre	2581–2572
Chephren (Khafre)	2572–2546
Mycerinus (Menkaure)	2539–2511
Shepseskaf	2511–2506

5th Dynasty

Userkaf	2504–2496
Sahure	2496–2483
Neferirkare	2483–2463
Shepseskare	2463–2456
Neferefre	2456–2445
Niuserre	2445–2414
Menkauhor	2414–2405
Djedkare	2405–2367
Unas	2367–2347

6th Dynasty

Teti	2347–2337
Userkare	2337–2335
Pepi I	2335–2285
Merenre (Nemtyemsaf)	2285–2279
Pepi II	2279–2219
Nemtyemsaf II	2219–2218
Nitkoris	2218–2216

7th Dynasty (70 days only)

8th Dynasty 17 kings 2216–2170

First Intermediate Period

9th–10th Dynasties (in Herakleopolis)

18 kings	c. 2170–2020

Middle Kingdom

11th Dynasty

Mentuhotep I	2119–?
Intef I	? –2103
Intef II	2103–2054
Intef III	2054–2046
Mentuhotep II	2046–1995
Mentuhotep III	1995–1983
Mentuhotep IV	1983–1976

12th Dynasty

Amenemhet I	1976–1947
Sesostris I (Senusret I)	1956–1911/10
Amenemhet II	1914–1879 /76
Sesostris II (Senusret II)	1882–1872
Sesostris III (Senusret III)	1872–1853
Amenemhet III	1853–1806/05
Amenemhet IV	1807/06–1798/97
Queen Sobeknefru	1798/97–1794/93

Second Intermediate Period

13th Dynasty 50 Kings	1794/94–1648
14th Dynasty (in the Delta)	(?)–1648
15th Dynasty (Hyksos)	1648–1539
16th Dynasty (vassals of the Hyksos)	
17th Dynasty (in Thebes)15 (?) kings	c.1645–1550

New Kingdom

18th Dynasty

Ahmose I	1550–1525
Amenophis I (Amenhotep I)	1525–1504
Thutmosis I	1504–1492
Thutmosis II	1492–1479
Queen Hatshepsut	1479–1458/57
Thutmosis III	1479–1425
Amenophis II (Amenhotep II)	1428–1397
Thutmosis IV	1397–1388
Amenophis III (Amenhotep III)	1388–1351/50
Amenophis IV (Akhenaten)	1351–1334
Semenkhkare	1337–1333
Tutankhamun	1333–1323
Ay	1323–1319
Horemheb	1319–1292

19th Dynasty

Ramesses I	1292–1290
Sethos I (Seti I)	1290–1279/78
Ramesses II	1279–1213
Merenptah (Merneptah)	1213–1203
Amenmesse	1203–1200/1199
Sethos II (Seti II)	1199–1194/93
Siptah/Queen Ta-usret (Twosret)	1194/93–1186/85

20th Dynasty

Sethnakht	1186 - 1183/82
Ramesses III	1183/82–1152?51
Ramesses IV	1152/51–1145/44
Ramesses V	1145/44–1142/40
Ramesses VI	1142/40–1134
Ramesses VII	1134–1126
Ramesses VIII	1126–1125
Ramesses IX	1125–1107
Ramesses X	1107–1103
Ramesses XI	1103–1070/69

Third Intermediate Period

21st Dynasty

Smendes I	1170/69–1044/43
Amenemnesu	1044/43–1040/39
Psusennes I	1044/43–994/93
Amenemope	996/95–985/84
Osorkon the Elder	985/84–979/78
Siamun	979/78–960 /59
Psusennes II	960/59–946/45

22nd Dynasty

Sheshonq I	946/45–925/24
Osorkon I	925/24–ca. 890
Siamun	ca. 890–877
Sheshonq II	ca. 877–875
Osorkon II	ca. 875–837
Sheshonq III	ca. 837–798/785(?)
Pami	ca. 785–774
Sheshonq V	ca. 774–736

Upper Egyptian House

Harsiese	ca. 870–850
Takelot II	ca. 841–816
Pedubastis I	ca. 830–805
Iuput I	ca. 816–800
Sheshonq IV	ca. 800–790
Osorkon III	ca. 790–762
Takelot III	ca. 767–755
Rudamun	ca. 755–735
Iuput II	ca. 735–730

23rd Dynasty (in the Delta)

Pedubastis II (at Tanis)	ca. 756–732/30
Iuput II (at Lentopolis)	ca. 756–725 (?)
Osorkon IV	ca. 732/30–722

24th Dynasty (at Saïs)

Tefnakht	ca. 740–719
Bocchoris (Bakenrenef)	719–714

Late Dynastic Period

25th Dynasty (Kushites)

Piyi (Piankhi)	ca. 746–715
Shabako	715–700
Shebitku	700–690
Taharqa	690–664
Tanotamun	664–ca. 655

26th Dynasty (Saites)

Psammetichus I (Psamtik I)	664–610
Necho (Nekau)	610–595
Psammetichus II (Psamtik II)	595–589
Apries (Wahibre)	589–570
Amasis (Ahmose II)	570–526
Psammetichus III (Psamtik III)	526–525

27th Dynasty (1st Persian period) 525–401

28th Dynasty

Amyrtaeus	404/401–399

29th Dynasty

Nepherites I (Nefaarud I)	399–393
Achoris (Hakor)	393–380
Nepherites II (Nefaarud II)	380

30th Dynasty

Nektanebo I (Nakhtnebef I)	380–362
Teos (Djedhor)	364/362–360
Nektanebo II (Nakhtnebef II)	360–342

31st Dynasty (2nd Persian period) 342–332

Macedonians	332 –305
Ptolemies	305–30 BC

Coloured Stones and their Sources

In their jewellery and amulets the Egyptians exploited not only semi-precious stones but also 'common' stones for their colour and structure. The specific magical powers ascribed to different types of stone were also important in ancient Egyptian medicine, in which precious stones were often prescribed as remedies in powder form. Greek alchemists from Alexandria transmitted the recipes to mediaeval Europe, where they continued to be used in medicine and as 'birth stones'.

After its invention, coloured glass often replaced coloured stone in jewellery, and can hardly be distinguished from the stones it imitates except by chemical analysis. Whether glass or stone, the important thing was the colour. The types of stone generally used in Egyptian jewellery can be categorized as follows, and their sources are indicated where these have been established.

Agate
Translucent, of various colours. Wadi Abu Gerida in the Eastern Desert and Sinai.

Alabaster
(Greek, after the Egyptian city of Alabastron; geological calcite) white or yellowish, partly translucent, often with golden-yellow veins. Eastern Desert.

Almandine
Blood-red or sometimes violet or amethystine tinted variety of garnet .

Amethyst
Translucent purple. Wadi el-Hudi, south-east of Aswan, Nubian Western Desert near Abu Simbel, in Roman times Gebel Abu Diyeiba on the Red Sea.

Beryl
Transparent green. Mined only during the Ptolemaic period near Sikait-Subara on the Red Sea.

Chalcedony
Whitish grey with bluish lustre. Wadi Saga and Wadi Gerida in the Eastern Desert, the oasis of Bahrija and north-west of Abu Simbel, at Fayum and in Sinai

Chrysoprase
Translucent apple-green variety of chalcedony.

Feldspar
Translucent green. Gebel Migif, Wadi el-Rusheid, Wadi Nugrus, Wadi Higelig in the Eastern Desert, the Nubian Western Desert north of the Tibesti mountains.

Garnet
Dark red to reddish brown. Aswan, the Eastern Desert, Sinai

Haematite
Metallic lustre, dark steel-grey. Found in the Eastern Desert.

Jasper
Strong colours, red, green, black or yellow. Red jasper from the Wadi Saga and Wadi Abu Gerida in the Eastern Desert. Green jasper from the Wadi Hammamat. Brown jasper found in the form of desert gravel.

Carnelian
Translucent red. Found in the form of gravel in the Western and Eastern Deserts.

Lapis lazuli
Dark blue with veins of iron pyrites. In his *Description of the Earth* of 1154, al-Idrisi mentions a mine near the oasis of el-Kharga. The present author was shown great lumps of this semiprecious stone by Bishari boys at Aswan in 1955. As it was used in Egypt from pre-dynastic times, it most likely originated in the country. The main source for lapis lazuli in the ancient world was Badakshan in the mountains of the Hindu Kush in Afghanistan.

Malachite
Opaque green. Found in the Eastern Desert and Sinai. Ground into powder on palettes and used for eye make-up, but never in jewellery.

Obsidian
Black volcanic glass. Found in the Eastern Desert, probably also imported from Asia Minor and Abyssinia.

Olivine
Pale green. Found in Nubia.

Pearl
From mother-of-pearl, known from pre-dynastic times. Except during the 18th Dynasty, actual pearls were only ever used in Egyptian jewellery during the Ptolemaic period.

Quartz
After feldspar, the most common mineral, occurring in three different colours:

white quartz: from quartz veins, often auriferous. Aswan and Eastern Desert;

colourless transparent rock crystal: Eastern and Western Deserts, Sinai;

purple (amethystine) quartz: found in the diorite quarries of the Western Desert, Wadi el-Hudi, and the Eastern Desert.

Sard
Translucent blackish brown. A gravel in the Western and Eastern Deserts.

Turquoise
Sky-blue to apple-green. Found at Wadi Maghara and Serabit el-Khadim in Sinai.

Maps: Egypt and Nubia

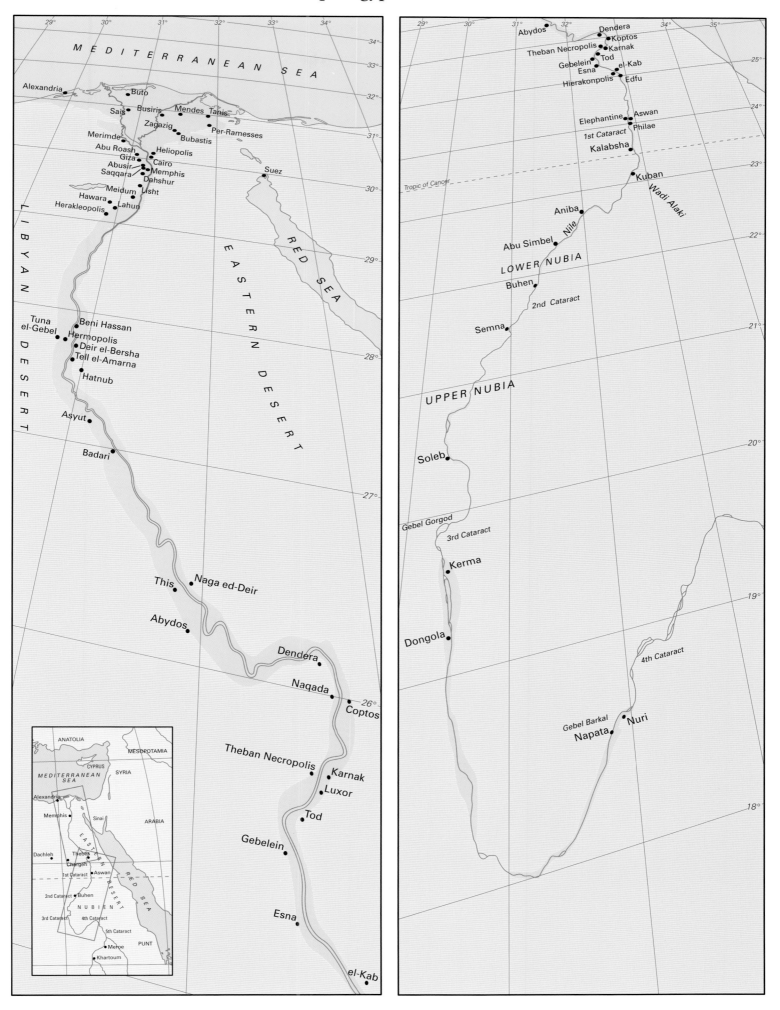

Left map (Lower Egypt and surrounding region):

MEDITERRANEAN SEA

LIBYAN DESERT

EASTERN DESERT

RED SEA

- Alexandria
- Buto
- Busiris
- Sais
- Mendes
- Tanis
- Zagazig
- Per-Ramesses
- Bubastis
- Merimde
- Abu Roash
- Heliopolis
- Giza
- Cairo
- Abusir
- Memphis
- Saqqara
- Dahshur
- Meidum
- Lisht
- Hawara
- Lahun
- Herakleopolis
- Suez
- Tuna el-Gebel
- Beni Hassan
- Hermopolis
- Deir el-Bersha
- Tell el-Amarna
- Hatnub
- Asyut
- Badari
- This
- Naga ed-Deir
- Abydos
- Dendera
- Naqada
- Coptos
- Theban Necropolis
- Karnak
- Luxor
- Tod
- Gebelein
- Esna
- el-Kab

Inset map:

ANATOLIA

MESOPOTAMIA

MEDITERRANEAN SEA

CYPRUS — SYRIA

- Alexandria
- Memphis
- Sinai
- ARABIA
- Dachleh
- Thebes
- Chargeh
- 1st Cataract
- Aswan
- 2nd Cataract
- Buhen
- NUBIEN
- 3rd Cataract
- 4th Cataract
- 5th Cataract
- Meroe
- Khartoum
- PUNT
- EASTERN DESERT
- RED SEA

Right map (Upper Egypt and Nubia):

- Abydos
- Dendera
- Koptos
- Theban Necropolis
- Karnak
- Gebelein
- Tod
- Esna
- el-Kab
- Hierakonpolis
- Edfu
- Elephantine
- Aswan
- 1st Cataract
- Philae
- Kalabsha
- Tropic of Cancer
- Kuban
- Wadi Alaki
- Aniba
- Nile
- Abu Simbel
- LOWER NUBIA
- Buhen
- 2nd Cataract
- Semna
- UPPER NUBIA
- Soleb
- Gebel Gorgod
- 3rd Cataract
- Kerma
- Dongola
- 4th Cataract
- Gebel Barkal
- Nuri
- Napata

Hieroglyphs, Insignia and Emblems of the Gods

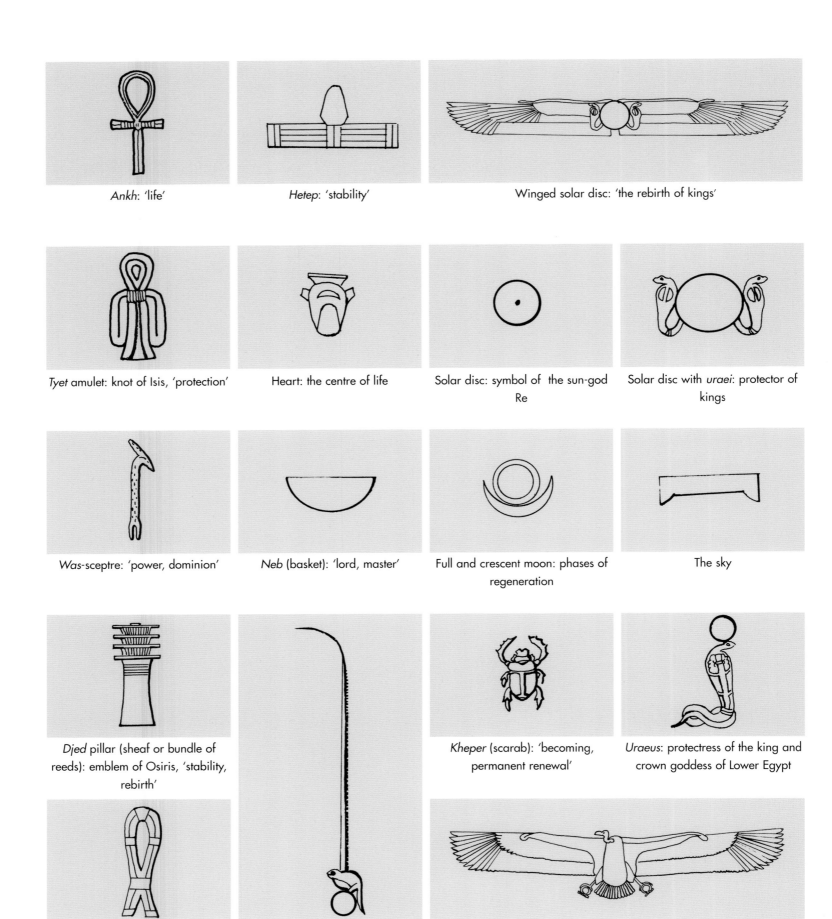

Ankh: 'life'

Hetep: 'stability'

Winged solar disc: 'the rebirth of kings'

Tyet amulet: knot of Isis, 'protection'

Heart: the centre of life

Solar disc: symbol of the sun-god Re

Solar disc with uraei: protector of kings

Was-sceptre: 'power, dominion'

Neb (basket): 'lord, master'

Full and crescent moon: phases of regeneration

The sky

Djed pillar (sheaf or bundle of reeds): emblem of Osiris, 'stability, rebirth'

Kheper (scarab): 'becoming, permanent renewal'

Uraeus: protectress of the king and crown goddess of Lower Egypt

Sa-loop: 'protection'

Palm rib ('year') plus tadpole ('millions'): 'millions of years'

Vulture-goddess Nekhbet: protectress and defender of kings and of Upper Egypt

Hieroglyphs, Insignia and Emblems of the Gods

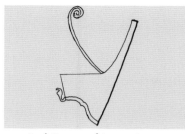

Red Crown of Lower Egypt

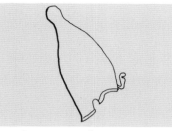

White Crown of Upper Egypt

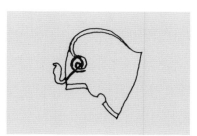

Khepresh: Blue Crown (war crown)

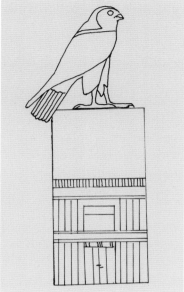

Serekh (Horus over the palace façade): emblematic frame for the king's name

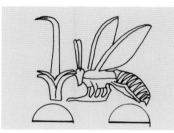

Nsw-bt: title of the king of Upper and Lower Egypt

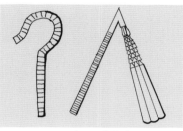

Sceptre (crook) and flail: 'power'

Falcon: symbol of Horus, god of the sun and the sky and of his incarnation, the king

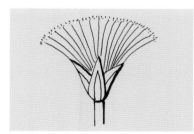

Papyrus: emblem of Lower Egypt and symbol of regeneration

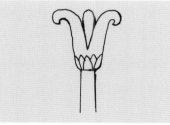

Lotus: emblem of Upper Egypt

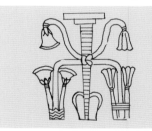

Lotus and papyrus entwined around lungs and windpipe: Upper and Lower Egypt united

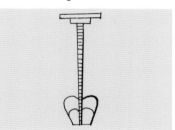

Lungs and windpipe: 'union'

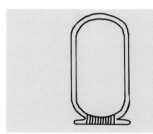

Cartouche: frame for the king's name

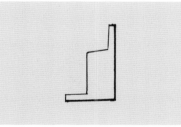

Throne: symbol of the goddess Isis; 'protection, magic'

Wedjat-eye: symbol of Horus, the god of the sky

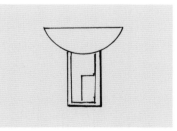

Emblem of the goddess Nephthys, sister of Osiris

Emblem of Bat, the goddess of the heavens

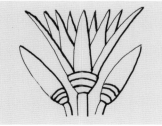

Lotus flower and buds: 'eternal rebirth'

Shen-ring (the world): the pharaoh's realm, 'eternity, strength'

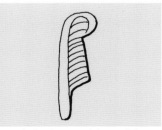

Ostrich feather: emblem of the goddess Ma'at; 'order and stability'

Select Bibliography

Aldred, Cyril *Jewels of the Pharaohs* London 1971, rev. ed. 1978

Andrews, Carol A. R. *Ancient Egyptian Jewellery* London 1990

— *Catalogue of Egyptian Antiquities in the British Museum VI: Jewellery* London 1981

Baines, John and **Malek**, Jaromir *Atlas of Ancient Egypt* Oxford 1980

Brunton, Guy *Lahun I: The Treasure* London 1920

Carter, Howard *The Tomb of Tut-ankh-amun* (3 vols.) London 1923–31

Clayton, Peter A. *Chronicle of the Pharaohs* London 1994, repr. 1996, 1998

De Morgan, J. *Fouilles à Dahchour, mars–juin 1894* Vienna 1895

Desroches-Noblecourt, Christiane *Tutankhamen: Life and Death of a Pharaoh* London 1963

Edwards, I. E. S. *Tutankhamun, His Tomb and its Treasures* New York 1976

— *Tutankhamun's Jewelry* New York 1976

(Exhibition catalogue) *Sudan: Antike Königreiche am Nil* Munich 1997

Faulkner, R. O. *The Ancient Egyptian Book of the Dead* London 1985

Forbes, R. J. *Studies in Ancient Technology* VII and VIII, Leiden 1966

Gale, N. H. and **Stos-Gale**, Z. A. 'Ancient Egyptian Silver' *JEA* 33, 1947

Galeries Nationales du Grand Palais *Ramses le Grand* (exhibition catalogue) Paris 1976

— *Tanis: L'Or des Pharaons* (exhibition catalogue) Paris 1987

Goyon, Georges 'Le Papyrus de Turin dit »Des Mines d'Or« et le Wadi Hammamat' *ASAE 49* 1949

— *La Découverte des Trésors de Tanis* Persea 1987

Harris, J. R. *Lexicographical Studies in Ancient Egyptian Minerals* Berlin 1961

Higgins, R. A. *Greek and Roman Jewellery* London 1961

Hoffmann, Herbert and **Davidson**, Patricia F. *Greek Gold: Jewelry from the Age of Alexander* (exhibition catalogue) The Brooklyn Museum, New York 1966

Kaiser, Werner *Ägyptisches Museum Berlin, Staatliche Museen Preußischer Kulturbesitz*, Berlin 1967

Lilyquist, Christine 'The Gold Bowl naming General Djehuty, a Study of Objects and Early Egyptology' *Metropolitan Museum Journal 23*, New York 1988

Lucas, A. 'Silver in Ancient Times' *JEA* 14, 1928

— *Ancient Egyptian Materials and Industries* London 1962

Mace, A. C. 'The Caskets of Princess Sit-Hathor-iunit' *Bulletin of the Metropolitan Museum of Art* New York 1924

Mace, A. C. and **Winlock**, H. E. *The Tomb of Seneb-tisi at Lisht* New York 1916

Maryon, H. 'Metal working in the Ancient World' *AJA* 53, 2, 1949

Maxwell-Hyslop, K. R. *Western Asiatic Jewellery c.3000–612 BC* London 1971

Montet, Pierre *La Nécropole royale de Tanis I: Les Constructions et le Tombeau d'Osorkon II à Tanis* Paris 1947

— *La Nécropole royale de Tanis II: Les Constructions et le Tombeau de Psusennes à Tanis* Paris 1951

Moustafa, A. Y. 'Reparation and Restoration of Egyptian Antiquities: The Belt of Prince Ptah-Shepses' *ASAE* 54, 1957

Müller, Hans Wolfgang *Staatliche Sammlung Ägyptischer Kunst München* Munich 1972

— *Ägyptische Kunst, Monumente alter Kulturen* Frankfurt am Main 1970

Ogden, Jack M. 'The so-called "Platinum" Inclusions in Egyptian Goldwork' *JEA* 62, 1976

Petrie, W. M. F. *The Royal Tombs of the First Dynasty* London 1900

Priese, Karl-Heinz, *Das Gold von Meroe* (exhibition catalogue) Berlin/Munich 1962

Rabi, Hassanein 'The Financial System of Egypt AH 564–741' *London Oriental Series 25*, Oxford 1972

Reeves, Nicholas *The Complete Tutankhamun* London 1990

Reisner, George A. *A History of the Giza Necropolis II, completed and revised by William St. Smith: The Tomb of Hetep-heres the Mother of Cheops* Cambridge, Mass. 1955

Saleh, Mohammed and **Hourig**, Sourouzian *The Egyptian Museum Cairo: Official Catalogue* Mainz 1986

Simpson, William Kelly 'The Vessels with Engraved Designs and the Repoussé Bowl from the Tell Basta Treasure' *AJA* 63, 1959

Smith, William Stevenson *The Art and Architecture of Ancient Egypt* London 1958

— *Interconnections in the Ancient Near East: A Study of the Relationships between the Arts of Egypt, the Aegean and Western Asia* New Haven/London 1965

Staehelin, Elisabeth 'Untersuchungen zur Ägyptischen Tracht im Alten Reich' *MÄS 8*, Berlin 1966

Stierlin, Henri *Das Gold der Pharaonen* Paris 1993

Stierlin, Henri and **Ziegler**, Christiane *Tanis, Vergessene Schätze der Pharaonen* Munich 1987

Vercoutter, J. 'The Gold of Kush: Two Gold-washing Stations at Faras East' *Kush: Journal of the Sudan Antiquity Service VII/VIII*, Khartoum 1959

Vernier, Emile *Bijoux et Orfèvreries: Catalogue Général des Antiquités Egyptiennes du Musée du Caire* Leipzig 1907

Vilimkova, Milada and **Abdul-Rahman**, Mohamed *Altägyptische Gold-schmiedekunst* Prague 1969

Wenig, Steffen *Africa in Antiquity: The Arts of Ancient Nubia and the Sudan* (2 vols.) New York 1978

Wilkinson, Alix *Ancient Egyptian Jewellery* London 1971

Williams, Caroline R. *Gold and Silver Jewellery and Related Objects* New York 1924

Winlock, H. E. *The Treasure of El Lahun* New York 1934

— *The Treasure of Three Egyptian Princesses* New York 1948

Wood, R. W. 'The Purple Gold of Tutankhamun' *JEA* 20, 1934

Zabkar, Louis V. 'Correlation of the Transformation Spells of the Book of the Dead and the Amulets of Tutankhamun's Mummy' in *Mélanges offerts à Jean Vercoutter* Paris 1985

Zoffilli, Ermanno *Kleidung und Schmuck im Alten Ägypten* Berlin 1992

List of Illustrations

Where photographs were taken by photographers other than Eberhard Thiem, the source is given in brackets after the entry. Sources for illustrations in the boxes follow at the end of the list.

1 Statue shrine. Wood, covered with gold foil. Height 20in (50.5cm), width 10½in (26.5cm), depth 12½in (32cm). From Thebes, Valley of the Kings, KV 62, tomb of Tutankhamun. 18th Dynasty. Cairo, Egyptian Museum JE 61481

2 Head of Hathor. Gold. Height 1½in (3.5cm). From Memphis, tomb of the high priest and prince Sheshonq. 22nd Dynasty. Cairo, Egyptian Museum JE 86781

3 Statuette of Tutankhamun. Wood, gilded; bronze, glass. Height 23¼in (58.8cm). From Thebes, Valley of the Kings, KV 62, tomb of Tutankhamun. 18th Dynasty. Cairo, Egyptian Museum JE 60713

4 Vulture pectoral. Gold, lapis lazuli (blue glass?), carnelian, obsidian (for eyes). Height 3in (7.4cm), width 4½in (11.7cm). From Thebes, Valley of the Kings, KV 62, tomb of Tutankhamun. 18th Dynasty. Cairo, Egyptian Museum JE 61895

5 Seated king. Gold. Height 2¼in (5.4cm), length of the chain 21¼in (54cm). From Thebes, Valley of the Kings, KV 62, tomb of Tutankhamun. 18th Dynasty. Cairo, Egyptian Museum JE 60702

6 Royal circlet. Lapis lazuli, obsidian, glass. Diameter 7½in (19cm), height of gold band 1in (2.5cm). From Thebes, Valley of the Kings, KV 62, tomb of Tutankhamun. 18th Dynasty. Cairo, Egyptian Museum JE 606084

7 Osiris pectoral. Gold, carnelian, glass. From Thebes, Valley of the Kings, KV 62, tomb of Tutankhamun. 18th Dynasty. Cairo, Egyptian Museum JE 61948

8 Counterweight with figure of eternity. Gold, carnelian, glass. Width 3¼in (8.2cm). From Thebes, Valley of the Kings, KV 62, tomb of Tutankhamun. 18th Dynasty. Cairo, Egyptian Museum JE 61462

9 Scarab bracelet. Gold, lapis lazuli, carnelian, turquoise, quartz. Diameter 2¼in (5.4cm). From Thebes, Valley of the Kings, KV 62, tomb of Tutankhamun. 18th Dynasty. Cairo, Egyptian Museum JE 62360

10–11 Double receptacle. Gold, silver, semiprecious stones, glass. Height 6¼in (16cm), width 3½in (8.8cm), depth 1¾in (4.3cm). From Thebes, Valley of the Kings, KV 62, tomb of Tutankhamun. 18th Dynasty. Cairo, Egyptian Museum JE 61496

12 Scarab bracelet. Gold, lapis lazuli, carnelian, electrum, quartz, glass. Length of scarab 2½in (6.6cm), length of bracelet 4¼in (10.7cm). From Thebes, Valley of the Kings, KV 62, tomb of Tutankhamun. 18th Dynasty. Cairo, Egyptian Museum JE 61917

13 Clasp or counterweight. Gold, silver, lapis lazuli, calcite, glass. Height 2¾in (6.8cm), width 2¼in (6cm). From Thebes, Valley of the Kings, KV 62, tomb of Tutankhamun. 18th Dynasty. Cairo, Egyptian Museum JE 61979

14 Scarab pectoral. Gold, lapis lazuli, carnelian, turquoise, glass. From Thebes, Valley of the Kings, KV 62, tomb of Tutankhamun. 18th Dynasty. Cairo, Egyptian Museum JE 61885

15 Metamorphosis pectoral. Gold, green feldspar (?), carnelian, glass. Height 6½in (16.5cm), width 9½in (24.4cm). From Thebes, Valley of the Kings, KV 62, tomb of Tutankhamun. 18th Dynasty. Cairo, Egyptian Museum JE 61948

16 Bracelet. Gold, lapis lazuli, carnelian. Diameter 2¼/2½in (5.9/6.6cm). From Tanis, tomb of Psusennes I. 21st Dynasty. Cairo, Egyptian Museum JE 55781

17 Bracelet of Sheshonq I. Gold, lapis lazuli, carnelian, turquoise, faience. Height 1¾in (4.6cm), diameter 2¾in (7cm). From Tanis, tomb of Sheshonq II. 22nd Dynasty. Cairo, Egyptian Museum JE 72184B

18 Rigid bracelet. Gold, lapis lazuli, carnelian, turquoise, glass. Height 2¾in (7.3cm), diameter 2½in (6.6cm). From West Thebes, tomb of Ahhotep. 17th/18th Dynasty. Cairo, Egyptian Museum CG 52068

19 Bead bracelet. Gold, lapis lazuli, almandine[?], carnelian. Width 1in (2.5cm), diameter 2¼in (5.9cm). From West Thebes, tomb of the 'Three Princesses'. 18th Dynasty. New York, Metropolitan Museum of Art 26.8.146 AB

20 Emblem of the falcon Gemhesu and statuette of the god Amun. Wood, gilded. From Thebes, Valley of the Kings, KV 62, tomb of Tutankhamun. 18th Dynasty. Cairo, Egyptian Museum JE 60746, 60734

21–22 Throne of Princess Sit-Amun. Wood, bronze, gold, silver. From Thebes, Valley of the Kings, KV 42, tomb of Juja and Tuja. 18th Dynasty. Cairo, Egyptian Museum CG 5113

23–24 Scarab pendant of Tutankhamun. Gold, lapis lazuli, turquoise, green feldspar, calcite, carnelian. Height 3½in (9cm), width 4½in (10.5cm). From Thebes, Valley of the Kings, KV 62, tomb of Tutankhamun. 18th Dynasty. Cairo, Egyptian Museum JE 61886

25 see 44

26 Sunrise on the Nile

27 Predynastic female figurine. Clay with white paint. Height 9½in (24cm), 4th century BC. New York, Metropolitan Museum of Art (H. W. Müller)

28 Predynastic and Early dynastic-period necklaces and armlets. Glazed faience, garnet, carnelian, bone. Length 27½in (70cm). From Tura. – String of beads. Faience, bone, stone, carnelian. Length 2in (5cm). From Tura. – String of beads. Stone, ostrich eggshell. Length 18½in (47cm). From Tura – String of beads. Faience, slate, carnelian. Length 15¼in (39cm). From el-Kubanijeh. – Bracelets. Grey slate. Diameter 6.5/6.6cm. From Tura. – String of beads. Quartz, calcite, agate,slate. Length 39cm. From Badari. – String of beads. Carnelian, quartz. Length 47cm. From el-Kubanijeh. – String of beads. Carnelian, haematite. Length 21cm. From Tura, Pre-dynastic period to Early Dynastic period , around 3000 BC, Vienna, Kunsthistorisches Museum ÄS 6898, 6912, 9192, 6907, 7154, 6925, 6927, 9615, 7141, 6897

29 Relief in the rock tomb of Ibi at Deir el-Gebrawi. End of the Old Kingdom, around 2000 BC (N. D. G. Davies, Deir el-Gebrawi, I, pl. XVII/XIV)

30 Umm el-Qa'ab, tomb of Dewen. 1st Dynasty (G. Dreyer)

31 Umm el-Qa'ab, tomb of Khasekhemwy. 2nd Dynasty (G. Dreyer)

32 Umm el-Qa'ab, tomb of Qa'a. 1st Dynasty (G. Dreyer)

33 Ointment jar. Breccia, gold. Height 2in (5.2cm), diameter 3¾in (9.5cm). From Umm el-Qa'ab, tomb of Khasekhemwy. 2nd Dynasty. London British Museum (K. Flimm)

34 Ointment jar. Carnelian, gold. Height 1½in (4.2cm), diameter 2½in (6.5cm). From Umm el-Qa'ab, tomb of Khasekhemwy. 2nd Dynasty. Cairo, Egyptian Museum JE 34941

35 Ointment jar. Breccia, gold. Height 2¾in (7.2cm), diameter 4in (10.5cm). From Umm el-Qa'ab, tomb of Khasekhemwy. 2nd Dynasty. Cairo, Egyptian Museum JE 34942

36 Knife. Flint, gold. Length 8½in (21.7cm). Early Dynastic period. From Gebel-Tarif. Cairo, Egyptian Museum CG 14265

37–38 Palette of King Narmer. Slate. Height 25in (64cm), width 16½in (42cm), depth 1in (2.5cm). Dynasty 0, around 3000 BC. Cairo, Egyptian Museum JE 32169 (J. Lipe)

39 Tomb relief. Limestone. Height 14in (36cm). From Saqqara. 2nd Dynasty. Antiquities Service store, Saqqara (D. Johannes, DAI Cairo)

40 Bracelet. Gold, turquoise, amethyst. From Umm el-Qa'ab, tomb of Djer. 1st Dynasty. Cairo, Egyptian Museum CG 52010

41 Bracelet. Gold, turquoise, lapis lazuli. From Umm el-Qa'ab, tomb of Djer. 1st Dynasty. Cairo, Egyptian Museum CG 52011

42 Pistil of lotus flower (Expédition en Egypte. Histoire Naturelle Botanique III, 2, pl. 60, 1822)

43 Forearm of the body of a woman, with the four bracelets. From Umm el-Qa'ab, tomb of Djer. 1st Dynasty. (Flinders Petrie, Royal Tombs, Vol. II, Frontispiece, 1902)

44 Bracelet links with Horus-falcon over the palace façade (serekh). Gold and turquoise. From Umm el-Qa'ab, tomb of Djer. 1st Dynasty. Cairo, Egyptian Museum CG 52008

45 Bracelet. Gold, lapis lazuli, turquoise. From Umm el-Qa'ab, tomb of Djer. 1st Dynasty. Cairo, Egyptian Museum CG 52009

46 Small stone 'basket'. Slate. Height 2in (4.8cm), length 9in (22.7cm), width 5½in (13.8cm). From Saqqara, 2nd Dynasty. Cairo, Egyptian Museum JE 71298

47 Necklace. Gold. Length of shell ½in (1.5cm). From Naga ed-Deir. Early Dynastic period. Cairo, Egyptian Museum CG 53802

48 Stone relief with emblem of the goddess Neith. Slate. Early Dynastic period . Brussels, Musée du Cinquantenaire

49 Amulet in the form of a beetle. Gold. Length 2¼in (6cm). From Naga ed-Deir. Cairo, Egyptian Museum CG 53821

50–51 Pectorals in the form of animals. Gold with stucco infill. Length of the oryx antelope 1½in (4cm), length of the bull 1½in (3.8cm). From Naga ed-Deir. Early Dynastic period. Cairo, Egyptian Museum CG 53824, 53825

52 Horus falcon on the hieroglyph for 'gold'

53 Seth, squatting over the hieroglyph for 'gold'

54 Sarcophagus of Queen Hatshepsut. Sandstone. Height 39¼in (100cm), width 34½in (87.5cm), length 96½in (245cm). From Thebes, Valley of the Kings KV 20, tomb of Hatshepsut. 18th Dynasty. Cairo, Egyptian Museum JE 37678, 52459

55 Fragment of relief. From Heliopolis. 3rd Dynasty. Turin, Museo Egizio

56 Second coffin of Tutankhamun. Gilded wood, glass. Length 204cm. From Thebes, Valley of the Kings, KV 62, tomb of Tutankhamun. 18th Dynasty. Cairo, Egyptian Museum JE 60670

57–59 Details of wall painting. From West Thebes, T T 63, tomb of Sebekhotep. 18th Dynasty. London, British Museum EA 920–2

60 Huts of pharaonic miners near the Fawachir gold mine (R. & D. Klemm)

61 Horus name of King Djet. Rock inscription in the Wadi Barramiyeh. 1st Dynasty

62 Mortar for grinding gold ore. Wadi Margh. New Kingdom (R. & D. Klemm)

63 Nugget. 4th Dynasty. Cairo, Egyptian Museum

64 Wadi Barramiyeh gold-mine. New Kingdom (R. & D. Klemm)

65 Gold-bearing quartz, mined in ancient times. Around Um Ud (R. & D. Klemm)

66 Gold-washing installation at Faras, Nubia. Presumably 4th century AD (J. Vercoutter, The Gold of Kush, 1959)

67 Wall painting. West Thebes, T T 181, tomb of Nehamun and Ipuki. 18th Dynasty

68 Stone weights for weighing gold. Found near the Nubian fortress of Semna. 12th Dynasty. Khartoum, National Museum 248 1

69 Bead collar. Gold, electrum, glass. Length of terminals 3½in (9cm). From Thebes, Valley of the Kings, KV 55, tomb of Smenkhkare. 18th Dynasty. Cairo, Egyptian Museum CG 52674

70 Ring. Gold, lapis lazuli. Height ¾in (1.9cm), diameter 1in (2.2cm). 18th Dynasty. Private collection

71 Girdle. Gold, amethyst. Length 23½in (60cm), length of panthers' heads 2in (5.3cm). From Dahshur, tomb of Mereret. 12th Dynasty. Cairo, Egyptian Museum JE 30879

72 Scarab bracelet. Gold, lapis lazuli, carnelian. 18th Dynasty. London, British Museum EA 65616

73 String of golden shells and ducks. Length of ducks ½in (1.1cm). 18th Dynasty. London, British Museum EA 14696

74–75 String of beads. Gold, carnelian, pendants in the form of dates alternating with lizards. 18th Dynasty. London, British Museum EA 3081

76 Necklaces. Gold and carnelian. Late Ptolemaic period. Private collection

77–82 Necklace with pendants, earrings, bracelets. Gold. Ptolemaic period. Private collection

83 Bracelet. Gold. Ptolemaic period. Cairo, Egyptian Museum

84 Foundation plaque. Gold. Length 4¼in (10.9cm), height 2in (5.1cm). From the Serapeum, Alexandria. Period of Ptolemy IV Philopator (222/1–205/4 BC). Alexandria Museum P 100035

List of Illustrations

List of Illustrations

List of Illustrations

List of Illustrations

506 Ibis, made of silver, wood and inlaid glass

This edition published by Barnes & Noble, Inc., by arrangement with
Thema media GmbH, Germany

2005 Barnes & Noble Books

M 10 9 8 7 6 5 4 3 2 1

ISBN 0-7607-7079-4

German edition designed and produced by
Thema media GmbH, Germany
Layout and design: Sabine Dohme, Thomas Steinkämper

English-language edition
Project editor: Simon Hall
Editors: Moira Johnston, Elizabeth Tatham
Typography and additional design: Christopher Howson
Translated from the German by Pierre Imhoff and Dafydd Roberts

Consultant Peter A. Clayton

Printed in China by Midas